Gift of
Harold and Mary McCurdy

D0561031

GINGRICH LIBRARY
ALBRIGHT COLLEGE

PRESENTED BY

Harold and Mary McCurdy

VISIONARY APPROPRIATION

VISIONARY APPROPRIATION

by
John Derrickson McCurdy

Philosophical Library
New York

ALBRIGHT COLLEGE LIBRARY

Copyright, 1978, by Philosophical Library, Inc.
15 East 40 Street, New York, N.Y. 10016
All rights reserved

Library of Congress Catalog Card No. 78-50530
SBN 8022-2227-7

Manufactured in the United States of America

194
M133v

182199

TABLE OF CONTENTS

PREFACE

We cannot possess the world, cannot make the earth our own, unless we let the world possess us, hold us spellbound. When the sensible externals inspire us, make our soul ecstatic, we do possess the world; we do get a grasp on the things which grip us. Unless our vision becomes visionary, we are dispossessed; we lack mental possession of our material property; we are deprived of our proper spirituality. When the world inflames the senses, the earth becomes my world, our world. The visionary beholds the public, outside, world; he does not, or need not, withdraw to his private enclosure. Perception demands the active glance which weaves a spell while recording the spectacle. Primitive perception is already visionary; prosaic sight is germinal poetry. Because our phantasies are not delusory, we can appropriate the world without dispossessing our subjectivity, without expunging our prepossessions. The external world is a human realm, a seductive surrounding which invites our exploration. Visionary sight sees the world, not merely an imaginary retreat, because the perceived exterior is already imaginary. We receive sensations, but cannot perceive a substantial habitat unless we go beyond the given. We must interpret the data; we must discover how the sensory impacts are to be humanly taken. Dispassionate vision, objective scrutiny, sees a world without man, and thus obliterates the original world which calls for human participation. The inhuman externals become properly a world only when humanized. Visionary sight possesses the world because the world demands our personal appropriation.

The present work follows Merleau-Ponty in tracing the first lines of an existential naturalism, a thought which lives the external world from the inside. Phenomenology does not objectify the natural things, but participates in their apparitional genesis; we do not speak about the things so much as we speak with the things, using the things for articulating the things, while the things employ our glottis, putting our dispositions at their disposal. We have our being in a world which surrounds us, an environment whose density is ventilated with circumambient media. We grasp the things through those atmospheric qualities which engage our interest, those indiscreet textures which invade our body and solicit our intentional activity. The things unfold their inner essence through the properties which call for our personal seizure; but we can take possession only if the world itself appropriates our body; only if we are possessed, taken over from within, can our body proper have property; in original perception, personal appropriation requires a surrender to our surroundings, requires that our body unbind itself, loosen its limbs, and let its gaze go astray. Primitive experience depersonalizes our body, so that we no longer know who perceives the world; someone sees, from I know not where; from somewhere over here a vision, a touch, perceives something sensible located somewhere out there, not positioned in the objective world but oriented toward this body whose passions provide the light. The inner man exits from his enclosure and becomes bound up with the things. No longer does consciousness confront lighted and colored surfaces yonder; consciousness, through its body, espouses the things, and becomes a living color, a visionary light, whose vibrations establish themselves as the level at which we live. The outer light is the prehuman gaze which leads our look into the clearing, and then into the background, whence the earth radiates ghostly secrets, dark dreams which first see light in human perception, then disappear from sight and become operative invisibles, become a transparent musculature, a phantom body which haunts our habitat, beclouding our spirit. Our exterior interiority is closer to us than we are to ourselves, and yet is not a private consciousness. When the inner man opens his closet and steps forth into the world, he works his way through an intersubjective nature. The phenomenal body becomes depersonalized so that my properties become public possessions through interpersonal appropriation; the personal becomes interpersonal through the impersonal world whose mute denizens hold us all fascinated, making each subject ecstatic, making each an oracle who speaks in his own tongue, and yet in a language we all understand. Glossolalia contains its own glossary. The world already speaks in prehuman tongues, and itself creates the appropriate audience; nature makes itself understood by making us stand outside ourselves on the common soil where we all congregate, making us stand under the outer light here below, on the earth, in the world which assembles in our vision when we work our way forward, into the background.

We wish, then, in this book, to describe the interface betwixt our own face and the external surfaces, to describe the interchange at the interface, an interpenetration at the interval which makes nature existential, our existence natural, our vision a visionary possession of the external world. We divide the book into five chapters, describing, first, synergetic perception. The visual sensibles are distinct from the tactile sensibles, and each eye sees a separate visual sensible. But binocular vision is synergetic. When our eyes focus, and work together with our hands, the separate sensibles overlap and merge upon solid reality, a density with depth beyond the present appearances. Our senses intercommunicate within a common sensorium and through the intersensory thing. The various senses are interchangeable, and correspondingly the various sensibles are systematic equivalents within the world horizon. Our living body is a natural symbolism whose perceptual gestures express our habitat. The sense organs generalize themselves as they explore the perceptual field, producing a habitual body. Always looking for something, our body captures a fleshly generality, an apparitional style, which leads us into depth while the background decompresses in layers. The second chapter describes apparitional reality. Unless things originally inscribed themselves in our flesh, we could never experience illusion as perceptual. Hallucination is experientially distinct from perception, but perception is invisibly imaginal, as becomes evident in disillusionment, when something real becomes a phantom, exhibiting the negativity hidden in positivity. We cannot withdraw from the world and begin with a doubt which seeks certitude, or probability. Despite error, our perceptual faith is justified, because the world never undeceives us without replacing the illusion with an apparition which convinces. Perception is always teleperception through images, operative invisibles. Nonimaginal reality is a potentiality for perception, while raw sensations are mere surface phenomena. If we strip away the intermediate layers, we confront just another surface; and we cannot discover pure intelligibles, unless we strip away our body. We never see reality all naked, because our body garbs the things with its own flesh. Reality conceals itself while revealing itself, clothing its body with the organs which rend its veils. Never naked, nature is a nude, a bodily reality whose skin is a sensuous flesh, a covering which can tear loose in our grasp, as in diplopia. Thirdly, in the third chapter, we describe the sensory media. Fundamentally, we do not face the things across a void, but possess them longitudinally through a surrounding atmosphere. We perceive through media which solicit our activity and draw us into the earth along leading elements. Light guides our gaze, while bodily motion leads our touch. Light is a level, a sensible which becomes invisible, becomes a lighting which lets us see lighted surfaces across the clearing. Light has a natural style which articulates the scenery, showing us the sense in the sensible. The fourth chapter describes the sensuous intermediaries. The lighted and shaded things can themselves become lightings, as their shining surfaces efface themselves before our prospective gaze. Letting the figured surfaces act as lightings, our illumined eye creates a face which assembles flashing facets into a single surface, a shining visage which shows us solid reality. Immersed in the media, the things reflect upon themselves in pools and shadows. Our eyes are sensible things which see themselves reflected in the mirror, and reflected again in the eye; the human eye is a mirror which sees. Humanity steps into the instrumental network already prepared, and lets nature perceive itself in us. The fifth, final, chapter describes the interchange between inside and outside. We have an inner life which draws the external world inside, and then turns inside out, pressing out carnal essences. Man is a flesh whose interiority has an outside, which we perceive from the hither side.

Flesh folds back upon itself, as our right hand touches the left hand, and then turns around, as the left hand touches the right, reversing the sensed to the sentient but never quite touching its touching. Interchange at the interface creates a sensuous visage which is jointly our own face, lived from the inside, and the face of the world, seen from the outside as an alien external, but lived now as our personal possession.

We produce descriptions; throughout this work we simply describe; but description is not simple, because we must delve beneath the surface. We describe not merely the superficial evidence, the obvious facts, but the deeper patterns which lie hidden in the most manifest phenomena. The secret structures become visible only when our gaze labors upon the passively received impressions; phenomenological structure is disclosed in poetic construction. We employ a phenomenological method which makes evident the figurations hidden in the obvious phenomena. Though our descriptions go beyond the surface, we do not go behind the surface; we do not begin with the visible panorama and, by ratiocination, go behind the scenes to the nonperceptual. We do not remain on the surface, producing trivial descriptions, nor do we go behind the surface, producing arguments which no longer describe; we go beyond the surface, through the surface; we dwell in the visible until surface opens toward depth. As Whitehead says, "Philosophy is mystical. For mysticism is direct insight into depths as yet unspoken."[1] Philosophy, though not poetry, is "akin to poetry."[2] Both poetry and philosophy perceive forms which lurk beyond literalistic speech; poetry is allied "to metre, philosophy to mathematical pattern."[3] The philosophic visionary wants structural rigor, but a rigor which is rhythmical, an aesthetic logic.

Primitive speculation about nature was mythopoeic;

myth was a poetry in which art was not yet distinguished from science. Strange phenomena startled untutored sensibilities, and nature came alive with divinities, cosmic forces as mutable as the imagination. Philosophy arose when western man roused himself from his stupor, raised himself to his full height, and made the wondrous stand in broad daylight; man stepped into the waking world, where we still struggle for full consciousness. Philosophy, by tradition, has been an intellectual activity operating with concepts, opposed to the imaginative activity which uses images, metaphors. Myth, even if regarded as thought, is, at best, pictorial thought, and philosophers have always wanted to discard the pictures. Philosophers, of course, are writers, and as literary men they have usually employed metaphor, but the fanciful phrase is an adventitious ornament. Or, if the metaphor is less frivolous, and expresses an essential doctrine, that doctrine, when intelligible, can be translated into plainer talk. Hardly ever has philosophy admitted that the truth about nature is intrinsically apprehensible through myth, and such an admission, in most eyes, converts philosophy into something like theosophy. We do not overlook that Plato often employed myth for communicating his deepest intuitions, but the myth is merely an expedient. Likewise, Aquinas allows that we must speak about ultimate reality in images, since sacred scripture is imaginative; but our language is inadequate, and expresses mostly our human limitation. Reality in itself is completely intelligible, and from the divine viewpoint is fully understood. Philosophy, then, even when employing myth, has never supposed that reality is mythic, and thus has employed myth as seldom as possible. Each philosopher, because he is a writer or a speaker, has a peculiar style, his personal tone, but the proper literary device would be a styleless style, a dry academic discourse, devoid

A necessary pastime)

of images, and appealing to no human passion except the desire for total clarity. Thought about nature has developed from the primitive poetic style toward a refined technical prose which can be manipulated in thinking machines. And sense organs are no longer required for empirical access to nature, since recording instruments operate more accurately.

Having noted the general stylistic evolution, we can look again and see, not only that philosophy has often employed hyperbole, but that the most literal literature has assumed many forms, some highly unsuitable for computer programing. Parmenides proclaimed that reality is intelligible, but couched his proclamation in verse and presented himself as the mouthpiece for a goddess. Heraclitus, notoriously obscure, expressed his philosophy in aphorisms. Socrates never wrote, but pursued his thought as a public dialogue, a conversation which exposed error in conventional opinion, without revealing truth. Plato adopted the dialogue format for his writing; the conversation is often inconclusive, and the reader is never altogether sure which disputant expresses the author's own thought. Moreover, Plato employs irony, which disguises the intended meaning. Aristotle is more exoteric; his surviving writings are mainly lecture notes, didactic treatises containing sober argument and careful observation. The model for correct reasoning is the syllogism, but Aristotle rarely uses syllogistic demonstration outside his treatises on logic. Medieval philosophy perpetuated the classical styles, and also developed its own. Augustine philosophizes while commenting upon scripture, so that his philosophy is often indistinguishable from theology; also he ruminates about his personal history, fashioning his philosophy in a confessional before the Christian god; philosophical insight and mystical illumination become inseparable. Anselm, an Augustinian, elaborates the most rigorous logical arguments within a prayer. Aquinas clearly distinguishes philosophy from theology, but his theology remains philosophical; his predominant style reflects the scholastic debate, in which metaphysical reasoning was augmented with appeals to ecclesiastical authority. In the later medieval schools there emerges a neutral analytical style, especially in the controversy about universals. In the Renaissance appear the first analytic and synthetic writings in the modern mode, but the early innovators often hold Plotinian, and even alchemical, beliefs, just as the later Newtonian science was influenced by theological convictions. The myths perished, the gods died; a methodology remained. Natural philosophy was both ideal and empirical, employing deduction which draws logical consequences from concepts, and using induction which draws conceptual conclusions from empirical facts; through induction and deduction, natural laws were formulated, the deductions continually being harmonized with the inductions, the mathematics with the practical experiments. Writings which exhibited this scientific method became the models for intelligible discourse, although philosophers adopting these models have not always avoided bizarre locutions. Consider Wittgenstein, a figurehead for contemporary analytical philosophy. Wittgenstein, in his early writings, proclaimed that everything sayable can be said clearly, and he created a logical language which ensured clear speech. Utilizing this new linguistic tool, Wittgenstein discovered that his proclamation was meaningless; we cannot say clearly that everything meaningful can be said clearly, because we cannot use the logical language for speaking about the language itself. A computer speaking the universal calculus would lack the inexpressible insight that its speech was true about reality. This insight Wittgenstein called the mystical, and he declared that the mystical calls for silence. Discursive thinking is fundamentally mute, and thus has no literary form at all, unless silence itself breaks the silence, becoming a significant silence, so that silence becomes literature. Wittgenstein requires a style which insinuates what cannot be said; if not silence, he wants words which convey the insight and then unsay themselves.

The mystical and imaginative influences in philosophy and science show that the human investigator is not a mere calculating and recording apparatus; discovery requires creative imagination. But creativity in science concerns only our subjective access to the natural object, does not concern the object itself; objects are not affected by our knowledge. Expressive art, however, presupposes that nature itself is perspectival, presupposes that nature has its being precisely in our knowledge; novelty in our knowing is novelty in the thing itself; art exhibits a knowing which is a making; aesthetic reality emerges within human experience. Phenomenal nature therefore calls for a literary style found nowhere in traditional philosophy; the style must be phenomenological.

Phenomenology as an independent philosophy originated with Husserl, who conceived philosophy as an ideal science, like logic. Phenomenology was originally intended to describe the essences which empirical science uses while investigating nature. Philosophy brackets the facts, suspends empirical reality, and investigates the meaning of the facts. Husserl developed a highly technical language which he employed with great precision in his quest for evident intuitions. While seeking scientific exactitude, Husserl uncovered a new theme for philosophy, a theme which contemporary phenomenologists have taken as their sole subject. Husserl thematized the life world, a realm more primitive than the objective world; the life world contains sen-

sible phenomena which have not yet appeared as certified facts. Contemporary thinkers have made the
phenomenological reduction into an operation which sets
aside the prejudices arising from science and common
sense, and lets us return to primitive experience. The language which expresses this preobjective life cannot have
the scientific exactitude that Husserl desired. Literary art
lets us see a world which science obscures, whether the
science be empirical or ideal. Foremost among the
phenomenologists after Husserl is Heidegger, in Germany.
Heidegger described the human being as the place where
being as a whole has its meaning, and described being as the
significance which takes place in human time. The cultural
world he described as an instrumental system which disguises being, and thus hides from man his own being. In
France, Sartre interpreted Heidegger as an existentialist,
and described man as a being who gives nature its meaning
through free decision. Destined perhaps to be a thinker
more important than Sartre is Merleau-Ponty, recently
dead. Merleau-Ponty was personally acquainted with
Sartre, was thoroughly familiar with Heidegger's thought,
and made a careful study of the entire Husserlian corpus.
Merleau-Ponty described how we have our being in the
world through a living body whose orientation is more
fundamental than the directedness established by personal
consciousness. He discovered a passivity in our embodied
intentionality; our bodily movements let us possess a world
which possesses us, fascinates us, suggests to us how the
world is to be taken.

The present book is a phenomenological work which
follows Merleau-Ponty. In my writing I employ two styles,
the one prosaic, the other more poetic; the one style blends
with the other. I provide a colorless academic exposition of
Merleau-Ponty's view, without adding any intuitions of my

own; but increasingly, as my author's views become clear, I abandon mere representation and capture in my work the productive style which animates my authority. Color suffuses the neutral prose; the reader realizes that I am using metaphor literally; the color is not a decorative coloration. In phenomenology, understood as a literary description of the life world, philosophy rejoins myth, from which scientific philosophy parted at birth. Myth is no longer a primitive science, a superstition. Phenomenology does not abolish rational knowledge or empirical knowledge; however, there is also a sensuous knowing. The primitive sensory world exhibits magical connections, oneiric meanings. This original nature finds expression, not in science primarily, but in the arts, insofar as these imaginative techniques do not simply represent empirical objects, or illustrate ideas. The world accessible through our senses and sensibilities has a sense, a meaning. We originally experience no logical or factual necessities, but the world has a discernible aesthetic necessity. Natural perception has the rigor displayed in a symphony; each note calls for the notes which follow, and yet each note without logical contradiction can be conceived not to exist, and factually can fail to be played; there is no causal connection between the first notes and the last, as there is between the bow stroke and the sound which issues from the violin; the symphony has an inner necessity which can be understood only by entering into the work. The reader of this book should not expect logical arguments, though he will find these, where Merleau-Ponty argues against opposing viewpoints; nor should he expect ordinary empirical descriptions, though he will find these also, where Merleau-Ponty cites scientific facts. Fundamentally, philosophy is not concerned with empirical details, but with essences, the deeper significance of factual triviality.[4] And the philosopher is not concerned with proof, but with evidence; philosophy makes the essences obvious. Even logic presupposes intuition, if logic has any importance, because "logical proof starts from premises, and ... premises are based upon evidence."[5] Argument merely articulates our metaphysical insights, rendering our mysticism rational. The reader should adopt an aesthetic attitude, as if he were reading literature. He should suspend his disbelief, and discover the perceptual faith which precedes dubitation. Only thus can the reader gain access to untamed nature which, mutely, is already literary, already musical, even before men join the chorus and prolong natural perception in creative expression.

In my work I am indebted to Alphonso Lingis whose thoughtful gaze has illuminated those passages where my author is still underway toward the unthought.

NOTES

[1] Alfred North Whitehead, *Modes of Thought* (New York: Cambridge University Press, 1956), p. 237.
[2] *MT*, p. 237.
[3] *MT*, p. 238.
[4] See *MT*, pp. 58-66.
[5] *MT*, p. 67.

Chapter I

SYNERGETIC PERCEPTION

I see things out there in the world with my two eyes, and those same things I touch with both hands. This thing here which I hold in my right hand I can also touch with my left hand, and this very same thing I can see with my right eye and also with my left. The eyeball too is something which my hands can touch, and the hands which touch the eye can touch each other. My hands are touching tangibles which are also visible. My hands are seen through my eyes, which are seeing tangibles. And my eyes see themselves, when I look in the mirror. If we interrogate these everyday phenomena, we can understand imagination and sense perception. When perception does its work, the world becomes an imaginal reality.

SENSUAL INITIATION

What do I see out there? Where are the visible externals located? And who is the person viewing these apparitions? I

1

am the one who sees, and I see what we all see, though I am situated here while other persons are centered elsewhere, and see from a different standpoint. The visionary is a living body; I see with these eyes here which I can touch with my hands. With these fleshly orbs I see something. But where? Outside me, and round about me; out there in the world, or in that external depth which becomes a world while I look. I look through my eyes, and see out there— something. But what?

Confronting the Externals

I see a vague field, an indistinct ground, a background which confronts me, and surrounds me. This undeciphered scenery presents me with figures, questionable apparitions, whose significance I must figure out. I unmistakably see something sensible yonder, but the "something" is not yet a "thing." Solid reality does not appear already assembled, but shines through ciphers. The thing emerges from the sensible manifold during creative perception; substance emerges during hermeneutic construction. My body dwells in a perceptual field traversed with routes, running in every direction. As my body makes its way along these paths, the thing appears as the goal toward which I travel; and the goal shows itself through the sensible appearances which I confront along the way. My way of moving adjusts to the way in which the thing appears, as my body moves toward a reality which lies always farther on. Perception is a bodily activity which uses my sense organs as instruments for moving through the world; the embodied mind goes beyond the given. Along my path I confront sensations, but because I experience these on the way toward the thing, I do not normally experience the sensations as, themselves, things; sensations are something which I encounter on my way toward the thing, when the thing

2

comes forth to meet me along the way. Sense receptivity is not distinguishable from perception, because sensation takes place within the perceptual field. Ordinarily we do not sense sensations; we sense sensible things which appear in a certain way. A sensible appearance is a mode in which the thing appears; we encounter sensations when we take the mode as itself a thing; sensation becomes distinct from perception when we take the sensible appearances out of their original context, when we isolate the parts from the whole. The vague background becomes more specific as we move forward, and the sensational foreground becomes more generalized, generating definite substances in the middle range. The sensible something which we see out there is an uncultivated world, which has a vague background, a sensational foreground, and sensible things which gradually emerge as we make our way forward, back into the background. The bewildering world, this wilderness, is already being cultivated in natural perception.

Appearances present themselves during a continuous perceptual activity, and already have a direction and a meaning, since they come forward on the path along whose length we are toiling. We are always already on the way. We are not first given raw data from which we afterwards produce things useful for daily life. Following Merleau-Ponty we shall argue against the intellectualist philosophers, who say that the living subject constructs external objects through intellectual judgment. We do not deny that we can construct an objective world; we only insist that thought presupposes an original experience in which sensibles already have a sense not imposed from above. Merleau-Ponty argues also against the empiricist philosophers, who say that in perception objects assemble automatically through association. We do not deny that the subject can experience sensations associating and dissociating with a certain regularity; but we insist that our body knows how to make its way through the world, even when the disembodied mind knows nothing except ideas. The passive spectator knows only the phantasmal atoms that flit before his eyes. When we put our mind in gear, and gear in with the externals, we learn what our body knows already; our mind learns on the job, as we bodily work our way into the world. We experience the things longitudinally, or transversally. Both empiricism and intellectualism are wrong when they suppose that we originally experience the world as a mass of raw sense data. Consequently, neither does our mind actively judge these data, nor is our mind passive while the data associate themselves. Originally our mind is embodied, and our body is already underway. Original experience is engaged speculation.

The Sensation

Do we ever encounter sensations? Is there, distinct from perception, a sensory experience where sensibles appear without a perceptual field? We could cite empirical studies which demonstrate that a stimulated subject experiences discrete sensory impacts, but these perceptual situations are artificial. The psychologist conducting the experiment contrives to isolate the subject from his normal field of operation. The denatured experimental subject is like the diseased person who sees spots before his eyes, or hears ringing in his ears. We experience sense data when we stumble in the dark, or receive a blow on the head; we experience sense data as modifications in the body subject. A pure sensation would be something like that greyness which surrounds me when I close my eyes, and that buzzing which sounds make in my head when I get drowsy. Such phenomena have no place in the objective world; sensations are located on the hither side of perceived qualities. Qualities are normally experienced as outside my body; two colors cannot be distinguished unless they are seen as forming a picture before me, even though their place within the picture is not precise.[1] The only sensibles that we experience without a perceptual field are modifications in our body beneath the skin, but empiricists and intellectualists have understood the sense datum as paradigmatically a color patch or a lighted surface hovering before our eyes, not something in our eyes. Even if the datum is objectively a retinal stimulus, we do not experience the sensation as internal. Everything which we see before our face already figures against a background, and thus already has a meaning, because the sensible seen in context leads our gaze beyond the focal figure. The background, or field, is not just a vacuous space or a neutral backing. The sensibles located within this space display their contours against the ground, and establish directions through the surroundings. A movement in one place shifts vectors throughout the entirety, because the whole surpasses the sum of its parts.[2]

The sensation understood as a bodily modification is something which we experience daily, but, understood as something yonder which confronts us, the sensation is not so familiar. We frontally experience sensational surfaces during organic breakdown, and also when a scientific technician artificially isolates us from our normal environment. Also, there are techniques whereby we can manipulate ourselves, cutting ourselves off from our habitat and breaking the world up into parts. We can reflect analytically upon our original experience and separate the sensible figures from their ground; analysis breaks down the originally perceived things and lets us reconstruct them as objects; analysis also breaks down my body into special senses. Sense perception is originally unspecialized; I perceive the same

5

world through all my sense organs. Suppose however that I localize my perceptual activity in my eyeballs, and thereby specialize perception as vision. Suppose that I am seated in my study, looking at the white paper scattered over the desk top; some sheets lie in the light shed through the window, others lie in shadow. "If I do not analyze my perception but content myself with the spectacle as a whole, I shall say that all the sheets of paper look equally white."[3] However, within the whole, I see a contrast between those white sheets lying in the light and those in shadow; hence I wonder whether the shaded sheets are not less white than the rest. I look more closely and fix my gaze upon the sheets in question; the visual field narrows down to my fixed focal point; perhaps my eyelids close to a slit, or perhaps I look through a match-box lid which separates the sheets from their surroundings, or through a window in a cardboard, called a "reduction screen."[4] Whether I use a mechanical device, or simply manage my body so that the naked eye assumes an analytical posture, the paper under scrutiny changes its appearance. "This is no longer white paper over which a shadow is cast, but a grey or steely blue substance, thick and not definitely localized."[5] We now see an external sense datum. If we again look over the whole visual field, we see that the shadowed sheets never were quite the same color as the sheets lying in the light, nor yet were they a different color; the shadowed whiteness cannot be fixed precisely along an objective scale graded from dark to light; the shadowed white was originally experienced as indeterminate. The determinate color appeared when I fixed my gaze upon a single point within the visual field. "Then and then only have I found before myself a certain *quale* which absorbs my gaze."[6]

Originally my gaze surveys the whole scene. I see the overall lighting, and see the various sheets in light of this illumination. My gaze stops wandering over the scene along the light when I direct my mind toward my gaze and ask what precisely is envisioned; the visible becomes precise only when I ask this critical question. I look at the world critically, either because I fear making a mistake, or because "I want to undertake a scientific study of the spectacle presented."[7] I experience "the quality, the separate sensory impact,"[8] only when I break the living bond between my body and the world. The visual ray is an umbilical cord which analysis severs. When the seer reflects upon his own body, and assumes the critical stance, "the world is atomized into sensible qualities."[9] The sensibles are separated from the perceptual field, just when the spectator himself is separated from his surroundings. The isolated spectator is no longer an embodied subject, but a pure vision.[10]

Original Sense Experience

Is sense perception our original experience? And does sensible apparition reveal original reality? Along with the empiricists and empirical realists, Merleau-Ponty believes that sense perception is psychologically primary. He would deny that our first experience is intellectual, and that we have fallen into bodies, where we must gradually recall our original condition. Most idealists admit that sense experience has psychological primacy, at least during embodied life; however, all insist that intellectual experience has prime importance for ontology. Initially our mind is entranced with the sensible surroundings, but this native environment is less knowable and less real than the ideal realm; the rationalist regards thought as a regressive movement from sense perception toward pure reason; the sensible world disguises an ideal reality which is fully actual in the empyrean; the thinker must withdraw from the delusory externals, and ascend to intelligible heights.[11] Though our author rejects this withdrawn interiority, he does admit a degradation which obscures our vision; we have not fallen from heaven to earth, but we do fall into everyday routines which conceal our native condition. Acquired habits make us forget our natural habitat. Repeated perception produces stereotypes, schemas, which we utilize without renewed insight; our easy competence in handling cultural accretion raises us above untutored experience. This artificial elevation explains the rationalist belief that ideas are primary. We fall into verbal routines which raise our mind to such a height that the return to original experience seems a fall from rationality.

Original experience is sense perception, but sensation embodies a primitive intelligibility. Hence original sense experience is not purely sensational; the empiricist analysis distorts perception. Analysis becomes a disease when we make artificial divisions in the natural continuum. Not every division is unnatural, since nature solicits some distinctions while discouraging others, but expressive analysis becomes perverted if we isolate the parts from the whole where they arise. The straightforward analysis which cuts nature into artificial segments is one disease, and reflexive analysis is another; reflection takes the natural segments into the mental closet and shuts the door. The straightforward and the reflexive maladies are mutually reinforcing, since an artificial division within nature cuts us off from nature, and something cut off from nature becomes artificial even though the division was once spontaneous. Also, analysis requires that we confront the world, and confrontation requires that we draw back from our environment; this withdrawal can easily become a pathological shrinkage in the phenomenal body. Sickness is unnatural, in the sense that the organism goes against nature; disease is natural only in the sense that pathological phenomena take place

8

within nature; disease is natural contingency gone astray. Galloping analysis has its being within nature, but not according to nature; analytical reflection breaks nature down into parts, and this operation is a pathological breakdown within the life world. Diseased empiricism divides nature into sensations and isolates these particles from the original background. Intellectualism takes the psychological atoms and discovers within our ego the intelligibles which harmonize the sensibles. The intellectualist move is fallacious, because sensations are cultural artifacts not often found in nature. Within a healthy natural life, sensations make sense; they are not senseless fragments which require an intellect to impose intelligibility from above, nor do they require an empirical mechanism for assembling them into a world, a fanciful assemblage which we instinctually suppose to be intelligible. Philosophical sickness is not incurable, because organic breakdown is a natural event which nature itself can conquer; nature is a doctor which doctors itself, sometimes through scientific agency. In our natural habitat we do make mistakes, and experience doubt; science then pieces together our fragmented experience, in the hope that the shards will coalesce. Or science, having experienced doubt, and fearing future errors, takes apart our experience in advance, repairs any defective parts, and reassembles the organism, hoping that no damage has been done during analysis. Also, when we have time on our hands, we sometimes experience a healthy curiosity about how things work. If we understand health not negatively as the absence of its negation but positively as the ability to overcome disease, we see that scientific thinking represents a primal urge. The doctor does not simply bind up wounds; he is a pioneer who actively risks breakdown, in order to discover latent powers.

How would analytical reflection be possible, if our

healthy organs did not sometimes experience the world as sensational? Does not nature sometimes call for impressionist painting, which analyzes the world into color patches? Empiricism would not be so plausible unless the world spontaneously exhibited phenomena like the empiricists manufacture. We rightly reject the thoroughgoing empiricism which analyzes the originally experienced world into a sensational chaos, leaving the wandering troop to shift for itself, and against the thoroughgoing intellectualism which puts the parts together in an objective whole constructed according to concepts. But we would wrongly conclude that original experience is thoroughly synthetic. We may justifiably learn to see the world as a picture, or an art work. How indeed would artistic expression be possible if we did not sometimes experience the world as possessing sensuous coherence? But the world is not always an aesthetic whole; sometimes the center does not hold, and things come apart; we are confronted with bits and pieces which make no sense, and we can make of them what we will. The empiricists are considering the evidence when they talk about sense data, but not all the evidence; plainly we do experience relations and relational fields. Our empiricism must be more radical, and not uproot those organic sensibles which evidentially do have roots running through the earth.

How then should we describe original sense experience? Do the originally perceived sensibles appear in a void, or do they appear against a background? Do they float free, or do they have ties which bind them to the earth, and ground them? Both. We suggest that original experience is both sensational and sensuous. Sometimes the empiricists do not manufacture their objects, but simply describe what they see, not through narrowed lids, but through wide-open eyes; the sensational chaos permits intellectual imposition, technical manipulation, and fanciful contrivance; psychological atoms are meaningless in themselves and call for organization from outside. Nonetheless, the perceptual field has some inherent sense, though it also possesses non-significance, where its paths work at cross-purposes; the meaning within the perceptual field is ambiguous; the inner organization never quite works itself out. Original experience includes both sensuous ambiguity and sensational chaos. Thus imagination is sometimes a fanciful activity; the idle mind puts together sensations in irrational combinations which amuse us during mental holidays. But imagination is sometimes serious work; artistic expression lets us thread our way through the perceptual field so that we take root and live there. Because he ignores creative imagination, the empiricist never inhabits the land, never takes personal possession, nor does the rationalist. The thinker is an exile on earth, a stranger in a land which he never appropriates. His art object is a toy which entertains our lower faculties, while we while away our life imprisonment, doing easy time. The artist however is more than a craftsman, a scientific investigator, or an edifying illustrator. Artistry is a work in which meaning emerges from the soil; art is a creative expression which makes this body mine, and makes this house my domicile. Earthly art prolongs nature, utilizing a natural body which is already at home in the world. This productive insight which makes things mine, and makes me a thing, is imaginal perception.

Without denying the possibility of chaotic upsurge, we shall follow Merleau-Ponty in his affirmations, describing sense perception as a coherent activity which makes a human pathway through the sensible world. We shall encounter sensations along the way, lighted surfaces which block our gaze; benumbing obstacles will trip us. But we shall press forward, watching for the moment when the opaque becomes pellucid. We want to keep our feet on the ground,

11

and see what can be done with these hands, and understand what can be seen with these eyes down here, which behind their lids hide from the things, and then seek them out. A world in which we do not blink, a world without doors that open and shut, a world without perspectives, is not the world in which we live, when we resolve not to take flight, but to get a view through.

Sensory Specialization

We want to describe in isolation the various layers which decompress from the background and come forth from the horizon, so we can afterwards describe how they overlap and lead us back into depth. Perception slices reality in many ways; we experience temporal layers, and spatial layers; we get glimpses from close up and from far away, from this angle and that. Moreover, each sense organ has its own way of modulating the field, its characteristic perceptual operation, its proper perspective; we want to describe the special sensibles isolated by the different senses; this description will enable us to understand all sensory specialization. What does speciality mean when we speak about the sensibles and their senses? A special sensible is "special," meaning that the common sensible is specialized as a particular appearance. But also, "special" means that the sensible is specific to a particular sense. The sense too is "special," meaning that it is a specialization of a more common sense, and meaning also that the sense is specific to a special sensible. A special sense specifies a special sensible; the special visual sense specifies, or picks out, all the various visual sensibles. A particular special sense or sensible is always a species which could be more specialized than it actually is. We see colors and shapes, and among colors we see red and blue; a blue sensible is a particular within the species of visual sensibles. The blue sensible is itself a species; this particular species is a present blue patch which incorporates absent blue patches; the blue sensible therefore is seen everywhere, whenever we see anything blue. Blueness can indeed be further specialized as just this present blue patch, but even this particularized patch is potentially a species, since our vision can be made more precise, when we look through a microscope and see blue specks which were previously invisible, but which an insect can pick out with his native optics. In everyday life we often specify whether we touch something, or see it; but we seldom specify whether we see with the rods or the cones, or see it with the right eye or the left. However we can easily imagine a situation in which a distinction between dexter vision and sinister vision would be practical; for example, we might be testing binoculars. Every special sense and sensible is a species separate from every other species at that level, but the level shifts constantly: one moment I perceive something just through the visual sense, but the next moment I perceive that thing also through the tactile sense, so that vision and touch merge as a more common sense; simultaneously, the special visual sensible merges with the special tactile sensible, and the experienced sensible becomes less specific.

How should we number the senses? Everyday opinion specifies five: we have a visual sense, a tactile sense, an auditory sense, an olfactory sense, and a gustatory sense. This enumeration is obvious, and adequate, though a more profound consideration would note the kinaesthetic sense which operates in all the sense organs. The five senses are specializations of the living body; the body serves as the common sense which unifies the various receptors. The fact that we perceive through a single body is ordinarily too obvious for comment, but we do comment, almost daily, upon the distinction among the senses, as when we see a

13

blind man. The normal subject in his everyday experience lacks no human sense, but he does experience his senses as separable, since he cares for his eyes and ears, and fingers. We all experience momentary blindness when we blink, and a momentary paralysis when our hands are tied up in a task; when we shut our eyes we cannot perceive color, and when our hands are tied we cannot touch the texture which we see across the room.

Certain sensibles, such as size and shape, can be perceived through more than one sense. We can see large square things, and also touch them; we see size and shape when we see large square color patches, just as we feel size and shape when we touch large square textured surfaces. Moreover, we can see texture, though texture can be reduced to size and shape, if we regard roughness as miniature shapes spread with a certain pattern across a surface. Size and shape mediate between sight and touch whenever we see the surface that our fingers feel. Since extension is not specific to sight or touch, we could postulate a sixth sense, somewhere behind our hands and eyes, which perceives the common sensibles, with our hands and eyes as intermediaries. The additional sense would be a mental faculty, since the mind is the organ for form, but would be a lower mental faculty, since the forms here are sensible. The eyes and hands, without the sixth sense, would perceive altogether formless visual and tactile sensibles, or else would perceive specialized forms; our eyes would perceive specifically visual shape and size, while our hands would perceive specifically tactile forms; only the sixth sense would be able to perceive the formal likeness between seen and touched form. Or perhaps we need not postulate an additional sense; seen form and touched form simply associate themselves in our experience until their conjunction becomes habitual; after a while, we blindly anticipate a

14

tactile form whenever we see a visual form; sure enough, our expectation is usually fulfilled. Visual shape and tactile shape we call "shape," because the two are constantly conjoined in our experience, and breaking a habit is difficult. But does associationism render intellectual insight otiose? Surely we perceive a certain likeness between visual shape and tactile shape; these two sensibles have in common at least their likeness, and then their shape.

SYNERGY

When we stand at the threshold of the world, confronting the externals, we perceive specialized apparitions, disconnected profiles; but, when we enter the world, we see that the sensible externals appear in layers, ranging in depth from the special to the common. All sensibles, without exception, appear within the natural world, a showplace whose boundary is the outermost horizon. This outer limit binds the apparitions into community, making them all exhibit a unitary nature. Located within the widest horizon are numberless specialized worlds, which have their own horizons. Each sense has its distinctive world, a place which displays the sensibles specific to a single sensory mode. All the specialized spheres interpenetrate within the most global world, and their horizons overlap within the horizon of horizons. Also, the various sensibles overlap, and pile up in layers; sensibles appearing in one world overlap upon sensibles appearing within another; one world overlaps its horizon with another world horizon and penetrates into the foreign sphere, merging alien sensibles as common impressions. Within the most comprehensive world, there is continual compression and decompression: special sensibles pile up and compress themselves into a single slice, while common sensibles decompress into separate layers, slices which diverge from their backing and wander aimlessly in the foreground. Some sensations settle down and take root, establishing routes which disappear into depth; when the forward sensibles press against the earth for support, the background becomes a perceptual field. Once we are initiated into the world, once we traverse the field before us, our initial perceptions acquire coherence; our sense organs find a common aim, and work together with a single purpose.

Communion Among Species

Man himself is a "*sensorium commune*,"[12] says Merleau-Ponty. Doubtless we can connect isolated sensibles by intellectual synthesis, and by automatic association, but originally we inhabit nature without employing these rational and empirical faculties. "My body is a ready-made system of equivalents and transpositions from one sense to another. The senses translate each other without any need of an interpreter...."[13] The body does not merely connect tactile shape with visible shape; vision communicates with all the senses. In my body "the visual and auditory experiences, for example, are pregnant one with the other."[14] Visual sense experience is a potentiality for auditory experience, and audition is already vision. However, these potentialities reside in my body, not in my eyes and ears considered in separation; the specifically visual sense experience is the potency for another specific sensation only insofar as visual experience is a specialization of sense experience as a whole; vision is equivalent to another special sense only because the visual sense specializes the common sense; the sensorium is reversibly visual and auditory. This interchangeability means that the sensorium can withdraw from

16

specialization as visual and become specialized as auditory; the sensorium is sometimes specialized as a single sense, but not often; normally it is differentiated as five senses, entering into each sense in different degrees; the visual and tactile senses are more sensitive than the others, more so, certainly, than smell and taste. When the sensorium is normally differentiated, it is only potentially reversible; it is simultaneously present in all the special senses, but has the ability to fluctuate among its modes. The common sense is reversible, and is also a system through which its specializations convert themselves into one another; our body is a reversible interchange through which the specializations are systematically interchangeable.

The sensorium commune faces a cosmos, not a chaos of specifics. Indeed, the special senses are specifiable "only against the background of a common world."[15] When I try to perceive through a single sense, and try to perceive through that sense a single sensible within the species specific to that sense, the special sensible suddenly disappears as figure and appears as a ground from which the sensing is no longer distinct. For example, suppose that through the visual sense I perceive the sky above, and try to see only its blueness; just as I succeed, the blue dome is no longer a sensible, but has become my momentary world. And just then, I am no longer aware that my seeing is sight; when perception is totally specialized as vision, sight becomes total perception.[16] Ordinarily the world displays its solidity through sensibles specific to various senses, and this sensible specialization enables me to specify vision as separate from other perceptual modes. We can understand the interchangeability among the special senses as an equivalence within a common world, but communion in the world requires a corresponding communion in the body. For example, the special visual sense is interchangeably auditory, since I can see auditory sensibles; looking at this goblet held in my hand, I can see the crash and tinkling which I will hear when I let the glass drop; the visual sensible activates the body, which systematically equates the seen sight with the heard sound, and enables us to see the noise. The noise might be invisible if we lacked ears, but because we have auditory organs, vision is transformed. The sensible thing is reversibly visible and audible; consequently the common sense equates vision with hearing. The special senses are equivalent to one another, not when isolated, but when united within a system, a bodily interchange for intentional energy. The body is a common percipient which makes the senses into a community. Within this societal system, the senses are equivalent to one another; they have equal value as specializations of the sentient body, and they perceive sensibles which have equal value as specializations of the sensible world.

This equivalence, this equal value, does not mean identity; when we say that the visual sense is equivalent to the tactile sense, we do not mean that vision is indistinguishable from touch. The visual and tactile senses can be isolated so that each perceives a distinctive species. One special sense is different from another, but the common sense remains identical with itself in all its specializations; in each mode the common sense is the same, but with a difference. The common sense which is specialized as vision is identical with the sensorium which is specialized as touch; the common sense is nonidentical with itself only insofar as it is specialized, and it is not specialized far enough to destroy the primitive communion; the body preserves its identity despite the differentiations. Seeing is different from touching, even though we can see a cube as well as touch it; a cube is not exclusively tactile, but its visibility is different from its tactility. Seeing a cube is not identical with touching a cube, and a cube as seen is not identical with a cube as touched; yet the cube we see is the very same cube we touch. A seen cube is a touched cube transposed into another key; a viewed cube is the same as a handled cube, and yet different, just as a melody played in another key is the same as that melody played in the first key, and yet different. Identity in difference we can also describe as translation: a seen cube is a touched cube translated into another language; the visual language expresses the same cube that the tactile language expresses, but differently, in a different language. A translation from one language to another, and a transposition from one key to another, is systematic. The common sensorium incarnates the system of equivalents, or the system of exchanges.[17]

The cube, then, appears interchangeably through visual sensibles and tactile sensibles, while our body perceives interchangeably through the visual sense and the tactile sense; perception requires an interchange in the thing, in the world, and a corresponding interchange in the body. This communion among the special sensibles, and among the special senses, operates when we perceive the cube, and also when we perceive the cubical shape. Analysis clearly differentiates "tactile shape" and "visual shape." How can we unify these two sense data as a single phenomenon? Empiricism notices that the two presentations are similar, and notes that the similar givens are constantly conjoined in experience; this repeated joint presentation produces a habitual association; finally we ignore the difference between the two and carelessly identify them, calling both by the same name, "shape." The rationalist says that the two sense data are similar because they have a common property; "tactile shape" is "tactile," and "visual shape" is "visual," but "tactile shape" and "visual shape" are similar because both are "shapes"; the universal "shape" is identical in

19

both data, but different because of the sensory specialization. Through sight and touch we perceive only the difference, but our mind notices the identity; the formal identity is not merely nominal, but real, at least in the mind. Merleau-Ponty, however, would reply that our senses differentiate touched shape and seen shape only within a perceived unity; we perceive the identity in the difference and the difference in the identity. Once we have reflectively isolated the tactile datum from the visual, we can no doubt discover a sensible similarity, or find an intelligible universality; but we originally experience tactile shape as shape, while perceiving visual shape as shape exhibited in another mode; because we do not originally isolate tactile shape from visual shape, we do not require an empirical association or a rational insight to identify them. Analysis demands a middle term for its identification, but originally the human body is the middle term which mediates the extremes; the body is a living syllogism whose leading principle is its behavioral style.

Vision communicates with touch when we perceive the cube, and also when we perceive the cubical shape. Because the cubical shape is the shape of the cube, some thinkers have concluded that the cube is essentially shape, or figure and extension. Vision and touch intercommunicate when we see shape, but vision does not communicate with hearing, or taste, because we cannot hear shape, or savor it. Objective thought says that sight and touch show us the material object while hearing displays only detachable properties, the nonessential sensibles. Admittedly, sight and touch are the most objective senses, because they locate the object at a definite distance from our face, whereas hearing, and smell, show us qualities which surround us, and penetrate our body like a flavor; sight and touch are the senses which can objectify the thing before us, eliminating

20

the atmospheric qualities which escape a circumscribed location. But why should we suppose that the objectifying senses show us the essence of matter? Though we cannot hear shape, we can hear the sounds which issue from cubes, and from other solid objects which are sonorous when struck; the material thing appears as truly through auditory sensibles as through the tactile and visual. A thing which is heard seems more solid, more substantial, than a thing which is merely seen and touched; substantiality is essentially depth, apparitional plenitude; the auditory sensibles, the olfactory and gustatory too, show us the material essence. Moreover, color shows us the essence, even though we do not touch color; although color is intangible, sight communicates with touch when we perceive a colored polyhedron; we see the color and touch the hardness, or softness, but we employ the same body in both sensory operations, and the two senses disclose the same solid. The cube is interchangeably hard and colored; the tactile sensible and the visual sensible have equal value as disclosures of the thing before us; the hard shape and the visible color are equivalent; and likewise the color and the visible shape.

But is hardness, after all, invisible, and color intangible? Perhaps we can see a touched hardness just as we can see a touched rectangularity; perhaps we can see a bitter taste, or see a loud sound. If we lacked a common sensorium, this poetic vision would be impossible; we cannot see sound and taste when the visual sense is artificially isolated from the other receptors; a dissociated sense can perceive only its specific sensibles. But, because our senses specialize a unitary body, we can accomplish what prosaic science deems absurd. Our sense organs work together in a world whose apparitions communicate along tangled circuits, unsuspected pathways. We wish to describe synaesthesia, an ex-

21

perience wherein the synergetic body wanders freely through the backwoods, uncovering hidden affinities.

Synaesthesia

The body has specialized sense organs; each receptor perceives a sensible, or a species of sensibles, specific to that organ alone. The eyes see colors; the ears hear sounds; the fingertips feel temperatures. Each sensible property is appropriated by a specific sense; the visual sense appropriates visual sensibles, not tactile sensibles, and not auditory sensibles, while the tactile sense too has an appropriate operation. But hardness is not always invisible, and color not always intangible. We can see the same polyhedron that we touch; and a touched rectangularity can be seen. Our senses intercommunicate also through the superficial qualities; we sometimes can see the hardness that we touch, and touch the color that we see, or see the sound that we hear. When we are careless, or carefree, our senses violate the proprieties; our uncritical organs appropriate nonspecific sensibles, qualities meant specifically for other receptors.

Superficial and deep synaesthetic insight. Empirical psychologists have produced synaesthetic experience in the laboratory; one technique is to feed a person mescalin. The drugged subject uncritically submits to the things perceived; he cannot stabilize things as scientific objects; his gaze wanders about in submission to his bodily "vitality."[18] Under the influence of this drug, "the sound of a flute gives a bluish-green color."[19] The investigators call this odd experience "synaesthesia," but the name implies an empiricist understanding of the phenomenon if we mean "a conjunction between sensations." The empiricist would say that, under mescalin, the subject experiences a "flutish sounding sensible" together with a "bluish-green looking sensible,"

22

or, less specifically, an auditory sensible together with a visual sensible. This description is inadequate, "*for the subject does not only say that he has the sensation both of a sound and a color: it is the sound itself that he sees where colors are formed.*"[20] The person who hears the flute does not merely sense a special auditory sensible through the auditory sense and conjointly perceive a visual sensible through the visual sense. The empiricist has defined visual perception as exclusively the interaction between visual sense and visual sensible; Merleau-Ponty wants to revise this definition, "since the sight of sounds and the hearing of colors exist as phenomena."[21] The phenomena are not even unusual, says Merleau-Ponty; average everyday experience is synaesthetic; empirical science has altered our sensibility "so that we have unlearned how to see, hear, and generally speaking, feel."[22] Of course, we do not see sounds in the specific way that we hear sounds; eyes are not ears; rather, we see the sound through its color; we see a color in the place where we hear the sound; the color appears as a quality of the noise. We might say that the auditory quality and the visual quality both qualify the same spatial location and merge there as a single sensible, except for the fact that the sound is externally stimulated while the color is a hallucination arising through sympathetic vibration; because of this fact, the auditory quality appears as the substance; the sound occupies the spatial locus as a substratum for additional qualification. The sound evokes the color, because noise has a certain intensity, a certain vibratory energy, which stimulates the common sensorium and invades the nonspecific senses by contagion; the visual sense vibrates at the dominant frequency and generates the color which contains the same level of sensory energy. The hallucinatory color is perceived as the color of the sound because the green is the visual embodiment of the sensory

23

ALBRIGHT COLLEGE LIBRARY 182199

energy contained in the noise; auditory vibration is qualified as color through the sensorium which harmonizes the eyes with the ears.

Let us consider the synaesthetic experience produced in another experiment. Suppose we show a movie and provide background music. When the subject concentrates his attention on the lighted surface, the audible accompaniment is not definitely localized in external space, but becomes an atmospheric sound which ranges between the visible scene and the subjective body; the sound becomes an "accent"[23] which indicates the direction from which the stimulus emanates. "An audible rhythm causes cinematograph pictures to run together and produces a perception of movement whereas, without auditory support, the same succession of images would be too slow to give rise to stroboscopic movement."[24] When the auditory sensibles invade the common sensorium, their phenomenal intensity stimulates the visual sense, augmenting the rhythm already operative in the eyeball. Sound modifies motion, and also color: when we show consecutive color images, "a louder note intensifies them, the interruption of the sound produces a wavering effect in them, and a low note makes blue darker or deeper."[25] The common element which communicates between vision and audition is not shape, not external form, but rhythm, a patterned energy. The sensuous form, the material essence, is the apparitional style; the inner essence of matter is style, not extension or figure. Shape too appears with a certain style; shape is fundamentally the patterned presentation of shape; shape echoes the apparitional rhythm of qualities which possess no contours. More fundamental than external figure is presentational pattern.

When the drugged subject sees sounds, the auditory sensibles do not stimulate the eyes directly; the sensorium modifies the sound, changing the sound into a color that

24

vibrates at the same frequency. Science has taught us to ignore these sensory fringes which haunt the directly perceived sensibles, but synaesthesia is an everyday experience; the drugs merely amplify this experience to hallucinatory intensity. We daily hear bright sounds and dull sounds; we see muted colors, shrill yellows, screaming vermillions. Red is a loud color which a painter can tone down. We can tell a blind man that red is like the sound of a trumpet, because a trumpet sounds red. Further, we can see gustatory qualities: we see acid greens and sweet pinks; green and pink agitate our taste buds, which communicate their verdict to the eyes. The sweetness which we see is not quite the sweetness tasted; we taste sweetness directly, but we see the sweetness of a color indirectly through the weak hallucination that the pervasive kinaesthetic vibration generates in our tongue. Likewise, when we see a red surface, the visible loudness is not precisely the loudness that we hear when assaulted by a bugler; the loudness of a loud sound is the quality most properly called loudness, but we weakly hallucinate a loud sound when we see a sensational redness; the auditory image merges with the visual, and we hear the color; we hear the sound of the color in the place where the color is seen. A red flash and a trumpet blast exhibit the same level of sensory violence, a perceptual energy which the ears express as a sound and the eyes express as a sight, whether we see a loud color or hear a red hot sound, or a hot red sound. With our ears, functioning as specializations of the common sense, we hear loud colors and colorful tunes. We can hear colors without hearing a sonorous object which is also colored, though a trumpet viewed under ruddy illumination would sound louder, or warmer.

We have described a synaesthesia which delves into the world, but not very deeply; this superficial synaesthesia

25

does not disclose the essence of things, only the essence of qualities. We can see loud colors, but not everything that looks loud sounds loud: a loud red cushion sounds soft when I drop it on the floor; the cushion resounds softly, makes a soft sound. The sound is more deeply revealing than the color; the cushion feels soft when I touch it; the soft sound conveys the soft tactile properties. But not everything that sounds soft feels soft: a purring electrical motor is fashioned from hard steel. A lemon tastes acidic when we drink its juice, and the skin is acid yellow; but not everything colored like a lemon tastes acidic: a lemon yellow auto tastes metallic, or dusty, if we lick the fender. Despite the testimony of direct taste, we should not deny that the yellow paint looks acidic; we should not argue that the painted fender makes us pucker merely because the yellow is lemon yellow and we remember the taste of lemons while looking at the car, though such association doubtless can occur. Red looks loud whether decorating a pillow or a fire engine; the loud color may be conjoined with a loud siren, and acid yellow may be conjoined with acidic pulp. Cezanne said that "one ought to be able to paint even odors."[26] Of course, the painter uses smelly pigment, but the paint which we smell is not the smell which we paint. To paint an odor, a classical painter would select an odorous object and then represent the thing so accurately that the image evokes olfactory reminiscence. But a modern painter would select a color which activates our superficial synaesthetic faculty; if blue has a smell, we need not represent an object which is blue and smelly; the painter can discover the smell of blueness by spreading pigment nonobjectively within the visual field. However, the smell of blue might conceivably be displayed in a blue object which exhibits an identical smell when sniffed. Once acid yellow is conjoined with an acidic fruit, a deeper synaesthesia emerges, a perception which pene-

26

trates into the depths of the material thing. A lemon painted blue does not retain its natural taste, though a blue
lemon tasted with the eyes shut tastes the same as a yellow
lemon tasted with the eyes shut. Superficial synaesthesia
can deceive us about the hidden qualities of a thing, when
something has a hard look but feels soft, or looks soft but
feels hard, like a plaster layer cake. We are deceived because we let the surface qualities lead us into depth; but we
always develop expectations about inner reality, and we are
not always misled. When nature disappoints us, and reveals
the qualities as mere surface phenomena, we find other
qualities which suggest new routes into the world. When we
bodily explore a material reality, employing all our organs,
we develop a deeper synaesthesia which shows us the inner
essence; the superficial qualities give way before our body
and direct us toward the deepest truth.

Merleau-Ponty describes several everyday synaesthetic
experiences which reveal an inner essence. The empiricist
notices only surface color, and describes colored scenes as a
play across breadth. According to the empiricist, vision
perceives specifically color and light; lighted color displays
shape, which outlines the colored area; when extended and
figured colors change position, we see movement; the visible world is a panorama flitting across a screen. Merleau-
Ponty replies that we see some colors which are transparent,
others which are muddy; these sensibles we experience as
outward appearances of an inner structure. The visible
color reveals an intersensory reality; the outer visibility is a
special modification which reveals the qualified object as
richer than its mode. Merleau-Ponty says every color, if
deeply perceived, displays overtly the inner structure of
some definite object. "The brilliance of gold palpably holds
out to us its homogeneous composition, and the dull color
of wood its heterogeneous make-up."[27] Vision perceives

hard colors, hard surfaces, and hard objects; the objects are revealed through hard surfaces, and hard coloration overlaid with a hard sheen. "One sees the hardness and brittleness of glass, and when, with a tinkling sound, it breaks, this sound is conveyed by the visible glass."[28] Vision perceives tactile qualities such as softness and flexibility. "One sees the springiness of steel, the ductility of red-hot steel, the hardness of a plane blade, the softness of shavings."[29] Visual sensibles reveal the deeper reality, because the form or structure of an object is not its outer geometry; the structure is an inner specific nature which makes the object a common sensible, something accessible through all the senses; the geometrical shape is merely the outer manifestation of a secret constitution. "The form of a fold in linen or cotton shows us the resilience or dryness of the fiber, the coldness or warmth of the material."[30] Having described how colored light and lighted color, along with shape, show forth a hidden essence, Merleau-Ponty speaks about visible motion. "The movement of visible objects is not the mere transference from place to place of colored patches which, in the visual field, correspond to these objects."[31] The visual field opens our perception toward the tactile field, and discloses distinct regions of tactility. "In the jerk of a twig from which a bird has just flown, we read its flexibility or elasticity, and it is thus that a branch of an apple-tree or a birch are immediately distinguishable."[32] Motion within the visible panorama discloses "the weight of a block of cast iron which sinks in the sand, the fluidity of water and the viscosity of syrup."[33] Still speaking implicitly about movement, our author turns from visual sensation to auditory: through the special auditory sense I perceive tactile sensibles, just as I do through the visual sense. "I hear the hardness and unevenness of cobbles in the rattle of a carriage, and we speak appropriately of a 'soft,' 'dull' or 'sharp' sound."[34] The hard stones issue a sharp staccato when the hard steel rims strike sharply and repeatedly upon the paved expanse. The auditory field is less revelatory than the visual and tactile spheres; we "may doubt whether the sense of hearing brings us genuine 'things;' " nonetheless we are "certain that it presents us, beyond the sounds in space, with something which 'murmurs,' and in this way communicates with the other senses."[35] Even though sounds do not reveal the definite location of the sonorous object, these stimuli open the auditory field into the wider world, enabling us to locate and circumscribe the sound source by sight and touch. Touch, unlike hearing, does reveal genuine things when operating independently. "If, with my eyes closed, I bend a steel bar and a lime branch, I perceive in my hands the most essential texture of the metal and the wood."[36] Empiricists and intellectualists have believed that tactile shape and size, along with visual, give us unique access to the object, whose essential structure is extension. Merleau-Ponty replies that an object shows its structure in every appearance. Each sense has a perspective which penetrates the heart of reality.[37]

When a special sense is destroyed by external accident, or isolated by internal volition, we receive clear evidence that the senses intercommunicate through a common sensorium, because perception shows a structural change. For instance, when the special olfactory sense is lacking, the gustatory sense is transformed. Taste, of course, is secretly a taste plus an associated smell, but the combination alters the structure of the special senses which are combined. We witness a similar transformation when I voluntarily specialize one of my senses; the selected sense is cultivated at the expense of other senses, whose powers diminish. A merely seen sight is clearly visible, but does not look the same as something which is both seen and heard, because

29

isolated vision does not vibrate sympathetically with an auditory input. However, a visual artist brings other senses into play when he paints a spectacle; he may evoke auditory or tactile sensations; he does this by stimulating superficial synaesthesia, or he may trigger habitual associations. In a painting, something may look hard because the object is so realistically represented that our hands get ready to touch the depicted contours; we dimly hallucinate the tactile sensible which we would feel if we were actually able to reach into the picture. Fundamentally, though, painting does not evoke tactile values. Instead, "it gives visible existence to what profane vision believes to be invisible; thanks to it we do not need a 'muscular sense' in order to possess the voluminosity of the world."[38] The structure of vision is changed by our past tactile experience, so that vision shows us tactility even when the opportunity for touch is removed; because tactility has been structurally incorporated into vision, the pure visionary does not lament the absence of tangibles; vision retains its altered structure. However, Merleau-Ponty emphasizes, not the change in our body, but the interchange in the world. "This voracious vision, reaching beyond the 'visual givens,' opens upon a texture of Being of which the discrete sensorial messages are only the punctuations or the caesurae."[39] Manipulating surface phenomena, the painter activates the deeper synaesthesia; he depicts the visual qualities which lead us instinctively into depth; he spreads before our gaze the transparent colors and variegated surfaces which reveal the inner essence of glass or marble. When we see a travertine slab, our eyes see tactile hardness through a modulation in the visual field, and our hands anticipate touching something hard; but a depicted slab frustrates the tactile urge, and makes us a pure visionary who can appreciate visible tactility.

Untutored insight and visionary acquisition. More primitive than acquired knowledge is an untutored insight which discloses the absent properties of intersensory presentations. The visual sensibles located in the visible field originally guide us toward the tactile field, and toward the other sensory fields, where we touch tactile sensibles or hear auditory sensibles. A tangible object is also visible; we see its visibility directly with the eyes, while viewing its tangibility indirectly through the actually presented visual sensibles. The visual field mediates tangible sensibles, changing tactility into a visual phenomenon. The apparitional style agitating the visual field is interchangeably a style of tactile apparition. Visible glass shows us how glass feels, and we see the tactility of wood through its visible texture.

Visual sensibles originally lead us toward tactile and auditory sensibles; but intuition is not infallible; sometimes the visible evidence leads us astray, arousing tactile anticipations which are disappointed when we try to touch the thing we see. Hence the painter can show us intangible tactility; the paint displays visible glass and glassy tactile qualities where we can actually touch only painted canvas. The painterly artifact leads us toward tactility, and misleads us if we expect to touch the tangibles which we see. The artistic product is located in nature; the flat artifact is not the only surface that deceives; unless nature was already misleading, the artist would have no materials for producing illusion. When natural visions deceive us about the essence of an object, we can acquire knowledge by perceptual exploration. Using this knowledge, we correct our initial impressions, until the cultural acquisition seems natural. When something looks hard, but feels soft, we learn to see the hardness as the misleading surface of a soft interior, so that the material thing looks soft despite its superficial

31

appearance. We seek knowledge, not only when we are deceived, but also when our sense impressions are neutral, neither leading nor misleading us; some sensations are nondirectional, or suggest contrary directions with equal force. We may spy a surface which looks neither hard nor soft, but tactile exploration reveals something soft, or hard, in the spot where we see the neutral surface. Not all visual sensibles are suggestive; we see neutral sensations which fail to suggest a tactile or auditory orientation. And not all directional sensibles are trustworthy; some mislead us, arouse tactile anticipations which are disappointed. Perceptual error is frequent, but we should not conclude that sensation is always nondirectional or misleading. Originally I do not doubt that something which looks hard will feel hard; doubt arises when I am disappointed. But perception corrects its own errors through further exploration. Original synaesthesia overcomes its defects by an acquired aesthesis.

Immediate experience is corrected during an exploration whose results become immediately evident when our acquisition is naturalized. Associated sensations seem synaesthetically connected. This acquired vision into material essence demands a structural change in our body: when we see something colored, and afterwards discover a soft tactile quality, the touch communicates with the sight through the common sensorium, altering our eyesight so that we see the softness in the color. Genuine synaesthesia, though, springs from a natural interchange in the body which echoes an interchange in the world. A surface which looks hard feels hard, not because we have developed a perceptual habit, but because an object displays its inner essence through tactile and visual qualities. A hard sound may be the sound of something hard; the hard auditory quality leads our body toward tactile hardness. A hot color may be the color of something hot, so that the sight warns us of being burnt. Nature frequently exhibits this coherence between superficial qualities and deeper essences; we daily witness a structured depth which emerges in superficial sensations, or in the deeper surfaces. A hot color is perceived through our eyes as a color and perceived as hot by the touch which is stimulated through the common sensorium; sight evokes a phantasmal tactility. This synaesthesia might be superficial; perhaps our perception contacts only the qualities, and requires an interchange only in our body. The synaesthesia is deeper if the hot color reveals a tactilely hot object which displays its secret in the colored visual field. But synaesthesia is certified as merely superficial if we see something which has a hot color and looks hot, but which feels cold when we touch it with our hand. Our shallow and deceptive experience may become deep, if tactile exploration alters the structure of vision so that we perceive the hot color as the appearance of a cool object, and see coolness in the color despite its superficial warmth. The direct tactile experience modifies our visual perception of the color so that we see the deeper coolness, because our tactile sense communicates with vision through the common sensorium, and produces a unified experience of the object. This acquired vision, which seems synaesthetic, is not a simple association between qualities sensed separately; the qualities grow together, creating a global impression.

We do not innately know whether surface sensibles reveal the deeper essence; we learn through prolonged experience. Perceptual exploration tells us whether our untutored intuitions are correct. The deeper synaesthesia is always operative; we discover its operation by a trust which grows wiser after disappointment. Sense experience is sometimes unilluminating, and sometimes misleading, but

33

we should not therefore withdraw from the world, reject-
ing all sensory guidance. Error does not prove that the
perceived world is totally deceptive. Unless we let the world
guide us, we would never suffer disillusion, and could accept no sensory suggestions for correcting our errors. Naivity contains wisdom, even though our initial impressions
are not sufficient for life.

When describing sensory insight, how can we distinguish
genuine synaesthesia and the acquired aesthesis which
seems synaesthetic? How can we discriminate uncultivated
nature and naturalized culture? Spurious synaesthesia
arises from a habitual association between nondirectional
qualities, or between directional qualities whose suggestions are misleading. How can we tell whether our intersensory anticipations are derived from blind association? Suppose we perceive something which feels hard and also looks
hard, something whose visual appearance leads us to expect
that the object would feel hard if touched. Can we be sure
that the object originally looked hard? Perhaps the visible
appearance is a nondirectional surface which we have
learned to see as the exterior of something resistant. Does
the object naturally look hard, or have we routinized an
interpretation? We admit that we are often uncertain how
to tell the difference. Nonetheless, we insist that sometimes
we feel no doubt; when we look at a marble slab we plainly
see its hardness; and we plainly see the softness of fur. But
the lightness of an empty container is not obvious from its
external appearance; expecting a heavy weight, we raise the
box more abruptly than we intended. We need not doubt
the obvious just because some examples are doubtful; we
should not disbelieve obvious synaesthesia simply because
some connections are obviously learned. We learn,
perhaps, to see aluminum as light and lead as heavy, unless
at first sight they are sitting on sand where we see the lead

34

sinking. If we must learn to see aluminum as light, we need not argue that all synaesthesia is fraudulent. We should simply return to the phenomena and ask whether the particular object under study discloses an inner essence through its envelope. We will discover that some objects are revealing, others deceptive, and others inscrutable. When we describe natural phenomena we always have subjective associations; we always have prior acquaintance which influences our present perceptions; we must therefore seek the clear examples which leave us no practical doubts. If we have carefully examined the phenomena, we can dismiss the objections spawned by preconceived empiricist theories.

Synaesthesia demonstrates that our senses are synergetic. The various specialized organs work together in superficial synaesthesia when one sense stimulates another through the common sensorium. They work together in deep synaesthesia when surface sensibles give us insight into the essence of material objects. Again they work together in spurious synaesthesia, where we blindly explore the object, developing associations which alter the organism, until we possess a visionary habit which seems unlearned. Our senses work together, generating a behavioral essence. The thing acts upon our body, and our flesh acts upon the thing, sealing a pact with the world which permits perceptual entry. Our life style incarnates the pattern of the world, unless we lose attunement.

The lack and loss of original harmony. Originally we enjoy a concord between a hither interchange and an interchange yonder. In the body the specialized senses communicate through the common sensorium, while in the world the specialized sensibles communicate through the intersensory thing. The body harmonizes with the world when the

35

communication within the body corresponds with the communication located outside the body. Correspondence is vibratory union between unitary body and unitary world. The human communicant develops a behavioral style which incorporates the apparitional rhythm generated yonder. When the special sensibles intercommunicate through the worldly interchange, each sensible exhibits the same apparitional rhythm; when the special senses intercommunicate through the bodily interchange, each sense exhibits the same perceptual style; when the hither and yonder interchanges harmonize, the perceptual style joins the apparitional rhythm, and animates a joint corporeality. If this harmony between body and world is operative, a special sensible stimulates the appropriate sense and also evokes in other senses the sensations which those organs would perceive more strongly if they actually explored the intersensory thing standing outside the body. A special sense, when isolated from the others, does not arouse sympathetic vibrations, but the special organ dimly perceives latent appearances. In an artist, the isolated organ perceives the sensibles which would be evoked if the special sense communicated with the other senses, and feels remotely the sensibles which would be perceived if the other senses actually contacted the intersensory thing which is now perceived through a single sense. The artist, with his specialized sensibility, experiences the intersensory rhythm without alien data. Through a single organ he captures an apparitional style which leads toward absent apparitions.

This harmony between body and world does not always exist. Sometimes we witness a special sensible which fails to communicate with other sensibles through the worldly interchange. This isolated sensible stimulates the proper sense without evoking sensations in the other senses, or it evokes sympathetic sensations which do not correspond to

36

the sensibles which would be perceived if the other senses actually explored the world. Conversely, we sometimes witness an interconnected sensible while the special sense is isolated from the bodily interchange; the yonder sensible stimulates a sense which is disconnected from the common sensorium. Straining our attention, localizing our mind in a specialized organ, we may forget how to exercise global perception. If a special sense does not communicate with other senses through the bodily interchange, the sensory stimulus cannot evoke intersensory expectations. When the harmony between body and nature does not exist we confront unexpected sensations and learn their interconnections; when we lack untutored insight we gradually develop an association of ideas, an acquired synaesthesia, which perfects original experience, or restores lost perfection. Learning eliminates natural ignorance, but we must avoid the ignorant learning which obliterates our native knowledge. Beyond a doubt, we originally enjoy a synaesthetic perception whose evidence is not yet shadowed by dubiety.

Binocular Vision

Synergy, or sensory communion, can be understood through a description of binocular vision. Merleau-Ponty argues that the interchange, the communication among the various specialized senses, is the same communion that operates within the visual sense when we experience a unification between the visual sensation in our left eye and the visual sensation in the right. When several equivalent senses are directed toward the same sensible, their sensory fields overlap; the tactile field and the visual field are territories which superimpose themselves as we chart our course through the world. During binocular exploration, the visual rays, the intentional radiations, streaming from the two eyes meet upon a single sensible; the two fields overlap, and duplicate visions merge as a visible unity. Binocular vision is a perceptual synthesis; the word "synthesis" often indicates a rational operation, an intellectual assembly; but Merleau-Ponty wants to show that the various sensibles are assembled in original sense perception. The perceptual synthesis is not association. The empiricist would argue that, in binocular vision, two similar sensations appear together; the constant conjunction establishes a habitual association; we soon ignore the slight difference between the sensations and identify them as the same, unifying the duality with a single name; the nominal assemblage is an internal representation, which is sometimes mistaken for the external object. Both "association" and intellectual "synthesis" presuppose that sensations entering one eye are experientially isolated from sensations in the other, and generally that sensations in one sense organ are experienced as separate from sensations in every other receptor; these isolated sensations require unification; mere sense perception does not show us a common world with unitary objects. The presupposition is mistaken; before sense impressions become analytically alienated, we enjoy a primordial synthesis which already makes sense of our surroundings.

When my two eyes are fixed on something remote, "I have a double image of objects nearby. When I transfer my gaze to the latter, I see the two images converge on what is to be the single object, and merge into it."[40] The images are special visual sensibles, colored lights or lighted colors with a certain shape and outline; the double sensibles appear as twin images of a common object; the object appears when its images disappear as twins and emerge as a unitary vision. We put together the twin images by moving our eyes and transferring our gaze. Merleau-Ponty warns that such assemblage is not an intellectual process which conceives the twins as two images of a single object; an intellectual combination would be performed the moment I noticed that the two images are lookalikes; but I must wait much longer before the monocular images are put together as a single apparition of a single object; I must wait until I shift my eyes, and refocus. Moreover, once the twin images are combined, the newly emergent unity is obviously not a conceived conjunction between two images, because the duality disappears the very moment the single object appears in perception. Merleau-Ponty thus rejects the intellectualist explanation of binocular vision.[41]

At greater length he examines and rejects a scientific explanation. Intellectual synthesis is a psychological process, whereas the twin images disappear through a bodily instrumentality which is quite obvious: our eyeballs shift and focus. We are therefore prompted to consider the body as a sensible external; the body becomes an object for empirical science, and we adopt scientific realism. Speaking for physiology, Merleau-Ponty asks whether the images have been fused by some device in the nervous system. Does there exist, "if not on the periphery, at least in the center, one sole excitation mediated by the two eyes?"[42] Our author replies that "the mere existence of one visual center cannot explain the single object, since double vision sometimes occurs."[43] Likewise, "the mere existence of the two retinas cannot explain double vision."[44] because we always have two retinas and two retinal images. In normal vision we experience double images, despite the single center, and also experience a single object, despite the double retinas; consequently, anatomical structure cannot explain binocular sight; the explanatory factor is function, the use which the subject makes of his body.

Having shown why a single visual center in the brain cannot explain single vision, and why the two eyes with their two retinas cannot explain double vision, Merleau-Ponty discusses convergence, focusing, and especially the non-symmetrical, or "dissymmetrical,"[45] images on the two retinas. Speaking for physiology and psychology, Merleau-Ponty asks whether we should "say that double sight occurs *because* our eyes do not converge on the object, and because it throws nonsymmetrical images on our two retinas."[46] And should we say that the "two images merge into one because fixation brings them back to corresponding points on the two retinas," [47] making the images symmetrical? Our author replies negatively, raising a doubt whether convergence is "the cause or the effect of . . . normal vision." [48] When persons are born blind and operated on for cataract, we cannot say, during the period after the operation, whether their vision is hampered by ocular noncoordination, or whether the noncoordination is produced by confusion in the visual field; we cannot tell "whether they fail to see through failure to focus, or whether they fail to focus through not having anything to see."[49] Consider now the retinal images in a.person born with normal vision. When I focus on something in the remote distance and hold a forefinger near my eyes, the thing nearby looks double; the finger casts two images on nonsymmetrical areas of my retinas. This retinal arrangement "cannot be the *cause*"[50] of the focusing activity which will eliminate the double vision; for the disappearance of duality is not an objective event. "My finger forms its image on a certain area of my left retina, and on an area of my right retina which is not symmetrical with the former. But the symmetrical area of the right retina is also full of visual excitations. . . ." [51] The images must be distinguished from the surrounding excitations which compose the background; the appropriate physiological vibrations must be recognized as images; this discrimination can be performed only by the living subject who possesses the stimulated retinas. "On the retinas them-

40

selves, considered as objects, there are only two groupings of *stimuli* that cannot be compared."[52] The stimuli become images, and become visibly nonsymmetrical, only when an embodied visionary experiences something visible. Perhaps the empirical psychologist will reply "that, unless the eyes are focused, these two groupings cannot be superimposed on each other, nor give rise to the vision of anything, and that in this sense their presence alone creates a state of unbalance."[53] But Merleau-Ponty interprets the unbalance as a phenomenon experienced by the seeing subject, and insists that the subject can experience double vision as unbalance only with reference to an expected single vision. When I shift my gaze from the remote background to my finger in the foreground, I "experience double vision as an unbalance or as imperfect vision, and tend towards the single object as towards the release of tension and the completion of vision. 'It is necessary to "look" in order to see.' "[54]

This "looking" is an intentional activity wherein the gaze goes prospecting for objects; the gaze looks ahead to the single image where the object will appear. "Seeing" is the culmination of "looking;" sight is an achievement. Seeing is not merely the passively endured effect of an objective cause; convergence, focusing, and the superimposition of retinal images, are not the causes of single vision; these objective operations are the effects of seeing; the seeing subject is the agent. We could call the intentional act a "subjective cause," but Merleau-Ponty likes to reserve the term "cause" for the objective causes which scientific realism conceives as extended and spatially located objects which produce natural events by external operations. Ocular behavior is a "condition" for seeing, not a "cause"; there would be no vision if eyes did not exist, but, given eyes and ocular functions as conditions, vision requires intentional activity. We are already speaking about intentionality when we mention "function"; bodily behavior is not merely an objective movement between spatial positions. Conditions become functional when subjective agency is introduced, when the embodied subject directs pregiven instruments toward practical aims. For example, divergence between the eyes appears as a cause of double vision when my right index finger presses my right eyeball with the intention of causing duality. Likewise a convergence between the eyes causes single vision when I focus my eyes with the intention of seeing a single object.

Duality in binocular vision is a motivating phenomenon which impels our gaze toward its implicit objective. A "motive" is not a cause which drives us blindly from behind, nor is it an ideal whose brilliance draws us from ahead. A motive is "a sort of operative reason"[55] which resides in the events themselves. The convergence between our eyes, experienced as muscular strain, motivates single vision, because the strain is experienced as an urge toward something outside our body. The binocular image, when it appears, makes explicit the significance of the motivating phenomenon, so that retrospectively the muscular strain appears as aimed toward an object which was already present. "Through a retrospective illusion, we speak . . . about a natural geometry of perception. We place beforehand within perception a science constructed upon it, and lose sight of the original relationship of motivation. . . ."[56] Because seeing requires looking, because we cannot actually see unless we are looking for something, the unitary object in binocular vision does not result from an objective process which gradually produces a single image by fusing the two monocular images; the twins are not simply superimposed; they are replaced with a single object. The object is "incomparably more substantial"[57] than the two images seen side by side, or the two images seen superimposed. If "image" suggests insubstantiality, we should say that the two images disappear where the single object appears, instead of saying that a single image appears; the superimposition of the two subjective images is not yet single vision of an object. The superimposed images compose the apparition of an object only when the images are motivated. "The two images of diplopia are not amalgamated into one single one in binocular vision; the unity of the object is intentional."[58]

The unity is not conceptual; binocular synthesis is perceptual rather than intellectual. Perception is already mental; the distinction between the intellectual and the perceptual synthesis resides within perception. "We pass from double vision to the single object . . . when the two eyes cease to function each on its own account and are used as a single organ by one single gaze."[59] The body brings about the synthesis "when it escapes from dispersion, pulls itself together and tends by all means in its power towards one single goal of its activity, and when one single intention is formed in it through the phenomenon of synergy."[60] Binocular vision takes place in the "phenomenal body,"[61] which projects a "setting"[62] around the subjective center, orientating the subject within an organized environment. The corporeal synthesis "takes for granted all the latent knowledge of itself that my body possesses."[63] This latency, comprising experiences sedimented as habit, is the "body image."[64] The body image incorporates all the knowledge of which we are not explicitly conscious, but which we unconsciously employ in our consciousness of objects.

The body image, or the habitual body, is an open unity. We use our bodily habits whenever we perceptually put together the two visual images with the intention of seeing a single object. This function of the body image explains why the perceived object always appears as something transcen-

43

dent: the object is located outside the bodily subject, and the synthesis takes place on the object in the outside world, because the synthesis which unifies the object is an open unity, leaving the object open for further manifestations. The distinction between the perceptual object and the intelligible object resides in original experience as the distinction between a closed and an open imaginal unity; the perceptual synthesis closes the unity while the intellectual synthesis leaves the unity open. During perception the body subject uses its habits to put together the images which appear here in the present; but habits are general and can be used for putting together images which will appear elsewhere and in the future; habits can be modified and further generalized in future use; the generality of habit enables the body subject to anticipate future appearances. During the passage from monocular to binocular vision, we experience two closed unities opening toward a more inclusive unity where the double images are combined and absorbed. "On passing from double to normal vision, I am not simply aware of seeing with my two eyes *the same* object, I am aware of progressing towards the object *itself* and finally enjoying its concrete presence."[65] The double vision is comparatively insubstantial. "Monocular images float vaguely *in front* of things, having no real place in the world and are swallowed up in it, as ghosts, at daybreak, repair to the rift in the earth which let them forth."[66] The binocular synthesis seemingly reaches the object, but the perceptual synthesis contains successive binocular acts, and the series is never completed. Hence, the object itself is "never *reached*: each aspect of the thing which falls to our perception is still only an invitation to perceive beyond it, still only a momentary halt in the perceptual process."[67] Reality is a depth whose apparitions are never exhausted. "If the thing itself were reached, it would be from that moment arrayed before us and stripped of its mystery. It would cease to exist as a thing at the very moment we thought to possess it."[68] The apparitional surface is present, but the depth contains absent appearances; transcendence requires absence, and a presence which discloses unperceived depth. Faced with a transcendent object, the perceiving subject requires "the unity of the body image, which is itself open and limitless."[69]

The analogy between binocular vision and intersensory perception Merleau-Ponty summarizes as follows: "The intersensory object is to the visual object what the visual object is to the monocular images of double vision, and the senses interact in perception as the two eyes collaborate in vision."[70] Intersensory perception is synergetic, like binocular vision. And also, intersensory perception is synaesthetic. Synaesthesia is a synergy, but shall we say that binocular synergy is synaesthetic? Shall we say, not only that we see the tangibility of things seen, but that we see dexter visibility through the left eye and sinister visibility through the right? When I look at an object through my right eye, do I glimpse the view which I can see through my left eye? Yes, when I see an object, I often see the possibility of views not seen. And when I take new viewpoints, looking through the other eye, or through the same eye resituated, I actualize a latency which I perceived from my initial standpoint. The deep synaesthetic communion between one eye and the other is analogous to the synaesthetic communication between vision and the nonvisual senses. But surely, when we look around the corner of a polyhedron, we are sometimes surprised by what we see. If we therefore say that binocular vision is not synaesthetic, denying that we see a latent left-eyed view through the right eye, we still must say that binocular vision is synergetic. The dexter and sinister views converge upon a single focus, and merge as a single vision; likewise our visual perceptions and our nonvisual perceptions converge upon unitary objects in a common world. Even when our eyes do not see the tactility which we touch, we at least see the intersensory object whose tactile qualities become apparent if we employ our hands.

Fleshly Generality

Operating within the common sensorium, the specialized senses unify their distinctive perspectives and disclose a common object which unifies diverse apparitions. This community in the body and the corresponding community in the world are conjoined along a generality which develops in perception. When we move from a specialized apparition toward a more common sensible, we incorporate an apparitional style which leads us into depth. We grasp a generality which unifies the diverse apparitions as perspectival appearances of a common reality. Because the common object is never fully present, we must grasp it through its unifying generality. We grasp the thing through characteristic apparitions, sensible surfaces which come forward with a distinctive style.

Perception receives a sense presentation, then goes beyond the given, prospecting for presentations which display the same style, appear within a single community, and disclose a common reality. Through my left eye is seen a special visual sensible, specialized as a vision seen through the left eye only; through my right eye is seen another specialized special sensible, a sensible specific to vision, and further specialized as a visual sensible specific to the right eye alone. When my left and right eyes work together, the separate views converge, and merge upon a common visual sensible, an apparition still specialized as visual, but uniting the more specialized apparitions specific to the separate eyes. Through my two eyes is now seen a binocular image, but a moment later I see through my two eyes another

46

binocular image; the one image is a visual sensible specific to the present binocular act, the other image is a visual sensible specific to the next binocular act. When my momentary activities work together, the temporally separated views converge, and merge upon a more common visual sensible, a single apparition which persists during successive glances. Through my two eyes, during two binocular acts, I perceive a common sensible which is still specialized as visual; and through my two hands, during successive tactile acts, I perceive a common sensible which is specialized as tactile; when my eyes work together with my hands, the special visual sensible and the special tactile sensible merge upon a yet more common apparition. Through the specialized senses, operating at specific moments, I experience a continually growing community of apparitions. The proliferating presentations mutually elaborate upon a single theme. Perception moves always from the specialized toward the more common, but never reaches the hidden particular toward which the apparitions lead us. The specialized sensibles merge upon a particular object which reveals its solidity through a shared apparition. The momentary sensations communicate through a common particular which comes forth in a unitary image. But the particular thing withdraws into distance as we continue our exploration, and then comes forth in another image which unifies the newly emergent appearances. Always unifying our experience, whether the thing stands forward or retreats into the background, is an exploratory style, an apparitional rhythm which leads us toward a particularized absence. The style which unifies the special sensibles is an operative generality that specifies a particular object.

The originally perceived object is a general particular. When apparitions intercommunicate and compose a community, they display either a particular or a universal. The universal is always a particular universal; every general is some particular general and not a general in general; even the general "generality" is a particular general, since it is not, for example, the general "particularity." There are more and less general generals, but even the most generalized general is a particular general; a general must be particular so that diverse items can hold the same general in common. Note that we are not suggesting the idealist view that sensible particulars are the least general generals. Diverse items may have in common the same general, the same particular general, or they may hold in common the same particular, as we see when several apparitions are properties of the same thing. When diverse appearances hold the same particular thing in common, and exhibit the same reality, the particular acquires generality, becomes a general particular, an individual which proliferates apparitions with stylistic unity.

Enduring solids multiply their properties while my body multiplies its appropriations, its glances and graspings. An external particular exhibits its surfaces with a distinctive tempo; a temporal modulation distinguishes this individual thing from others; the thing is a stuff with a style. The material solid is a "flesh"[71] whose generality penetrates my body while my body explores the world. Fleshly generality, corporeal universality, is an "element."[72] An element is a "*general thing*, midway between the spatio-temporal individual and the idea, a sort of incarnate principle which brings a style of being wherever there is a fragment of being."[73] The fleshly polyhedron facing me yonder is a sensibly given particular which endures through experiential flux; fleshly generality runs through the appearances, whereas conceptual generality overarches the appearances, collecting data which have no inherent connection. Flesh is

48

a stuff which generalizes itself by multiplying appearances in time and space. That clay, that bronze, or that wood yonder, is not "a collection of colors and tactile data, not even their total *Gestalt*, but something from which emanates a woody essence; these 'sense data' modulate a certain theme or illustrate a certain style which is the wood itself."[74] The hand which palpates the multifaceted mass is also a flesh; like the tangible solid which I touch, I myself am a stuff with a style. The sensitive body, the common sensorium, is a general particular, a living individual which makes perception universal as the specialized organs exercise sequential perceptive acts. My body is a particular which lives its generality, whereas the yonder mass has a generality which is not yet alive; the wooden chunk, the brass box, the bronze cube, lies dead, waiting for me to live it in perception. As my hand explores the inert exterior, there emerges, between my own hand and the brazen mass, a thing which has been worked over in perception; each finger, each hand, each sense organ, works in a specialized mode, but together they create a cultural artifact which exhibits thematic unity.

The thing, the solid external, has perceptual generality which shines through its multiple apparitions, but the superficial sensibles display a universality of their own. A color patch directs my gaze toward a colored thing which is tangible, but also the color leads my gaze toward other specimens within that species. Apparitions have a surface generality; a red sensation is the presence of redness, a universal entity which appears in uncounted sensory impacts. A special sensible is a field phenomenon; a sensed red is a figure located within a field of unsensed, but potentially seen, red. A glimpsed red is not "an opaque *quale*,"[75] not "an atom."[76] The red which appears in a red dress is a "punctuation in the field of red things."[77] Hovering around the dress

49

I see blood, strawberries, fire hydrants, terracotta tiling, wet clay in the gullies that flank southern roads. The red figures also in the field of red garments, which includes the costumes of bishops and bellhops, figures also in the field of adornments, including rubies and rouges. The red impact figures within several overlapping fields; each area lends the datum a specific generality, a determinate vagueness. In various directions the datum has a potentiality beyond its actual presentation, a latency which enables us to sense red again, and elsewhere. Red is both particular and general, both this red and redness; in original sense perception, the particular and general are experienced together. This red is isolated from redness, and this red thing is isolated from other red things, by an artificial analysis; a "naked color"[78] is a "fossil drawn up from the depths of imaginary worlds."[79]

A special sensible, then, has an intrasensory generality. A single color, a highly specialized visual sensible, has a surface generality, a directionality which guides our gaze toward absence, toward peripheral apparitions located within the horizon of the specific field. Further, a special sensible has an intersensory generality, as in superficial synaesthesia. A color presentation guides perception toward special sensibles in other sensory fields; vision communicates with touch, and with hearing. "The sight of sounds or the hearing of colors comes about in the same way as the unity of the gaze through the two eyes: in so far as my body is, not a collection of adjacent organs, but a synergic system. . . ."[80] However, the sight when I hear a sound, or the sound when I see a sight, may be a hallucination produced in the sensorium. "When I say that I see a sound, I mean that I echo the vibration of the sound with my whole sensory being, and particularly with that sector of myself which is susceptible to colors."[81] A colorful tune, or a noise which sounds blue, shows nothing about solid reality if the synaesthesia

50

arises merely from bodily vibrations. But synaesthesia sometimes leads beneath the qualities; a special sensible may have an intersensory generality which delves into real depth. A hot color may be the color of a hot object which burns when we touch it; a red object may look hot, and not disappoint us when we put the tactile sense into play. This deeper synaesthesia joins with sensory communion; our sense organs work together, and the bodily interchange corresponds with an interchange in the world; our perceptual acts focus upon the things and disclose a stereometric reality. The deepest generality is an apparitional style which reaches into the background, toward the world horizon.

THE SENSORY RANGE

Generality is a generativity over here in my own body, and also yonder in the world, a generative style which joins perceptual energy with apparitional activity. When my body employs its sense organs synergetically, exploring the things over there in the outer world, the sensible presentations range hither and yon between my central interiority and the circumferential externals. Let us describe this sensory range.

When I fix my gaze upon an object or let my gaze wander within its contours, the color which I see appears as a superficial color extended over the surface of the thing, and it appears as located determinately in space. When however I do not control my gaze, but wholly submit to the thing, the same color appears as an atmospheric hue which diffuses itself around the object. Next the color appears simply as a vibration of my gaze. Finally the color may pervade my body so that I can no longer call it a color. Likewise there exists outside my body a sound which reverberates in a musical instrument; there is also an atmospheric sound which appears between the thing and my body; then there is a sound which vibrates in my ears; finally the sound appears as a pervasive bodily change which can no longer be distinguished as an auditory sensation. We see that a special sensible, such as a sound or color, appears along a range. At one end of this longitude, the special sensible is located in an object, and the common sensible which possesses this quality is located in a confined space: the color extends over the ashtray, the sound reverberates in the violin. At the other end of the range, the special sensible is taken into the body subject and is no longer a sensible, but the sense itself as modified during perception. In the body, the sound or color overflows the specialized sense toward all the other senses that modulate the common sensorium.[82]

In original sense perception, the sensibles range between the object and the bodily subject. The sensibles can be objectified only in the object or near the object. If we do not objectify the thing before us, do not confront it, but let the special sensibles range toward the subject, they cease to be sensible and become invisibly operative in the special senses, and finally in the common sensorium where we no longer face them. Sound becomes a living sonority; color becomes a sentient vibration in the eye. When the special sensibles yonder appear as a modification of a more common object, we see substantial things through the atmospheric properties. "Everything appears to us through a medium to which it lends its own fundamental quality...."[83] A chunk of wood becomes a ligneous essence which invades our body through the various woody colors and textures.

The traditional secondary qualities are primary; color gives us the inner reality, whereas shape is merely an "envelope."[84]

From over there in the world, the sensibles range all the way to the hither side. The world generates things, and the things decompress as layers; these laminations disperse into the atmosphere around the things and my body. The circumambient seeps inside; the atmospheric layers invade my inner space; I inhale the surroundings with the air I breathe. The overlapping layers shade from my body unto the things themselves, and from the things to my body. Layers unpile from the things, and float free, letting the things breathe. Inspirational nature heaves a sigh and becomes efflorescent with dreams. Our stimulated senses reach into the background, along the sensory range; in the middle distance we synergetically perceive a solid reality which incorporates the imaginal media.

NOTES

[1]Maurice Merleau-Ponty, *Phenomenology of Perception* (New York: Humanities Press, 1962), p. 3.

[2]*PP*, pp. 3-4.

[3]*PP*, pp. 225-26.

[4]*PP*, p. 226.

[5]*PP*, p. 226

[6]*PP*, p. 226.

[7]*PP*, p. 226.

[8]*PP*, p. 227.

[9]*PP*, p. 227.

[10]*PP*, pp. 226-7.

[11]Compare Maurice Merleau-Ponty, *The Visible and the Invisible* (Evanston: Northwestern University Press, 1968), pp. 28-49.

[12]*PP*, p. 235.

[13]*PP*, p. 235.

[14]*PP*, p. 235.

[15]*PP*, p. 225.

[16]*PP*, p. 225.

[17]*PP*, p. 235.

[18]*PP*, p. 228.

[19]*PP*, p. 228.

[20]*PP*, p. 229.

[21]*PP*, p. 229.

[22]*PP*, p. 229.

[23]*PP*, p. 227.

[24]*PP*, p. 228.

[25]*PP*, p. 228.

[26]Maurice Merleau-Ponty, *La prose du monde* (Paris: Gallimard, 1969), p. ii.

[27]*PP*, p. 229.

[28]*PP*, p. 229.

[29]*PP*, p. 229.

[30]*PP*, p. 229.

[31]*PP*, pp. 229-30.

[32]*PP*, p. 230.

[33]*PP*, p. 230.

[34]*PP*, p. 230.

[35]*PP*, p. 230.

[36]*PP*, p. 230.

[37]*PP*, pp. 229-30.

[38]Maurice Merleau-Ponty, *The Primacy of Perception* (Evanston: Northwestern University Press, 1964), p. 166.

[39]*PrP*, p. 166.

[40]*PP*, p. 230.

[41]*PP*, pp. 230-31.

[42]*PP*, p. 231.

[43] *PP*, p. 231.
[44] *PP*, p. 231.
[45] *PP*, p. 231.
[46] *PP*, p. 231.
[47] *PP*, p. 231.
[48] *PP*, p. 231.
[49] *PP*, p. 231.
[50] *PP*, p. 231.
[51] *PP*, p. 231.
[52] *PP*, pp. 231-32.
[53] *PP*, p. 232.
[54] *PP*, p. 232.
[55] *PP*, p. 50.
[56] *PP*, p. 50.
[57] *PP*, p. 232.
[58] *PP*, p. 232.
[59] *PP*, p. 232.
[60] *PP*, p. 232.
[61] *PP*, p. 232.
[62] *PP*, p. 232.
[63] *PP*, p. 233.
[64] *PP*, p. 233.
[65] *PP*, p. 233.
[66] *PP*, p. 233.
[67] *PP*, p. 233.
[68] *PP*, p. 233.
[69] *PP*, p. 233.
[70] *PP*, pp. 233-34.
[71] *VI*, p. 139.
[72] *VI*, p. 139.
[73] *VI*, p. 139.
[74] *PP*, p. 450.
[75] *PP*, p. 234.
[76] *VI*, p. 132.
[77] *VI*, p. 132.
[78] *VI*, p. 132.

[79] *VI*, p. 132.
[80] *PP*, p. 234.
[81] *PP*, p. 234.
[82] *PP*, p. 227.
[83] *PP*, p. 450.
[84] *PrP*, p. 172.

Chapter II

APPARITIONAL REALITY

Imagination generates illusion, and yet without imagination we could never perceive. The very power that cuts us off from the world also gives us access. Normal vision is latent diplopia. Only if we could manage to see without two monocular images would double vision be impossible. We must risk illusion, because we see the world less well when we close one eye. Through a single eye we see something, but something less solid than the thing which we see through both eyes working together. Only a thing which threatens to break up and appear double could look so solid when it appears single.

THE NATIVE HABITAT

Illusion is a phenomenon where we experience something as something else. Illusion becomes apparent in the phenomenon of disillusionment. When nature breaks our enchantment, we perceive that the vision we accepted as valid is not really real. We lose our faith in apparition; we can no longer repose our trust in a mere appearance. What we formerly perceived as a thing appears now as not a thing at all, but something shadowy which we can banish into outer darkness. Something else, something really real, has come to light; this newly illuminated surface dislocates the thing in which we previously believed. We cannot understand illusion unless we first understand what reality is. We must describe the sensible thing, and the natural world where the thing and our body have their being.

Perceptual Appearance

The undefined sensible which we experience out there in the world has numerous layers ranging into depth. We can locate, or localize, these layers at various distances. In the foreground are the countless "particular special sensibles," and behind these are the five "special sensibles"; these forward surfaces are the "qualities." Behind the qualities are the "things," and behind the things is the "world" appearing as a general "field" or "ground." Within this sensory range, the most "particular" sensibles appear in the foreground and the most "general" appear in the background. This generality is a sensible communion. The "common" ranges toward the back, while "specialization" ranges into the foreground. The things let our senses intercommunicate better than do the qualities, and thus are most properly called "common sensibles"; the things are more centrally "intersensory." The qualities, the things, and the world are all possible "appearances."

The apparitions along the sensory range exhibit opacity and transparency, a positivity and a negativity. The various sensible layers are arranged in depth so that the layers in front overlap the layers directly behind. A sensible at any distance can appear as an appearance of itself, blocking our view of the thing behind, or can appear as an appearance of something else, transmitting a vision of the hinterland. The most superficial appearances are experienced without any intermediaries except the naked sense organs and the invisible light. The appearances located farther in depth appear through specialized appearances of themselves, if the various species in front are sufficiently transparent. A particular special sensible may appear as just itself, or it may appear as the appearance of a more common sensible. Sometimes even the background appears through the foreground, not laterally around the forward figure, and the world emerges as an individual. The innumerable layers at various distances along the sensory range have the potentiality for both opacity and transparency. The sensible layer which initially obtrudes its own surface gradually becomes the appearance of something else behind; the foreground progressively disappears as it leads our gaze into depth. If the distant thing, toward which the transparent layer leads our gaze, suddenly disappears, then the transparent layer reappears as a "mere appearance" with a certain opacity. The deeper thing toward which the superficial layers led us was "merely apparent," because it existed only in its appearances. Each appearance led us toward another appearance, which, in turn, led us toward another; but suddenly, nothing further appeared, and we perceived that we had been led toward nothing at all; the solid thing, to which we looked forward, never materializes, and we are left with nothing but the transparencies which led us on, plus something else which appeared in the place where our objective disappeared. Sensibles at every distance, except the most remote sensibles in the farthest distance, are reversible between the real and the merely apparent. Something real can turn into a mirage, and a mist can solidify. This reversibility has degrees: the most superficial sensibles are the most reversible from the real to the apparent, and the apparent to the real; the deeper sensibles are less reversible; the things fluctuate less than do the qualities, and the natural world is the most stabile sensible. The world, within which everything else appears, is absolutely non-reversible; all reversal from the real to the apparent and back takes place within the world. The superficial sensibles are less real than the world, even when they reverse to the real, because the really real is a stability farther on beyond the fluctuating sensibles through which it appears.

The reversal between the real and the illusory is a reversal between the "apparent" and the "merely apparent," because the real is something which appears; reality is apparitional. The real appears through transparent layers which show forth something beyond themselves. The "merely apparent" or "illusory" is a sensible layer, or layered pile, which shows forth just itself, but which makes us anticipate something beyond. The illusory leads us on toward something which turns out to be nothing, or something other than we anticipated. The illusory has a "being-for-us," while we are on our way toward the apparent goal, but has no "being-in-itself." A "real being" is essentially that being which has "being-in-itself." Such beings are originally those things which we experience in the natural world; and an artifact, when experienced as having being-in-itself, is felt as fundamentally a natural being. A "real natural being" is something which appears, without appearing as "merely apparent." Nonetheless, a real being is in some sense "apparent;" the real as perceived has a "being-for-us;" the real is an "in-itself-for-us."[1]

An illusory or merely apparent being is a layered pile which leads us on, without leading us into that obscurity which it promises to illumine. A merely apparent being is "merely imaginary." Hallucination presents us with imaginary beings which lack solidity; figments are cloudy transparencies with no density backing them up. Even the most solid reality is "imaginary," since the real appears through intermediaries which efface themselves before its more factual surfaces; but solid reality is fundamentally "perceptual." The real is the "perceived" and the illusory is the "imagined." Often we can leave undecided the question whether something is "imagined" or "perceived," and call it "something experienced," since "experience" has both "perceptual" and "imaginal" modes. Or, the experienced sensible we can call simply "a being," since everything which can be experienced has "being" in some sense. "Real being" is "perceived being," and "illusory being" is "imagined." That naked reality which we confront without intermediaries is a "nonimaginal reality"; and the experience in which we intend such a being should be called "nonimaginal perception." Those transparent illusions which have no factual backing we should call "mere imaginaries"; and the experience should be called "nonperceptual imagination," or simply "hallucination" or "illusion." However, we, with Merleau-Ponty, want to describe that original experience wherein we enjoy "perceptual imagination" and "imaginal perception." Through this perception we experience an "imaginal reality."

Among those sensible beings which have enough reality to be called "things," some are more real than others. A thing is a common sensible, and thus is perceivable through two senses or more; a thing which is common to more senses is more real than a thing which is perceivable through only two; the most real thing is a common sensible upon which all five special senses overlap. This apple which I see, touch, smell, taste and hear, when I take a bite, is more truly a thing than the sky up there which I only see, and which has no visible figure of its own. The wind which touches my cheek is not yet a thing, but becomes real when I see a gust bend some trees. Further, among those sensible appearances which are specific to a single sense, there are certain appearances which are more real and more truly the appearances of the thing itself; certain appearances are experienced as the real, or true, appearances. A thing seems more truly a thing when we experience its real visible shape and size than when we experience its apparent shape and size.[2] Further, we more truly experience external reality through the visual and tactile senses than through the others.[3] Thus a more thinglike thing would not only be sensed through several special senses, but at least one of these special senses would be vision or touch. An animal with a keener olfactory sense would feel differently; but, like us, he would want to sink his teeth into things, or handle with his mouth what we touch with our hands.

When speaking about "reality," we should mark a distinction between "thing" and "object": the common sensible appearing in original experience is a "thing," whereas the common sensible analyzed and reassembled in reflective experience we may call an "object." This object may be the crude commonsense object in which the naive realist believes, or it may be the refined scientific object in which the critical idealist believes. The everyday object is supposedly sensible, but the scientific object has its sensuosity refined away, so that the common sensible is reconstructed as a pure intelligible. In contexts where a division between "thing" and "object" is not required, we can use the word "being"; in many contexts we may call a being indifferently "thing" and "object," whether that being appears in original experience or only in reflection. Broadly speaking, every being is a "thing," just as everything is a "being." And every being is an "object," in the sense that every being about which we speak is an "intentional object." In this sense, we understand "object" as a being which arises in the path of our intentionality. This being may appear along the path on the way toward the end, or may appear at the end of the path, standing over against our intentions as the end or goal. The terminal object is a being at which we aim, at which our intention stops; a being along the path of our intentionality may be a means through which we aim at the end, or it may be an obstacle upon which we stumble and stop on our way toward the end. In original experience we find that we ourselves have arisen on a path toward beings which we find already in our path as ends or means, or as obstacles. In reflective experience, we intending subjects actively throw the intentional objects which we find before us; reflexivity permits pure projects; in reflective experience we encounter no obstructions except those which we ourselves have constructed. Having defined "object" as "intentional object," we may distinguish between "object" and "objective," and then speak about an "objective object" and a "preobjective object." An intentional object may be imaginary, altogether unreal; such an object is not "objective," for the objective is real, although there are intentional objects which are real without being objective. In original experience there appear intentional objects which are real and which are properly called "things," but which are not yet "objectively real," not yet "objects" understood as objectively real beings. Objective reality is naked reality, a thing whose solidity has been certified, and presented without sensuous intermediaries. Something objective is an intersubjectively valid being constructed in reflection; the "objective object" is an "intersubjectively valid object," or an "object of knowledge"; these constructions are cultural, not natural. The natural thing which appears in original experience is intersubjective, but is not a being constructed during a reflective search for certainty. If we sometimes call

63

original experience "pre-objective,"[4] we do not mean that originally there appear no sensible things; we mean that we do not experience those "objects" constructed in "objectifying" reflection. We need not everywhere maintain the distinction between "object" understood as an "objective intentional object" and "thing" understood as a "preobjective common sensible," because "things" are the foundation for "objects." The preobjective things make "objectivity" possible.

Does the "thing" have any reality in itself? Is there a sensible "thing-in-itself?" Embodied perception allows a distinction between the reality which a thing has "in itself" and the being which it has "for us," if we understand this distinction as the difference between potentially and actually experienced reality. Reality in itself is the reality which could be experienced if we were otherwise situated in time and space. Only a body has a situation and a perspective; the intellect is everywhere and nowhere, like god. The originally experienced thing is an intentional object for a subject whose intentionality is bodily.[5] We dismiss the "thing-in-itself" if understood as something purely intelligible hidden behind the sensible appearances; even a pure intelligence could not drag the natural thing from its hiding place because the thing is bound up in its apparitional hide. Against intellectualism, Merleau-Ponty urges that we cannot even think about a thing which is neither perceived nor perceivable. We can indeed speak meaningfully about a thing which is not actually perceived, but we intend the hidden thing through our speech. A thing intended as not perceived has its existence for us as the intentional object of our thought; our intellectual intention intends the thing as at least potentially perceived through the bodily senses.[6]

We have failed to see that the thing has its being for incarnate subjectivity, because we are hampered by prejudices arising from objectifying reflection, which constructs the thing as an object. An object is an intelligible being which is intended by a pure intellect; through reflection the sensible thing becomes an intelligible object, and the bodily subject becomes a disembodied mind.[7] The intelligible object has its being only for us, but this subjective existence has being apart from the body. The empirical realists sometimes postulate a being-in-itself not intended even through an intellect, but the realist simply projects beyond all intentionality the object which science first constructed through reflection. The natural thing has its being only for embodied subjects, but nonetheless retains its own bodily reality. Unfortunately, once we have seen that the thing exists in subjective relation, we may fail to notice that the thing also has independent existence, because we are hampered by prejudices which arise from everyday experience, from life in the cultural context. Ordinarily we experience things as having their being-for-us as the ends at which we aim in our practical activity, or as a means toward such ends. Practical dealings employ the body, but they do not deal with things as beings within a natural world. Meditation, though, can suspend our practical activities and direct the mind toward things beneath culture. The things are revealed as uncanny, alien; our civility disguises undomesticated nature, and makes the strange familiar. When the practical man suddenly encounters nature, the world appears as a domain without man; when we lay down our tools and experience nature as an aesthetic whole, we at first feel anxious in the world whose power has not yet been stabilized in culture.[8] We experience the thing as having "being-in-itself" when theoretical activity constructs the sensible thing as an intelligible object; scientific theory forgets that the thing is originally something sensible which has its being for a body furnished with sense organs. We experience the thing as having "being-for-us" when practical activity constructs the sensible thing as something intended for our use; everyday practice forgets that the thing is originally something in nature. However, the thing originally has neither practical being-for-us nor theoretical being-in-itself; it has an independent and a relative existence more original than these practical and theoretical constructions. Original being-in-itself is an untamed potency for domestication in perception. Beneath culture, our natural body is already making itself at home in the wilderness.

Consulting embodied naivity, we say that "the world is what we perceive,"[9] and say that the thing is a "genuine in-itself-for-us."[10] These assertions are ambiguous; they can be uttered with an idealist accent or a realist accent, depending upon the circumstances. When arguing against idealists, Merleau-Ponty employs the realist accent, reminding us that the things have a being-in-themselves. When arguing against realists, he employs the idealist accent, reminding us that the things have a being-for-us. Combining both arguments he says that the natural thing has a "being-in-itself-for-us." This phrase reconciles idealism and realism, bridges the split between subject and object, inner and outer. We reconcile the conflict without eliminating the opposition. Beyond the being which a thing has for us there remains a being-in-itself; this transcendence is a potentiality destined for continuous actualization in human experience, a real potency, a latency which has being outside its experiential realization. Nature achieves imaginal reality without becoming a mere imaginary. During active perception we aim at something beyond our experience, and we perceive this absent potency as already possessing reality before it comes within our ken. We admit a transcendent material reality, and move from phenomenology to metaphysics. Increasingly we understand phenomenology as a thought which goes beyond appearances, without inferential leaps. We reach "transcendent" reality through a "transcendental geology."[11] We can go beyond experience, from inside experience, because we experience the material thing as withholding itself, as holding itself back from our gaze. Transcendent reality is a pure potency slumbering in darkness. Merleau-Ponty does indeed state that "the thing is inseparable from the person perceiving it, and can never be actually *in itself*,"[12] but our author means that transcendent materiality is not an actuality, not something actualized; he rejects the metaphysics of pure act. For the embodied soul, there is no daylight behind the lighted surfaces which confront us across the clearing; things come to light in the clearing where man stands. The luminous apparitions conceal only a pregnant darkness. Our metaphysics avoids the intellectualist idealism which understands the things as luminous intelligibles; and we avoid the empiricist idealism which understands the things as merely the sensible appearances that we actually perceive. We avoid also the empirical realism which naively supposes that things outside our sight have precisely the qualities we perceive when the things come into view. If we turn off the light, the things no longer have actual color and shape; but these qualities are still lurking about, ready for reappearance. The distinction between latent and manifest is the difference between "earth" and "world." The thing decompresses into the world, while pressing against the earth. Apparitional genesis decompresses compacted latency, and invades the mental vacuum. Human mentality is a clearing upon this earth, which grounds the things and our body.

When the background unfolds into the atmosphere, the thing appears across the clearing, and comes across, to our side, ranging from this side to the side yonder. The thing appears along the sensory range as a temporal relationship

67

among its sensible layers. Apparition is a temporal process, a visionary activity with a certain rhythm. Perceptual genesis is rhythmical, melodic, tonal. The invisible relation among the layered appearances is a "style"[13] of presentation, a level of apparition, an ordered agitation which we capture in our bodies. Because each layer appears within a stylistic nexus, each appearance, when present, is inseparable from other appearances. The present appearance symbolizes the appearances which are absent, as well as the other appearances which are effectively given. The perceived surface symbolizes absent sensibles that are specific to the sense through which the symbolic appearance is perceived, and also symbolizes absent sensibles specific to other senses. This styled and symbolic relation among the appearances of a thing is a sensuous structure, a sensory essence. Perceptual structure is flexible; sensory rhythm is an open coherence, growing organically as we utilize our exploratory organs. Each appearance figuring in a unitary network symbolizes all the other figures; an appearance which is present symbolizes the other appearances, whether they are present or absent. Symbolism draws absent apparitions into a field of presence. The thing is essentially the unified system in which diverse appearances are equivalent, and interchangeable. The equivalents are not alike; individually each apparition is irreplaceable; but within the total system each appearance has equal value, as an expression of the thing itself; the equivalence is systematic equivalence, metaphorical interchange. The natural symbol is a superficial reality with intentional reference. When we direct our mind toward an appearance which is effectively given, we are led through that surface toward latent apparitions. This structure, or system of intentional relations among the appearances, is the sense, or significance, of the sensible thing. The thing has depth beyond its presenta-

68

tional surface. When there no longer remain further appearances, when the apparitional possibilities are exhausted, the thing no longer exists. Each presentation draws our body toward absence, opens our organs toward material transcendence. We can reflect upon the sensible thing and construct a concept which verbally expresses the meaning of perception, but our speech cannot render all appearances present, cannot evacuate material plenitude. Our vocalizations never exhaust the meaning that we mutely sense in the thing itself.[14]

The material thing is a productive mass. The thing is a depth which generates superficial appearances, images which open our perception into depth. The natural background has an originative rhythm; depth exhibits a generative style, an essence which animates the apparitions. The thing is apparition, and style, and depth. Each perceived appearance is a symbol which opens into depth along the style, revealing the thing itself, making the absent present in a surface presentation.

Having described the real thing, we can describe the imaginary, by contrast. "The imaginary has no depth,"[15] or has only a shallow depth. Real depth is fathomless, whereas the depth in an image is easily plumbed. A sensation, a striking impression, is a superficial sensible, but most apparitions have a sensuous materiality; the imaginary has a minimal reality. A painted image, like the reality depicted, must be perceptually explored before we can understand its significance; and the deeper meaning of the paint cannot be exhausted in words. So far the image is like the thing. But the painted image is constructed through a mental act, and very little sensible material suffices for the embodiment of our intentions; the significance of the painted image already existed before the image was constructed. By contrast, the real thing fully embodies its significance; the significance and the sensible materiality are unitary; neither has being before the other. When I intend to perceive an imaginary being, I believe that I have already perceived it. An actually perceived imaginary being has enough materiality for me to perceive the being that I intend to perceive, but no more. A real being has more materiality, and more significance, than I intend to perceive; when I perceive the real, I must adjust my general intentions to the apparitions which emerge from yonder depth. My general perceptual intention, my mental predisposition, does influence the appearances; the way in which I look at the thing does influence the way the thing looks to me. Nonetheless, my mental power is not unlimited; I cannot actually perceive everything that I intend to perceive, if I direct my mind toward external reality. I cannot experience my own arbitrary constructions as realities, because they have no significance beyond the meaning which I project. A real being shows me unsuspected meaning in every perception aimed toward its density; from yonder depth emerges significance beyond the meaning which I had in mind. Real materiality progressively releases hidden meaning during our mental exploration.[16] A phantasm or a painting, regarded as a real thing in the natural world, is a fragile slice, whereas a natural thing is solid, something substantial appearing through a forward surface. If someone exits from a doorway into the dimly lighted street, I can imagine that the indistinct figure over there is the person whom I await, but the figure may turn out to be someone else, a stranger, a thing with surprising significance. If, however, I do meet the person for whom I am waiting, if my imaginative anticipation is satisfied, "the familiar figure will emerge from this nebulous background as the earth does from a ground mist."[17] A real personage advances from a solid backing. A painting shows us a vaporous world which is grounded only in the pigment and canvas. Or, if the painted image is grounded in a reality beyond the material surface, the image is grounded more tenuously than the familiar person who approaches from the doorway and grasps my hand in greeting.

We experience things within a world; things appear always against a ground; the world is grounded in the earth, the latent plenitude which gives things their backing, their background. The world has absolute reality, more reality than the thing. The common sensible fluctuates between the real and the merely imaginary; facts turn into fictions, figments become facts; but the world remains stabile, the unmoved stage of apparitional activity. A sensible is less reversible, it fluctuates less, the more depth it possesses. We experience a being as real while its appearances are emerging from depth; the real reverses to the imaginary when depth is emptied; we witness a figment when no further appearances come forth from the background. A thing can vanish, but the world ground is a depth which can never be emptied; the world can never be flattened into a mere surface. The world is not an assemblage of sense impressions, nor is it a collection of sensory things; the world is "the inexhaustible reservoir from which things are drawn."[18] Not a collection of things, neither is the world the systematic interrelation among things.[19] Originally the world appears as the background against which particular things figure; the things are interrelated against this ground in which they are rooted. If uprooted, things become phantasms, despite their interconnections.

Occasionally, the background itself comes to the fore, so that we experience the world as an "individual."[20] But usually, things stand before us, holding back the ground, coming forth from the background where earth witholds its secrets. Usually, the world is depth and ground, a background

71

which surrounds us, embracing our body and the things, enclosing us within a horizon. The world horizon retreats as we advance toward the distant backdrop; the horizon withdraws as we draw things forth from their backing. Natural things figure within the horizon, but direct our gaze beyond the visible boundaries, into the encompassing invisibility. Each thing has an individual horizon, a boundary which unites its manifestations. Everything appears within its own horizon, and also within the horizon of the natural world. "The natural world is the horizon of all horizons. . . ."[21] A thing has its inner horizon, the limit within which its own appearances emerge, but also a thing has outer horizons, and the natural world is the outermost horizon. The things and their environment direct our mental ray past every horizon, toward the next frontier. Penetrating into grounding depth, pushing past limits, we explore boundless surroundings, straining toward a last horizon which never appears. Apparitions emerge from absence with a certain style; layered reality advances from depth with a distinctive rhythm. Each thing has an individuating vibrancy, yet reverberates also with the mood of the world. Everything in the natural world appears with the same general style; the world is "the style of all possible styles."[22]

The world possesses the outermost horizon and the uttermost style. As prospective perception moves into depth, along a style, toward the horizon, we experience depth as openness. Our closed world, the enclosed clearing, breaks open, releases us toward the uncleared, a wild environs which will capture us anew. Our world opens and closes as the world discloses and conceals its latency, the external foundation of our earthly potency. The surrounding horizon encloses an encircling panorama. This broad expanse which spreads before our gaze is less fundamental than the depth hidden behind the scenes. The panorama is rooted in

72

the abyss; when a depth is exhausted, apparitions no longer array themselves before our face; the appearances which have already emerged become phantasms of a thing which no longer appears. The temporal thread is broken; we lose the animating style, the apparitional generality which led our gaze into distance. The universal is "beneath" the surface, and when we penetrate, the universal is located "not before, but *behind* us."[23] When we move into horizontal depth, generality transfixes our body and penetrates into our corporeal background. Our experiential horizon is a circle which expands into surrounding depth, a sphere whose center receives the rays of the world; we capture the style of the things which catch our attention. A real thing is a sensuous density whose horizons are open toward depth; we enjoy the reality of the thing while we move through its open frontier; when the horizon closes, the visible becomes imaginary.

If we regard the world as something which exists outside our experience, we will complain that we never quite perceive this world whose horizon is always opening into depth. But we do perceive this world, precisely as never quite perceived; the visible manifests the invisibility of the visible, the latency of the actual. The embodied subject is temporal; we can perceive the thing and the world only through time. For temporal subjectivity, external reality could never be totally present, just as we can never be fully present to ourselves. We intend the totality along its style; the style intimates absent apparitions; these presumptive presentations are never fully given. [24] The thing and the world exist for us as visions in our intentional field. The appearances which figure within the field could not foreshadow natural reality, if the background were merely a "field of presence."[25] The intentional field is horizontal; its boundary is open upon the appearances which are absent;

we intend the unperceived along the style which animates our present perceptions. If subjectivity could make the thing and the world completely present, we would no longer experience reality, because the real requires absence in depth.[26] A subject lacking the experience of reality would not be a real subject; the subject too has depth and obscurity. The reality of the subject requires an intentional field with open horizons; when the boundaries close, so that the subject becomes closed in upon itself, the subject is shut off from external reality, and loses its own reality; subjectivity requires external realization. Closure produces indrawn subjectivity, but beneath this pure spirit remains an embodied subject whose intentional field has open horizons, unless limited by a neurotic obsession, or contracted by hysteria.[27]

Usually we experience the world as abysmal background and surrounding horizon, but sometimes the world comes to the fore, and appears within its own horizon, against its own ground; the world sometimes appears as an individual. We can understand this event, if we see how individual things are worlds, within the world. Each natural thing, each common sensible, has a horizon embracing specialized apparitions which symbolize one another and the thing itself. The thing is the world where these sensibles appear; the world itself appears through the sensibles which appear within its horizon. A thing which emerges within the wide natural world has an inner horizon and an outer horizon; the natural world understood as an individual has only an inner horizon, and this interior is the outermost of the outer horizons possessed by things. The things are worlds, each sense has its own world, and qualities too are worlds; but all these specialized worlds open into the one universe from which they are uprooted.[28] How does the world manifest itself as an individual, like the things within its horizon?

74

We must not suppose that all the common sensibles disappear into nothingness, leaving only the background against which they once figured as things; an empty backdrop is not an individual. The world can no more appear without common sensibles than the things can appear without special sensibles; the thing appears when we experience the special sensibles as showing forth the common sensible behind them; when the common sensible appears as something real, we experience the world as just the background against which the thing stands while displaying its own individuality. If the world comes forward as an individual, the world appears through the common sensibles, and we experience these as appearances of the world. The special sensibles too would be appearances of the world, rather than appearances of the common sensibles figuring as things. Sensible manifestations of the world can be more or less transparent, just as qualities, or momentary glimpses, can be more or less revelatory about the thing which bears these properties.

In childhood we enjoy a monistic experience of the world as a huge individual; all apparitions are experienced indiscriminately as appearances of cosmic reality. Maturation brings concern with particulars, and we suffer disappointment when the things which attract us turn into phantoms. But precisely in disillusionment we experience the world as an individual that backs up the promises which the particular things have made; when one thing disappoints us, something else satisfies our desire for reality; in disillusionment we experience a huge individual withdrawing its support from one thing and coming forward in another thing instead. The world nourishes our illusions even while undeceiving us; we experience the world as an individual when we witness reversal from the real to the illusory.[29]

More vaguely we experience the world as an individual

when the world appears as a background. When I shut one eye, I see a specialized world; each special sense has its world. Each common sensible is a world, and each special sensible. The color "yellow" is a world, and yet only a partial world. This particular color becomes universal and gives us access to the totality when the yellow becomes an overall illumination and dominates the sensory field; at the very moment this particular sensible becomes dominant, it becomes invisible as a particular and functions as a universal. "The 'World' is this whole where each 'part,' when one takes it for itself, suddenly opens unlimited dimensions—becomes a *total part*."[30] Each partial world is "*torn up* from the whole, comes with its roots, encroaches upon the whole, transgresses the frontiers of the others."[31] Most usually we do not uproot the things and isolate them from the background; we experience the common sensibles as things which stand forth from a background in which they are still entrenched. Thus we are vaguely aware that we could experience the ground itself as an individual which further particularizes itself in the things. The things can be experienced as rooted in the earth, but also the earth can be experienced as branching into the clearing. If I am prompted to isolate a common sensible from its surroundings, the soil still clings to its roots, and this momentary world retains the possibility of being grounded again. We never quite break our natal bond with the earth, except in reflection or hallucination. Roots, too long exposed, wither away; we grasp dead wood in our hands, rags and tatters which cannot be stitched into place. Our terrestrial home becomes a madhouse.

The Nonperceptual Imaginary

Embodied perception is always imaginal, a perception through images, but imagination is sometimes nonperceptual. Illusions, dreams, and hallucinations are nonperceptual imaginaries. Most vivid is the hallucination, a waking dream which isolates us from the world even when the lights are lit, and our eyes open. Obsessional delusions block the outer light, and lock us into private enclosures. The asylum wall is more deceptive than a mural; the museum is an enclosure which we can escape, but our obsessions hover always before us, obstructing our gaze. We shall argue, with Merleau-Ponty, that visions and voices have alienating power because the real world gives us imaginal leeway.

Examining the clinical evidence, Merleau-Ponty asserts that a hallucinating subject usually experiences a distinction between his hallucinations and his perceptions. Admittedly this distinction is often ambiguous, but the uncertainty does not arise from a mistaken belief or judgment that hallucinations are perceptions; the abnormal subject does not intellectually blur a boundary which in itself is clear.[32] When Merleau-Ponty says that the lunatic does not intellectually believe or judge, he is arguing against the rationalist understanding of hallucination. With the statement that the abnormal subject experiences a distinction between hallucination and perception, he begins the argument against empiricism. Our author argues against empiricism, against intellectualism, and against the objectivism which both have in common.

The empiricist understanding of hallucination is a causal explanation. Delusion is caused by a stimulus inside the body; internal agitation stimulates certain nerves just as these nerves are stimulated during perception by a cause outside the body. The hallucinating subject experiences a sense datum identical to the sensible experienced in perception. The only difference between hallucination and perception is that, in hallucination, the experienced sensible is caused by an internal stimulus, whereas in perception the experienced sensible is externally stimulated. The bodily subject experiences the effect only, not the cause; the effect is the same whether the stimulus is inside the body or outside. Only the physiologist experiences the cause; he has an outside standpoint. The bodily subject cannot observe himself from outside, and hence he experiences no distinction between illusion and reality. But we have noted that the patient does experience a distinction. Hence the empiricist understanding is incorrect.[33]

The intellectualist understands hallucination, not through physiological research, but through reflective construction; he creates a concept of hallucination, and conceives hallucination as a conceptual operation. For the rationalist, the normal intellect is already closed in upon itself; the reflective subject has just that being which it has for itself; I exist in my own sight, and have no existence beyond my visible presence. The mental vision operative in the subject has no being in itself, but has just the being which this intentional activity intends. There exists in the reflective subject nothing which the subject does not intend; and every being which the subject intends is inside the subject, and has being only for the subject. All intention is intellectual. Intellection is an intentional activity where the subject is certain that the intended object is precisely what it appears to be. A true appearance is a being which is what it seems, while a false appearance is not what it seems. The intellectualist supposes that the reflective subject can distinguish between true and false appearances without relating the apparitions to a thing outside the subject, since the subject intends no being which is not just a modification of the subject. Now, hallucinations are false appearances; the intellectualist sees that hallucination is not perception, since in perception we experience only those beings which appear as what they are. The rationalist says that hallucination is the false intellectual belief or the false intellectual judgment that the false appearances are true appearances. Or perhaps the hallucinating subject falsely believes or judges that he intends true appearances when truly the subject intends no appearances at all. Whether we say that the hallucinating subject falsely judges that false appearances are true appearances, or say that the hallucinating subject falsely judges that there are true appearances, there exists anyhow a false judgment which emerges in the for-itself. Merleau-Ponty argues that the rationalist explanation of hallucination is incompatible with the intellectualist understanding of subjectivity. How can a reflective subject falsely judge? The rationalist might reply that hallucination is a mere intellectual belief upon which the subject has not yet reflected and seen as false. But then we ask how the reflective subject can possess a belief upon which it has not reflected. If the subject has reflected upon its belief and seen that the belief is false, how can the subject still falsely believe? The intellect holds a false belief only when we cannot reflect upon our belief and see that the belief is false. Merleau-Ponty therefore concludes that the thoroughly conscious mind cannot hallucinate; the rationalist cannot understand hallucination, because he misunderstands original subjectivity. A hallucinating subject who thinks that his hallucination is objectively a hallucination can no longer hallucinate; and if the objective thinker still hallucinates, hallucination cannot be understood objectively.[34]

The rationalist and empiricist accounts are quite different, but they have in common the presupposition that we can understand hallucination objectively; they both suppose that we have sole access to being through objectifying reflection; all being is objective. The empiricist however does not suppose that objects are constructed. Here Merleau-Ponty agrees with the intellectualists, and would say that the empiricist simply projects into the world the object he has constructed, and then forgetfully supposes that the objects which he scientifically intends were already in the world naturally. When the empiricist causally explains hallucination, the body about which he speaks is an object, and not the lived body. The intellectualist wants reflectively to construct hallucination, as an object within the subject. Merleau-Ponty says that we must abandon construction and simply describe hallucination as it appears in original experience before all objectification.[35]

Who should perform the description? Since we ourselves do not suffer delusions, perhaps we should let the madman describe his own experience, while we listen. So we let him talk, and we notice that the abnormal subject usually experiences a distinction between hallucination and perception; but sometimes he cannot distinguish. Shall we believe our witness when he describes hallucination as perception, or shall we believe him when he describes hallucination as nonperceptual? We should not simply believe the madman, since he contradicts himself; we should "understand" [36] him. We achieve understanding through reflection upon his naive descriptions. Is our critical comprehension an intellectual construction? When understanding original hallucinatory experience, we do construct hallucination in reflection; we are creating a concept, making experience conceptual; but we avoid "arbitrary constructions,"[37] like the scheme produced by the rationalist. The rationalistic concept was arbitrary, because the intellectualist conceives the subject as totally reflective, closed off from the world and other subjects. The naive subject is open toward the world; he enjoys an original experience which is not yet reflective.[38]

How can we understand original experience through

reflection? Surely our reflection separates us from the description, and thus from the experience which the hallucinating subject describes. Reflection does require distance, but the patient's description already introduces distance into immediate experience, though the abnormal subject is less separated from his naivity when he describes than are we, when we reflect upon his description. We describe with words, and speech is separation; but the verbal medium provides contact across distance. When we reflect upon prereflective experience, the original is present, despite its absence. Original experience has a meaning, and speech can express this sense, because a primordial speech, a gestural language, stirs within mute perception. Our reflections upon life seem natural; primitive verbalization is not felt as a rupture which alienates our immediacy. The abnormal subject is present to himself across distance even when he describes his hallucinations to himself.[39]

Because the abnormal subject contradicts himself when he speaks to us about his experience, we do not uncritically accept his reports, but seek understanding through reflection. Perhaps we do not require lunatic testimony for understanding of lunacy, since the clinical patient is separated from his experience just as we are separated from his descriptions; perhaps we normal subjects should simply describe our own experience, and use our description of perception for an understanding of hallucination. Unfortunately, we too are separated from our original experience when we describe it. Can we overcome this separation? Perhaps we should artificially produce hallucinations in ourselves, and take the lunatic standpoint. But we are in no better position for comprehension. If we hallucinate altogether nonreflectively, then we cannot describe our experience, even to ourselves; if we do describe, we are separated from ourselves, and can be reflectively under-

81

stood by other subjects who do not believe everything we say. When we regain normal awareness and rejoin the others who are normal, we ourselves will not believe all we said while entranced. The abnormal subject who talks about his experience is separated from his experience and from himself. He is separated from himself as a person who in the past lived his original experience without describing it; and in the future he will be separated from himself as a person who no longer describes, as he does now. In the future, the abnormal subject can reflect upon his present description and not believe himself, just as another person can now reflect unbelievingly upon this description.[40]

When seeking comprehension, we must consider the total context in which normal subjects develop their understanding of perception and hallucination. The context is social; our situation encompasses the abnormal subject and the normal subject speaking with one another about their immediate experience. The abnormal subject describes his hallucinations, while we normal subjects describe our perceptions. The abnormal subject is already separated from his hallucinatory experience when he describes it, but he is less separated than are we, who are separated also from his description when we reflect. However, we are already separated from our own perceptual experience when we describe it, and we are further separated when we reflect upon our description along with the patient's description. Having reflected upon his testimony and ours, we return to our own immediacy and again describe perception. We are now describing our original experience through our understanding of his hallucinations, and simultaneously we redescribe his experience along with ours. We understand our experience within a whole which includes the abnormal subject with his distorted perceptions, and therefore we can rightly approach his experience through an understanding of our own. When we speak with the madman, and he speaks with us, we are not closed in upon ourselves, and our final description will express original hallucination. Socially engaged speculation is a verbal mediation which expresses the immediacy lost in scientific language.[41]

Listening to the abnormal subject while he talks about his experience, I see that my world lacks the visions and voices which he describes. I call his private objects "hallucinatory," not simply because I myself do not experience them, but because I experience things which apparently have inter-subjective existence. If other persons are not present, if I am the only person perceiving the things before me, I experience these beings as having potential existence for others. The abnormal subject, however, experiences the beings which I call hallucinatory as having their existence only for himself; he does not experience his visions as essentially intersubjective. [42] Of course, the hallucinatory beings have potential existence for others in the sense that others too might hallucinate. But this potential intersubjec-tivity is not a real potentiality, or, if real, has its reality only in us. Others too could hallucinate, but, even so, the hal-lucinatory being would not be experienced as having being for others; the figment which others experience would not be experienced as having being for me. The possibility that others could hallucinate belongs to the other subject, and not to the hallucinatory subject matter. Hallucinatory being has no depth, or lacks the depth which the perceived being possesses. A being which has being for me, but no being for others, lacks the depth which I experience in a being that has actual or potential existence for other subjects. Still less does a sensible being possess depth, if it has actual existence for me now but no future existence. Perceptual depth is essentially potential intersubjectivity, since subjectivity is already intersubjective, a relation between past, present,

83

and future selves. The beings which I perceive, and which I call "things," I experience as having at least potential being for others; and the encompassing world I experience as a territory which I share with other percipients. I perceive other bodily subjects living amongst the things in the external world; and I perceive that the other subjects perceive the same things that I perceive. When the others do not actually perceive the things which I perceive, I perceive that they perceive things which have potential existence for me, and I see that they perceive me as a bodily subject who perceives things which have potential existence for them. Everything corporeal is situated in the same cosmos. My body situates me in a particular time and place, so that the things which I perceive are not present to me as they would be presented to another subject at another spatiotemporal location. Nonetheless, in the perceived thing present before me I experience potential presence to other subjects, just as I experience the potential appearances which the thing could generate in my presence if I moved to another location. I do not yet perceive the actual existence which the sensible thing will possess when I perceive it elsewhere, but I anticipate that existence; the future apparitions have an actual potentiality in the present. I anticipate that the thing before me will display further existence for myself and the others.[43]

Depth can be called "fullness."[44] The natural being possessing depth is filled with latent apparitions, full with appearances which have potential existence for future subjectivities. Through the appearances present to me, a perceived being directs my mind toward all the absent apparitions; my bodily intentions are solicited or "motivated"[45] by the intentions which I experience in the present appearance. A hallucinatory being does not motivate my bodily directionality toward absent appearances. A hallucination

lacks temporal "thickness."[46] Thickness is the distance between appearances which emerge from depth; thickness is
also the temporal distance which separates the percipient
subject from himself. The subject who experiences an appearance of a sensible thing is temporally separated from
himself as a subject who has already experienced an appearance of that being, and is separated from himself as a
subject who will later experience another appearance. The
perceived being, the reality, can be called "ponderous."[47]
The perceived is weighed down with the appearances
which fill its depth to overflowing.

The delusory visions and voices lack depth, fullness,
thickness and weight; these phantoms exist not in the world
among the substantial externals but in a bodily subject
which no longer exists in the world. The hallucinating
subject inhabits the human organism, but the body no
longer prolongs its life into the environment. A figment has
no depth, and thus exists not deep in the world but on the
surface; the hallucination floats on the hither side of solid
reality. If the madman envisions a person who speaks, the
visionary has already heard what the person says as soon as
the speech begins. This audible vision does not exist in
natural time; normally we have fully heard what a person
says only when he has finished speaking. The hallucinatory
personage is just the hallucinating subject experienced as
outside the subject in the world. We can experience our
subjectivity as outside the body, because our experiential
body is the experience of our situation in the world. When
the body subject no longer has its existential place in the
world, we experience our bodily situation as the world
itself. Our body is worldly, but is not the whole world; the
body subject is that part of the world which orients us within
the world as a whole; we experience our embodiment as
whole world when we no longer experience the w

side our body. Madness is a disturbance of our body image, our habitual body. Hallucination is not so much the experience of a positive existent as it is the experience of our intentional potentialities, possible mental acts which no longer reach reality. We do not deny that the abnormal subject intends a ghostly materialization, which we have called a "hallucinatory being." We do however affirm that the patient experiences as an actual being his disturbed potentialities for intending real beings. The abnormal subject often intends real externals through his disturbed potentialities, but the real beings thus intended become distorted, become hallucinatory. The inner image is normally transparent to outer reality. Hallucinatory beings are either more particular than perceived things, or more general. Most hallucinatory beings are apparitions which quickly vanish; they are sensations rather than things; the momentary figment is a particularized presentation with no temporal thickness. More rarely, a hallucinatory being thickens and perdures through several apparitions, but such a figment does not possess all the layers that a perceived being would have. The enduring hallucinatory being presents enough appearances to make evident its general style, but not enough for us to experience its full particularity; this hallucination is full of gaps. Hallucinatory beings, then, are sometimes experienced as appearances without a style of appearing, and sometimes are experienced as a general style of appearing with hardly any appearances. These vacuous entities can have no causal relationships among themselves; they possess only intentional interrelationships, which express the most general intentionality of the hallucinating subject; the intentional interrelations among delusory apparitions express the general orientation of the madman toward the world in which he no longer has his being. Hallucinatory beings express the general situation of the worldless body subject.[48]

Our description thus far supports mainly our argument against the empiricist, since we have been describing hallucination as experientially distinct from sense perception. Merleau-Ponty next supports the argument against the rationalist, by showing that hallucination is distinct from judgment. Through reflection upon the thing and the natural world we can construct the object and the objective world; then we can reflect again upon uncultivated nature and intellectually judge whether the sensible beings now before us can be conceived as objective realities. The rationalist regards hallucination as the false judgment that an apparitional entity is objective. Merleau-Ponty replies that the hallucinating subject is not disillusioned when we tell him that his visions and voices are nonobjective; we do not disillusion him, because he himself does not judge that his hallucinations exist in the objective world. The abnormal subject does not dispute our judgment, but he hallucinates regardless.[49]

The abnormal subject experiences hallucinatory beings as real, because he no longer perceives the real; the real world and the things within that world no longer express themselves; the expressive appearances of the body subject close up the soul within the bodily world. For the encapsulated subject, hallucinations have more existence than his perceptions. Hallucination is not simply imagination; it is an abnormalcy in perceptual imagination, a malfunction in the imagination normally operative within perception. The normal subject nonreflectively experiences a real world; but because he is situated in a body, and because his intentional field has a narrow horizon, he cannot be certain that further experience will not reveal as phantastical the being

87

which he now experiences as real. Rationalism incorrectly understands perception as originally a reflection upon perception, a reflexivity which seeks certitude. Objectifying reflection is a later development; we become objective after reality betrays our trust. When we experience a reversal from the real to the imaginary, our original belief becomes doubt; we reflect upon the beings which we originally experience as real, and ask whether they are really real. Are they certainly real, or probably real, or possibly real, or doubtfully real? The beings certified through such reflection we intellectually judge to be objective, but the normal subject originally experiences beings as real without any dubitation. The appearances of the body subject join with appearances of beings outside the body, so that the subject opens toward a real world which expresses external depth through all these interposed appearances. Nonreflectively the normal subject remains open upon the world, and maintains his being in the world. The abnormal subject withdraws from the world so that the body image no longer joins with the appearances of the world; the disconnected body schema becomes a delusory panorama. Cautious persons who fear deception construct for themselves an objective world; but objectivity arises through reflection upon a prior experience. Preobjective reality is the foundation for intellectually certified reality. Without this foundation, scientific objects would have no more reality than hallucinations. Natural dreams, however, do not arise through conceptual artifice; delusions are not theoretical constructs.[50]

Our intentional openness upon the real world Merleau-Ponty calls "faith" or "primary opinion."[51] This trust is mute, but when expressed in speech is a view close to common sense, except that common sense often includes opinions taken from science. Our natal openness we can call "perceptual faith."[52] When we speak about "faith" we indicate a contrast with the doubt which motivates the reflective quest for certainty. "Opinion" indicates a contrast with the knowledge which reflection gains through its mental constructions. Though we believe that we are open toward the world, we suspect that we have illusions; likewise the madman suspects that an outside world exists even though he cloisters his senses. In original experience there is no clear distinction between the imagined and the perceived, because we have never witnessed all the apparitions which would enable us to construct the world as an object. The child, or childlike subject who has not yet reflected, experiences a world which encompasses both the imagined and the perceived; in this most primordial experience the world presents itself as a single individual which shines through every apparition. Dreams are distinct from perceptions in that dreams appear only to sleepers; dreams nonetheless are appearances of the one primal world. Once we have reflected upon our experience, we mark the imaginary as not an appearance of the externals. But since we can never finally assemble an objective world, the imagined is always included within the perceived, and we can hallucinate.[53]

Perception is not certain, but we should not therefore suppose that the thing perceived is only possibly, or probably, perceived. The originally perceived thing is not a "permanent possibility of perception."[54] Original experience does exhibit a nonstatistical probability,[55] but objective possibility and probability do not emerge until something perceptual changes into a phantasm. From disillusionment arises doubt, and doubt evolves as reflection upon original experience. Exercising critical reflection, we calculate possibilities. But despite doubt, and without any calculation, we still experience things straightforwardly as real and perceived. Every naively perceived being can be "cancelled"[56] and emerge as merely imaginary, but the being which is no

89

longer experienced as real is replaced by another reality. Thus, even though every entity experienced as perceived can afterwards be experienced as uncertain, we are at least certain that we experience things and a world. We cannot meaningfully doubt that the world is real, because the world is not just a collection of things whose reality we can doubt; rather, the world is that whole from whose depth all things appear. When we consider that we originally perceive everything against the background of the world, we see that we are never altogether disillusioned, for the world with its open horizon leads us to anticipate disillusionment and further perception. In our primitive experience of the real world, we do not yet possess that objective realm which we construct as a protection against error. We do perceive the world, but we do not enjoy certified perception.

We have spoken about the intentional object, and have said this object is not objective; our perception is originally directed toward a preobjective goal. Correspondingly we may speak about the intending subject, and may assert that the naive percipient is not fully reflective, does not fully exist in his own sight. A person can experience hallucination as perception because he is not conscious of himself as a subject who is hallucinating. The hallucination which he experiences as a perception does not exist for him as a reflectively certified perception, nor has reflection designated the apparent perception as an illusion. A subject could construct a hallucination only if he did not reflect that he was doing so; whenever the hallucination exists for the subject as an explicit construction, the hallucination no longer deceives. The madman does not originally construct his phantasies; he still hallucinates even when he reflects that he hallucinates, because hallucination is an experience more original than reflection. We do not say that the naive subject is completely nonreflective, completely lacking self awareness; we do not entirely divide the nonreflective from the reflective subject. The subject who reflects that he hallucinates still hallucinates, but his hallucination does not have the same meaning that it would have without reflection. We insist only that the human subject is never totally reflective; the pure spirit, conceived by the rationalist, is an ideal goal which we never reach. Between myself, who has already intended a given being, and myself now, who reflectively intends that being precisely as already intended, there is a temporal thickness, such that I can doubt whether that being which I once intended was indeed intended precisely as I now intend it. Yet this doubt presupposes that I do indeed intend my past self; and my belief that through reflection I can intend a being without illusion presupposes the perceptual faith that in original experience I intend a real world within whose horizons I experience all disillusion and reassurance.[57]

The perceptual experience binding us to the world gives us imaginal latitude. Reality is always deep in distance, always coming forward, but remaining absent. The sensible thing is revealed through veils which, unannounced, become shrouds. Unless perceptual experience gave us imaginal leeway on the way toward the thing, we could never experience our illusionary drifting as perceptual prospection.

SCEPTICAL BELIEF

Natural reality emerges as a depth which is clear in the foreground but obscure farther back. The sensible things display lighted surfaces across the clearing, but hidden behind are further surfaces, and far in the background is the earthly density which has not yet become apparitional. Reality is obscure because the background has not come

91

forward and displayed itself in breadth. Again, reality is obscure because the surfaces in the foreground possess an opacity. These shining surfaces gradually become transparent; they make way before our gaze. We are always looking for something farther on, and the interceding surfaces slowly efface themselves before the things that we want to see. Although invisible, the layered transparencies remain as an atmosphere which lends the thing a radiance, a vital breath. The transparent layers pile up and overcast the very thing they reveal. Operative invisibility requires a secret opacity. During perceptual prospection we experience an opacity in the background, an opacity in the foreground, and an opacity on the way back into the background, a triple obturation which gives depth its obscurity.

Natural obscurity pains the eye that strains for clarity. We want to strip away the veils and see the thing all naked before our gaze. We want the bare facts, the stark truth, not sorcery; we struggle to dispel this stupor; we want to see the things laid out before us in broad daylight. But total revelation would disembody our spirit; total clarity would eliminate our senses and sensitivities. We already possess all the light we need for making our way through life, and the world promises us more illumination, when we need it. We need only the inexhaustible promise and its gradual fulfillment. Without the promise we would confront a chaos. Instead, our perceptual organs work within an ambiguous wilderness, where the wandering shades haunt solid reality. The primordial world is atmospheric, not the airless earth of pedestrian positivism, yet not the aetherial world of disembodied intellectualism. Nature cannot be understood as breadth and clarity. Naked reality is beyond our grasp, while we possess hands and eyes. Our perceptual organs are the instruments of a waking dreamer.

We have a natural desire to behold reality, but whence arises the demand for naked reality, a reality without apparitions? The demand arises from doubt, from the negativity which afflicts our mind when we grapple with vacuous materiality. The originally perceived world is positive, packed full with existence. This positivity is verbalized in naive realism, but if the realist suffers sufficient disillusionment he becomes sceptical, and original faith is transmogrified into a Pyrrhonian doubt which expresses the world as a simple lack. The Pyrrhonist condemns the world as an apparition which lacks convincing solidity. Doubt becomes encapsulated; reflecting upon illusion we develop a total distrust, and no longer abandon ourselves to the environment which could restore our confidence. Natural doubt is exacerbated as an unbelief which calls for naked reality, and denies that we can satisfy our desire; the demand is absolute, and deception total. The denial inflames our frustrated desire; total scepticism stimulates a totalitarian thought which annihilates doubt by constructing an objective world, a realm deprived of illusionary power. Thought forgets our native habitat; the soul has already withdrawn from the world when doubt becomes uncompromising. We cannot remain naive, because the original world generates deception; positivity engenders a modulating negativity. But we cannot become totally sceptical, if we remember our origins. Reality has degrees: the world is not an unmodified positivity, nor is subjectivity an unqualified negativity. External plenitude shades into the subject. Consequently, we can never withdraw into Pyrrhonian nothingness, and we cannot lunge forward and catch things all naked behind the scenes. Merleau-Ponty proposes an interrogative philosophy which doubts while believing. Interrogation is a thought which remains primordial; the natural

93

things cast themselves into doubt while promising further revelations; this sensory dialectic becomes articulate in human thought.

Total Scepticism

"We see the things themselves, the world is what we see. . . ."[58] These words express our native realism, which the more reflective philosopher must question. Who are "we?" What is "seeing?" What is the "thing," and the "world?" These puzzles disorient the natural man, making him stagger where once we stood flat footed. Our questions obscure a reality which seemed perfectly clear; even the clearest answers seem obscurantist, because they imply a prior ignorance. Philosophy is a sophisticated naivity which the untutored primitive can never understand. "It is at the same time true that the world is *what we see* and that, nonetheless, we must learn to see it. . . ."[59] We can learn only if we know nothing, and yet we want to learn what we already know without verbal articulation. Our ignorance is a pretense which makes a space in which the world itself can speak; the philosopher wants to talk about the world which everyone mutely understands. The thinker doubts the world because he, like everyone else, believes in the world; he believes that the world is real enough to overcome his doubt, and give him verbal knowledge where once he and the world were speechless. "But philosophy is not a lexicon. . . ."[60] The philosopher does not shrink back into another world where he knows merely the meaning of words; he wishes to express the things themselves, "from the depths of their silence."[61] Philosophical interrogation is not a doubt which annihilates reality so that we can construct our world from within. Material reality already contains a negativity which appears in the imaginary, and finally in philosophical thought, which operates with verbal images.[62]

94

Annihilating doubt often arises through reflection upon disillusionment, but we can reach total scepticism also through inner reflection upon images which have never deceived us. Suppose that, sitting in my study, I look at my desk, upon which I am writing. I experience this furniture as a perceptual reality; the desk is an opaque depth filled with potential appearances; the latent apparitions are packed together as a dark opacity which halts the probing gaze; my visual ray stops short at the density positioned before my face. Suppose that, while looking at the desk, I imagine a factory, which I have frequently seen, but which is now located beyond my visual field. Even though the building is outside my periphery, I believe that I experience the factory itself just as surely as I do my writing desk. My intentionality does not stop at an image of the factory; the imaginative intermediary does not block access to the factory itself. Also I believe that, encompassing the desk which I perceive and the factory which I imagine, there is a world, a surrounding horizon from whose depth I myself emerge.[63] Centering myself in the world, I imagine the factory without hallucinating; my visual image does not appear before me as a solid reality comparable with the furniture in the room. I am not disillusioned if someone tells me that the factory is not in my apartment, and not in my head. Nevertheless, I may lose my belief that I experience the factory and the desk, if I reflect that I myself have my existence in the world, and reflect that the factory and the desk have existence for me. In reflection I direct my mind toward my intentionality, and become aware of things in the world as my intentional objects; I no longer experience being itself but only being for me. My intentional objects have their being only for the intending subject, and they have precisely the being that I intend. The subject who reflects upon himself experiences himself as intentional

95

activity, and sees being itself turn into being for us. I turn back upon the mental directionality along which I straightforwardly reach the world; the reflective belief that I myself intend the world takes away the belief that I intend the world itself. Snatched from the real world in which I was naively centered, I inhabit a dream world whose apparitions center themselves in me.[64]

This egocentric scepticism, this Cartesian doubt, which reflects that everything has being for me, is different from the Pyrrhonism which argues from disillusionment. When deceived, we experience a natural reversal from the real to the illusory; something in the world turns out to be something else; this reversal is a practical experience, and not a theoretical operation. Meditating upon our disillusionment, the Pyrrhonist argues that everything may be illusory, since the things which disappointed us seemed once as real as the things in which we still believe. The Pyrrhonist doubts that anything which has being for us has being in itself, but his doubt is produced naturally, not by an artificial operation where we turn back upon ourselves. Pyrrhonism does not start from solipsism, but this ancient scepticism has assisted the modern return to the self.

Without becoming Cartesian, what shall we say against the Pyrrhonist? From "dreams, delirium, or illusions" [65] the ancient sceptic argues that all the sensible entities in our experience may be merely imaginary, or "false."[66] We must reply that the sceptic presupposes the perceptual faith which he distrusts. If we did not sometimes experience truth, we would not understand what "false" means; falsity requires for its significance an experiential contrast with truth. The sceptic tacitly postulates a true world which has its being in itself, and this veracious realm he covertly contrasts with perceptual entities, categorizing the perceived with the imaginary as subjective existence. The sceptic categorizes the perceived with the imaginary, simply because we once experienced the imaginary as perceived; he forgets that we experienced a particular being reverse from the perceived to the imaginary, and thereby reveal its falsity, only within a global experience which still exhibits some things as perceptual. The sceptic regards himself as more sophisticated than the rustic who believes that we perceive things themselves; but the doubter is equally naive, because he too postulates a being in itself, albeit a being beyond our experience. Once we have discarded this spurious postulate, we can simply describe the difference between the real and the illusory. The perceived appears as an open series of coherent appearances, and solicits from us an open series of coherent perceptions. The imaginary does not generate this open coherence, and we cannot bodily explore or "observe"[67] the imaginary being; the dream appears as an apparitional series which is full of gaps, riddled with incoherence. This experiential distinction between the imaginary and the perceived adequately answers the sceptical doubt that we ever perceive. Of course, we can still raise particularized doubts; naive realism should become critical; but we can become cautious without becoming catatonic.[68]

Particularized doubt is a negativity which nature itself eliminates as we perceptually explore the thing which we distrust. But there still remains a problem, even when we have answered the Pyrrhonian doubt, and even when nature answers our particular doubts. There remains a problem about our access to the world, and we begin to see this difficulty only when the ancient dilemmas have been dismissed. The modern sceptic wonders how the imaginary can ever be experienced as perceptual. How can we experience a dream as the true world? Our dreams are rags torn from a closely woven fabric; and yet, while dreaming, we experience the rags as the whole cloth. How can we, when fascinated, experience the unconsciousness of not having perceived as the consciousness of having perceived, or observed? Suppose we admit that the imaginary is shallow and empty, quite different from the perceived, which has a depth crammed full with apparitions; and suppose we admit that our belief in the imaginary is quite distinct from our belief in the perceived; and let us admit that the hallucinating subject no longer possesses our discrimination between the imaginary and the perceived, and no longer has in his private world any discriminative standard. If there emerged within the diseased soul a single entity from the publically perceived world, the patient would again know the difference between dream and reality; and he would no longer hallucinate, or he would recognize the dream as deceptive. Despite our admissions, we must note that the living subject can lose his intuitive criterion, even while he believes that he possesses it. Should we therefore argue that we are never certain that we have possession? If we can withdraw from the real world unawares, "nothing proves to us that we are ever in it, nor that the observable is ever entirely observable, nor that it is made of another fabric than the dream."[69] This is the argument of the modern sceptic who turns back upon his subjectivity and seeks internal criteria. This reflective route "begins well beyond the Pyrrhonian arguments."[70]

The Pyrrhonist argues from practical disillusionment whereas the modern sceptic argues from theoretical uncertainty. Practical uncertainty easily becomes theoretical, but nonetheless we can separate the ancients from the moderns, the empirics from the idealists, whether the idealists be empiricist or rationalist. The ancient empiric would be convinced if the external things would only appear without sensible apparitions; a trustworthy nature should reveal

98

itself without any being-for-us. Theoretical uncertainty, purely hypothetical doubt, must be overcome by an internal reality which appears as the law regulating the sensible apparitions; intelligible reality has its being only for us. The idealist sceptic wants consistency with himself; he wants to avoid saying anything about the world which contradicts what he has already said; thus he wants essences. The empiric is close to the naive realist, who wants consistency with the world; he wants to avoid saying anything which contradicts the facts; he wants straightforward facts, and withdraws into himself only when the world cuts him off with natural illusions. Disillusioned, the Pyrrhonist argues that I cannot be sure anything sensible is nondeceptive, because the only relevant empirical difference among the items which I experience is that some have deceived me whereas others have not; I cannot conclude that the items which have not yet betrayed me are trustworthy. The Pyrrhonist departs from naive realism when he postulates a reality beyond experience. Every adult has experienced disillusionment, and has reflected upon the illusions which betrayed him; and thus we all admit that some entities experienced as real are untrustworthy. But each particular illusion has some distinguishing mark, beyond the simple fact that it has betrayed us. Our realism becomes critical; we believe that, by recalling the various marks of illusion, we can discover at least some beings which are trustworthy. If we ask whether this or that particular perception is non-reversible, nature itself answers our doubt, though not with absolute finality. Even the wisest person can make mistakes. Seeking practical wisdom, the critical realist attempts to differentiate between the nonreversible perceived and the reversible, by making comparisons with those particular items which have already reversed from the perceived to the imaginary. When this attempt is continually defeated,

99

the defeat may lead to despair, and the despair may be expressed in Pyrrhonian arguments. The disappointed empiric entirely overlooks the "problem of the world," [71] which arises when we notice that the criterion for reality is depth. Our problem is how we can lose the criterion and withdraw from the world, while we believe that we still have our bearings. The idealist sees the problem, but withdraws into himself for the solution; he becomes locked up with his representations. The correct solution, however, lies beyond our representations, but not beyond our experience. The natural world lies somewhere between the reflective inner life and the straightforward exteriority which speaks vaguely about the really real, and then, disillusioned, counts "the perceived and the imaginary indiscriminately among our 'states of consciousness.' "[72] We can solve the problem of the world, if we simply describe our original sense experience, without assuming that we already understand the subject, the world, the thing, and the imaginary.[73]

Interrogation

Holding firmly the perceptual faith that we perceive the thing itself, and not some "representation"[74] which exists only for us, we may begin our description of the problematic world by adding to our faith the statement that "the thing is at the end of my gaze and, in general, at the end of my exploration."[75] My gaze plays over the desk located within my visual field, and I notice that intentional activity is a temporal exploration, a bodily interrogation of a perduring presentation. My gaze interrogates the desk concerning the appearances which this thing can present to my body along the temporal dimension. The thing is the objective, the target, at which my intentional act now aims, the goal which attracts my intentional activity. Though I modify mute perceptual faith with the statement that I myself am the person who sees the thing before me, I do not yet introduce the understanding which I gain through reflection upon other bodily subjects, or upon my own body experienced as the body of another. Even without reflecting externally upon my body, I must allow that the thing which I see has a singular being for me, because I experience my own body along with the things which I perceive; when I see things in the external world, my own body is always in the foreground. "With each flutter of my eyelashes a curtain lowers and rises, though I do not think for an instant of imputing this eclipse to the things themselves. . . ."[76] Each footstep jars the cameras held in my eyesockets, and "with each movement of my eyes that sweep the space before me the things suffer a brief torsion, which I also ascribe to myself."[77] We would badly express these organic events, if we said that my body covers, or hides, or distorts the things, or interposes a veil between the things and myself; I do not experience my body as something "subjective" or "corporeal"[78] which blocks my external access. The nearby apparitions of my body do not isolate me from the things; likewise, monocular images do not isolate me, when my eyes function together.[79] My body appears as a garment which dresses the things without concealing them.

The monocular image is an appearance of my body; the binocular image is an appearance of the thing beyond my body. The thing outfits itself with the monocular images and wears them as a unitary flesh; the double vision disappears, and the thing exhibits its solidity through a single apparition. The thing which we see with both eyes is not something constructed from two monocular images; we do not consciously assemble the unitary thing from separate facets. The monocular appearances do not have existence in the same sense that the thing perceived with both eyes has existence. The monocular appearances are "phantoms"[80] which vanish when we use both eyes synergetically; in the place where the phantoms disappeared, there materializes the thing, which alone is "real."[81] The sensibles experienced through a single eye are "pre-things." [82] The binocular presentation we experience as the thing itself, whereas the monocular appearances are only a certain "divergence"[83] from the real appearance. The monocular appearances are intentionally related to the real appearances from which they diverge; in vision we experience the monocular appearances continually converging upon the binocular real appearance, and then diverging again. The monocular visions have merely imaginary being; when the double images converge upon the real appearance and disappear there, we experience a reversal from the imaginary to the real; when the two monocular appearances reappear and diverge from the binocular appearance, which we experience as the thing itself, we experience a reversal from the real to the imaginary.[84] The thing dresses and undresses before our eyes; but unclad reality may hide behind its robes; the garments become curtains which look as if they would be revealing, if worn.

We cannot put the two monocular appearances beside the one binocular appearance and compare the two with the one; the monocular appearances and the binocular appearances are not comparable, because the two and the one do not have being in the same sense; we cannot compare imaginary being with real being, except to distinguish them. We can however put the two monocular appearances beside one another and compare these. But because the monocular appearances and the binocular appearances are incommensurable, we cannot construct a binocular appearance by putting the two monocular images together as a single apparition; the perceptual event where the monocular images converge, and merge upon the thing, does not result from an intellectual synthesis. Lest the perceptual synthesis be confused with the intellectual, Merleau-Ponty calls the convergence a "metamorphosis."[85] "Each perspective *merges into* the other and, in so far as it is still possible to speak of a synthesis, we are concerned with a 'transitional synthesis.' "[86] The metamorphosis takes place in "synergic perception."[87] We can put together the monocular appearances only "*by looking*;"[88] we cannot make them converge by thinking. When we look, we do not simply pile up garments; we pile them upon something which bodily assumes these layers, and wears them.

In visual sense perception, the sensible thing is located farther beyond the monocular images; these imaginary appearances intend the absent reality, and the thing from afar is present in its images; the monocular images disappear when they converge upon the binocular image, which appears as the reality which the monocular images always intended. The perceived thing, when it appears, must maintain in its depth all the intentional interrelationships among the vanished images; likewise the percipient subject must retain in its depth all the intentional interrelations between the binocular image and the vanished monocular images. I gain access to the perceptual world by looking with my eyes; the same bodily eyes through which I see two monocular images are just a little later eyes through which I perceive a single binocular image, when the two eyes function in unison. My bodily intentionality exhibits a quite remarkable relation with external nature; sometimes my body closes me off from the things, and sometimes it opens me outward; sometimes I remain closed up in appearances, and sometimes I gain access through my body to the things themselves. Our ability to reach the yonder externals is a power which becomes manifest along with our ability to remain closed up with phantasms; we experience our access to the things as just the other side of our ability to withdraw; and we experience our retreat from the things as the reverse side of our natural ability to enter the perceived world. Untutored realism believes both that we have perceptual access to the things themselves and that appearances of the things have their being within our body. We hold both these beliefs when engaged in practical affairs; but, when we verbally express our tacit experience, the two beliefs sound theoretically incompatible. If we ignore the verbal contradiction and return to original experience, our phenomenological description of binocular vision shows that perceptual faith is justified.[89]

We have mitigated the excessive scepticism which arises when I reflect that I myself experience the things. We may now deal with the doubt which arises when I reflect that other embodied subjects also have experiences. Binocular vision shows me that I sometimes perceive things in the world, and not just appearances inside my body; but now I doubt whether the other subjects perceive things in the world as I do. I perceive a thing out there, and I perceive that the other has eyes which converge upon the thing, but I do not perceive the apparitions which he experiences; therefore his images must be somewhere inside his body. But then I reflect that the other perceives me just as I perceive him; he does not experience the appearance that I do, and for him even my binocular image is somewhere inside my body. Again I doubt whether I really perceive things in the world; or else I doubt whether my world is the real world. Should I, after all, speak about the beings which I experience as "things," and should I call my experience "perception?" Should I call the background against which these sensibles figure a "world?" If I speak about a "world," I mean a special realm which has being only for me; but the "world," properly speaking, is a common world.[90] Against this excessive doubt which arises when I reflect upon other persons, we may argue that my binocular image and the binocular image which the other possesses operate like the monocular images which I possess. The various binocular images converge upon an intersubjective apparition which we subjects experience communally as a thing in the public world. My private world and the other private worlds are divergent perspectives upon a common reality.[91]

The common sensible has enough depth to be called a "thing" because it is common to all my special senses, and also because it is common to all bodily subjects. The special senses within my own body overlap one another in the same way that the special visual sense overlaps itself through the two eyes; the common sensible is common to the various special senses in the same way that it is common to the two specialized organs which incarnate the visual sense. The two eyes are organic specializations of a sense which itself is a specialization of the body, understood as a generalized sense organ. The various special senses all possess the body subject as common property. The visual sensibles overlap on the common sensible which we intend through the two eyes; the body subject, through all the various special senses and their organs, overlaps its perspectives on the common sensible. Now, the body subject, or common sense, is a specialization of our common humanity. Man is a general subjectivity which perceives the world from multiple standpoints; individual visions converge and exhibit a common sensible located in a communal world.[92]

Our reflective interrogation has restored the perceptual faith that we experience the real world. Restoration converts belief into certainty; before doubting, we enjoyed belief; after doubt was conquered, we regained our habitual peace. Certitude is an examined belief which we cannot doubt, because certitude has overcome the doubt which overcame untested assurance. Certitude emerges in the reflective questioning of original belief. Doubt is unbelief, a loss of naivity; and doubt is uncertainty, a lack of the certitude which restores our lost innocence. If we lose our certitude, and fall again into uncertainty, losing our loss of lost innocence, we can only reflect once more upon prelapsarian experience, and recapture our hard-won comprehension. Reflection generates a rational belief which internalizes doubt; certitude remains shadowed with uncertainty. We rest assured in a sceptical belief; our confidence is interrogative. Reflection upon perceptual faith makes us confident that nature is deceptive, but we trust that nature will continually undeceive us. The world is illusionary, but disillusionment renews our confidence, because nature could not undeceive us without engaging our trust in a newly emergent reality. When we let nature question itself in human language, our thought negates the immediate, but produces a second immediacy. Mediation negates immediacy and negates its own negation; thought is the positivity of double negation, a negative position which returns us to the positivity which speech negated. The untutored realist does not suffer the generalized doubt; and the positivist rejects doubt; but the reflective philosopher abandons himself to the suffering of the negative. He lets nature raise the generalized doubt, the totalizing nihilation. In the night of human denial, nature overcomes negativity, simply by exhibiting its plenitude in the space that doubt evacuates. Human language is a natural expressivity which sounds in the void; a resounding medium emerges in the vacuum, mediating the distance between man and world.

When we voice our doubts, reality becomes interrogative. The apparitional world emerges in the place where man reflects, the locus where human images cultivate brute positivity. Humanized nature can never be spread out in breadth, its skin exposed beneath our gaze, all its depth a pellicle, all its guises stripped away. Our own body is pressed against the world; the things clothe themselves in our flesh; reality hides its nakedness in our perceptual embrace. The hand covers the things discovered; the visionary conceals the things his eye reveals. And then we lose our grip; or the coverings come loose in our grasp; the things slip away, discarding their garments in our hands, leaving their imprint in this flesh which is now mine alone. The thing which pressed against my palm leaves an impression, and I mistake the imprint for something that presses. Suddenly, solid reality emerges among the phantoms, making a fresh impact; imaginal reality emerges among the nonperceptual imaginaries, and I experience disillusionment; a void opens between me and the world; I suffer the nothingness of nonperception. Disillusionment is the phenomenon which lets us see that we do not perceive. Nature abhors this vacuum, this annihilating distrust. This void, this gap, this hiatus, "is the zero of pressure between two solids that makes them adhere to one another."[93] The world rushes into my arms, and presses against my palms. My eyeball too is buried in matter; perception becomes a blind immediacy, an immersion which suffocates rationality. The contact makes me draw away; I stand back to get a look. But, if I remain immersed, sunk in the sleep of reason, nature soon leaves me standing alone; the things in my grasp withdraw into the background, and leave me staring.

Vision requires distance; yet we cannot see in the void. Speculation demands doubt; but, without trust, our thought cannot reach the world. Interrogative thinking is an engaged speculation, a detached practice, a practical involvement which evolves a visionary disengagement. Vision requires a medium, a mediating materiality illumined with spirit, a positivity modulated with mental nothingness. Visible nature has an atmosphere, a nimbus which bathes the animate body. Perceptual space is plenished with an aether which aetherializes the denser earth; the background decompresses its density and populates the air with ghostly intermediaries. My own body, so compact in its depth, becomes a transparency in the pile that prolongs my body into the world; my eye is the eyepiece of an invisible telescope whose layered lenses refract the gaze, and concentrate my attention upon the yonder visibles. Perception is "teleperception."[94] The sensible layers which guide my gaze are not images floating "free;"[95] the image is bound to the background, and opens me into the distance, like a lens. My own head, containing its optical equipment, looks opaque from outside, and yet the inhabitant who looks along the neural routes does not dream of plucking out his eyes for a better view. Because vision requires eyes, an optical medium, we cannot strip nature naked; we cannot see pure essences or bare facts, because we cannot strip away our own body.

When we haunt the native habitat, our soul is never naked; our fleshly outfit is the body of the mind. Sensate flesh is not an outergarment insulating detached interiority. The soul can disrobe, but the disembodied soul has lost access to the world; nature meanwhile can shed its images, but dispirited matter loses access to our mind. Indeed, the desirous grasp can undress the thing which inflames our curiosity; we can remove the concealing drapes, the patent trimmings, but we expose a reality whose skin can deceive. We unmistakably behold reality in the raw, undoubtedly we hold truth in our hand, but captured nature covertly escapes our captivated flesh, and clothes itself elsewhere. Dark solidity shifts behind moulting superficiality. Yet this resplendent surface is the reality we yearned to embrace; "the secret blackness of milk . . . is accessible only through its whiteness."[96] The nude emerges from enshrouding robes, but the milky flesh bared beneath our gaze becomes a visual impression which can rob our eye of reality. Bare skin arouses visionary caprice, rendering the body radiant, but obscuring unillumined solidity behind blinding revelation; exposed surface becomes a concealing carapace. Drawn into orbit, our dazzled orbs fix on the flesh; the mesmeric mass removes its clothing, sheds its skin, while our eyes are still fastened upon the fabric. The once living flesh retains its life only in our sight; then we see that the undressed flesh has died, has lost its inspirational presence; and our eyes lose their light. Illusion is gradual, a slow growth in a graduated medium, but disillusion is sudden. Our desire for truth reveals natural nudity, but possession is temporary; we enjoy but a fleeting satisfaction. Philosophical palpation is not clinical research; we do not achieve an objective result. A reality incapable of deluding us can never inspire us, can never evoke our admiration, can never kindle a flame in our vision; the unlit eye never alights on living reality. Nature is an inspirational nudity, a bodily reality which sets fire to its surroundings, making the environment a florescent garment which amplifies the flesh. Electrified, we visionaries enter the ambient; our bodies become invisible wrappings, as our glances caress the unconcealed figure. The nude holds the world in a charmed circle around its body, spreading a hypnotic influence which enlists our eyesight. Our visual rays become spokes radiating toward the hub, convergent perspectives focused from divergent viewpoints. The visible implicates the viewer, making the spectator a spokesman. The nude hides its nakedness in the surrounding reflections, the encircling admirations.

Wrapped with enraptured visionaries, reality escapes critical scrutiny. Our wheeling bodies enshroud primordial matter, repulsing the mind that seeks a reality unencumbered by apparitions.

NOTES

[1] *PP*, p. 322.
[2] *PP*, pp. 317-18.
[3] *VI*, p. 83.
[4] *PP*, p. xvii.
[5] *PP*, pp. 319-20.
[6] *PP*, p. 320.
[7] *PP*, p. 320.
[8] *PP*, p. 322.
[9] *PP*, p. xvi.
[10] *PP*, p. 322.
[11] *VI*, p. 259.
[12] *PP*, p. 320.
[13] *PP*, p. 327.
[14] *PP*, p. 323.
[15] *PP*, p. 323.
[16] *PP*, pp. 323-24.
[17] *PP*, p. 324.
[18] *PP*, p. 344.
[19] *PP*, p. 327.
[20] *PP*, p. 327.
[21] *PP*, p. 330.
[22] *PP*, p. 330.
[23] *VI*, p. 218.
[24] *PP*, pp. 330-31.
[25] *PP*, p. 331.
[26] *PP*, pp. 331-32.
[27] *PP*, pp. 330-34.

[28]See *VI*, pp. 217-18.
[29]See *PP*, pp. 327-28.
[30]*VI*, p. 218.
[31]*VI*, p. 218.
[32]*PP*, pp. 334-45.
[33]*PP*, pp. 335-36.
[34]*PP*, pp. 335-36.
[35]*PP*, pp. 335-36.
[36]*PP*, p. 337.
[37]*PP*, p. 337.
[38]*PP*, pp. 336-37.
[39]*PP*, p. 337.
[40]*PP*, p. 337.
[41]*PP*, pp. 336-38.
[42]*PP*, p. 338.
[43]*PP*, pp. 338-39.
[44]*PP*, p. 339.
[45]*PP*, p. 339.
[46]*PP*, p. 339.
[47]*PP*, p. 340.
[48]*PP*, pp. 339-41.
[49]PP, pp. 341-42.
[50]*PP*, pp. 342-43.
[51]*PP*, p. 343.
[52]*VI*, p. 14.
[53]*PP*, pp. 341-43.
[54]*PP*, pp. 343-44.
[55]See *PP*, p. 442.
[56]*PP*, p. 344.
[57]*PP*, pp. 343-45.
[58]*VI*, p. 3.
[59]*VI*, p. 4.
[60]*VI*, p. 4.
[61]*VI*, p. 4.
[62]*VI*, pp. 3-4.
[63]*VI*, pp. 4-5.
[64]*VI*, pp. 4-5.

[65] *VI*, p. 5.
[66] *VI*, p. 5.
[67] *VI*, p. 5.
[68] *VI*, p. 5.
[69] *VI*, p. 6.
[70] *VI*, p. 6.
[71] *VI*, p. 6.
[72] *VI*, p. 6.
[73] *VI*, pp. 6-7.
[74] *VI*, p. 7.
[75] *VI*, p. 7.
[76] *VI*, p. 7.
[77] *VI*, p. 7.
[78] *VI*, p. 7.
[79] *VI*, p. 7.
[80] *VI*, p. 7.
[81] *VI*, p. 7.
[82] *VI*, p. 7.
[83] *VI*, p. 7.
[84] *VI*, pp. 7-8.
[85] *VI*, p. 8.
[86] *PP*, p. 329.
[87] *VI*, p. 8.
[88] *VI*, p. 8.
[89] *VI*, p. 8.
[90] *VI*, pp. 8-10.
[91] *VI*, p. 10, note. *VI*, p. 216.
[92] *VI*, pp. 10-14.
[93] *VI*, p. 148.
[94] *VI*, p. 258.
[95] *VI*, p. 258.
[96] *VI*, p. 150.

Chapter III

THE SENSORY MEDIA

The imaginary is the depth on the hither side. As we penetrate into the world, the depth on the yonder side crosses over to this side, and the real becomes imaginal. We penetrate into the world through an elemental ambient in which our body and the things are immersed. In the atmosphere are directional elements which lead us across distance until we confront the things before us. Each sense has its own medium which becomes imaginary as we penetrate into depth along a leading element. We want to describe these media, and especially we want to describe how the light leads our gaze, how the surrounding luminosity leads our body into the background which awaits the light and our look.

LEVELS AND CONSTANCY

A medium is a level of sensory being. The light around us has degrees, grades, shades; we visionaries experience levels of illumination. A light is a degree of energy, a grade of intensity. A light becomes a lighting, a level at which we live while viewing our surroundings. The lighting level is a living norm, a neutral which organizes the deviant lights and darks. A level, then, is a degree of radiance which becomes an operative invisible when our gaze vibrates at the dominant grade; when our perceptual energies emerge from our body, and merge with the surrounding illumination, the level at which the light shines becomes the grade at which we see, the level at which our vision vibrates; the sensory degree becomes a sensitive degree. Not only does the light have degrees, it has directions; the light shines, it beams, traces routes through the clearing; while establishing a level, the light establishes routes. We never experience a luminous route without a degree of luminosity, and we never experience a lighting level without a directionality, but we nevertheless can distinguish levels from routes. Strictly speaking, perception moves "along a route, at a level," not "along a level," since a level is not a route. However, levels often operate as routes. The lighting level which confronts our face gradually draws our phenomenal body inside; and, once we inhabit this lighting, we are drawn along the interior rays, beams whose operation holds the level constant. Moreover, the lighting shifts levels, and the gradient between grades is a direction; when the lighting shifts from one level to another, the shift directs our vision toward a greater or lesser intensity. Grades involve gradients between grades, and a gradient is a direction, a graduated continuum. We experience this gradation, this gradual shift, at dawn and dusk, but also during the day, when the light shades around something lighted; the shading is a route which leads our gaze around the visible thing, rounding the bulk within our sight. Furthermore, when we describe the spatial, motile, and temporal levels, we shall speak about directional degrees. The spatial orientation which emerges between divergent directions is a level; and the overall motion which emerges between divergent motions is a level. Motion traces a route through space and time, and thus a level, or degree, of motion is a directional phenomenon. Motile and spatial levels are directions indeed, but they are graded directions, levels between conflictory vectors, grades which normalize a disorganized field. Essentially then, a level is a degree, a grade, a mean, a norm, and thus can be distinguished from a route, even though graded illumination has routes, even though the gradient between luminous grades is a route, and even though routes establish a routine directionality, a grade of orientation.

Spatial, Motile, and Temporal Levels

Merleau-Ponty is the author who provides the fundamental delineation; he first speaks about "levels" when describing directions in space,[1] and movement along these spatial levels;[2] then he describes movement along the directions in lived space and imaginary space, where the levels fully express our existential situation.[3] Describing directions in space, Merleau-Ponty shows that spatial orientation prolongs our bodily directedness; we situate ourselves in space, and this space expresses our lived body. The present spatial level is a living harmony between our own bodily directedness and the directions in things, and also an adjustment between a new bodily directedness and the old bodily directedness which is already sedimented in our body, and in the things which express our body. We become disoriented when a thing is turned in a new direction, because the thing turns our body against itself. The newly turned thing requires that we newly direct our body toward the thing, so that the thing expresses anew our bodily situa-

115

tion. Merleau-Ponty initially speaks about the spatial level as the adjustment between the old bodily directedness and a new bodily directedness.[4] But "we cannot dissociate being from orientated being, . . ."[5] and the things are experienced as having a directedness additional to that directedness which expresses just our own bodily orientation. This additional vector has a being in the things, insofar as the things are at least potentially perceivable. Against directedness in the things themselves, Merleau-Ponty argues only that there is no directedness which can be experienced by a disembodied mind.[6] Merleau-Ponty sometimes seems to deny directedness outside our body, because he argues against intellectualism which understands the subject as a disembodied intellect without directedness, and against empiricism which understands the things as having direction in themselves apart from a subject. Against the intellectualists Merleau-Ponty argues that underneath the intellect is an embodied subject who has access to the world through its own bodily orientation. Against the empiricists our author argues that a disoriented body subject cannot reorient itself toward an orientation in the things themselves, since the things and the body subject lose their directedness together. They regain their directedness when the subject directs his activities into the things, and when the things direct their activities into the subject. The directedness in the things can be experienced only by a bodily subject which itself has a direction. The overall directedness is an adjustment between the directedness in the body and the directedness in the things, and the body and the things have each their own directedness within the overall direction. The overall directedness is an orientation throughout the whole perceptual field.[7] This established vector guides our body when we prolong anew our bodily directions into space. Along the field orientation we direct our actual body, whose activities are sedimented in our potential body as habit. Using our habitual body, we direct our actual body toward a potential body which has not yet been actualized. Merleau-Ponty describes the directions "up" and "down," and describes how we reorient ourselves after the things are turned "upside down."[8] He describes the directions "vertical" and "oblique," and describes how we reorient ourselves after vertical things are slanted.[9] "Vertical" and "upwards" involve the dimension "height." Having described "height," Merleau-Ponty describes "width" and "depth."[10]

Next our author describes "movement" along the spatial directions. "Like top and bottom, motion is a phenomenon of levels, every movement presupposing a certain anchorage which is variable."[11] Every anchoring point can move when the anchorage shifts elsewhere. If we consider motion and rest in our own body, we can say that my bodily anchorage is the situation from which I move, and the place toward which I move. I experience as stationary the place which I have already reached, and the place which I have not yet reached; and I experience myself as moving between these two places, unless I reach toward my reaching, and rest in my movement; then the place which I have not yet reached appears as moving toward me, while the place which I have already reached appears as moving away. Or I may rest at the place which I have already reached. But resting can be an activity; rest may require that I actively direct my body through time, so that I remain in the same interrelation with other things which appear stabile. But time too can stop, or pause between temporal waves, so that I passively rest in space without directing myself toward a future. If we consider our body together with the things, we can say that there is an overall movement and rest which shifts within the whole field. Sometimes the overall movement is centered in my body, so that I experience myself moving with the whole. And sometimes the overall movement is centered outside my body, so that I experience myself moving against the whole. Or perhaps I experience myself at rest on something which moves with the whole, or against it. If my body prolongs itself into the moving thing, I experience myself as no longer at rest. Between absolute motion and absolute rest there are levels, and these levels are relative absolutes. I experience in myself the shift from one level to another, while I experience also a shift in the things, and in the whole field. Perhaps I experience myself as moving, but then something moves past me so quickly that I experience myself as standing still, and then I experience myself and the thing which passes me as moving past everything else in the perceptual field. Motion and rest shift over the field, while my body and the things undergo a shift from motion to rest, and back again. My bodily situation is the place where I rest, but I am not always situated; the ground shifts, or I shift my ground. Thus Merleau-Ponty says that rest and movement appear between the thing and my body, shifting from the thing to my body and back. Both the thing and my body can be experienced as either moving or resting.[12]

Spatial levels and motile levels exhibit the "level" as a directional grade. This phenomenon is a direction between directions, an overall direction, or a deeper direction beneath superficial vacillations. Consider spatial levels. If my body is directed rightside up, and the things are turned upside down, there appears between my old upside and the new upside in the things an overall upside from which my upside and the upside in the things diverge; the divergent upsides converge upon the overall upside, so that I experience both the things and my body as rightside up. Consider motile levels. If my body is moving toward a thing at rest, and the thing starts moving toward my body, there appears between my body and the thing an overall movement upon which the separate movements converge. A level then is a direction between directions, which diverge from the over-all direction, or converge upon it. We move toward levels, and away from levels, but along levels, except during dis-orientation. Along a level we move toward divergent and convergent levels, and away from them. The divergent and convergent lines crisscross the level along which we move; each crossing is a crisis. As we live through the crisis, the overall level shifts, and we move from the crossing along a newly emergent direction, a route toward newly divergent and convergent levels.

A direction between shifting directions is a temporal directedness. The overall level is a direction through time and space along which appearances present themselves with a certain style. Even when time stops and we rest in time at some place resting in space, we still move through time, since a temporal movement comes to rest between a past time and a future time, and the present recollects the past and anticipates the future. A temporal stop is just a rest within an overall temporal movement. The overall flow has "waves" and "pulsations."[13] Temporal movement always involves some spatial movement, although the movement may not be perceived. Even when we are located at a place resting in space, we enjoy a rectilinear movement in our glance, and a vibratory movement in our gaze. If I sit viewing a scene in which nothing moves, I see things at rest and I see my body at rest, but I do not see my eyes which move over the whole motionless scene. My gaze moves into the world, and the light moving through the world moves into my eyes. Even when my moving eye fixes its gaze upon something in the world, there remains an imperceptible vibratory movement. I do not see this movement, because the vibration is the level along which I look. This level is a spatial and temporal movement in which my body rests; my body rests in its perceptual activity. Experienced rest is a condition in which the bodily movement has become imperceptible, because my subjective body has become situated at the prevailing motile level. The imperceptible motion is potentially perceivable, and may become actually perceived, if the overall level shifts. Our bodily situation is the spatial activity in which our soul sits, but we may experience our bodily situation as moving, if the world does not sit in our lap. A level understood as an established direction through space and time is a directional life along which we experience sensible appearances which present themselves with a certain style. Each direction has its own style, which we experience from the inside when we live at that level. The motile levels involve motion and rest in space, and spatial rest is always motion through time. Time stops only within an overall temporal movement which never stops. The pauses within temporal movement are punctuations which give time its style. Temporal motion and rest understood as levels have their being within an overall motion which never stops while there is life. Every level is temporal. A level is the style with which time flows through space. This flow is temporal and spatial motion. Temporal movement always involves spatial movement, because we subjects are bodies. Our body directs itself through time along its postures and gestures. The various sensory levels are founded upon the spatial and motile levels, since perception is bodily gesture within a corporeal world. Always a level is a certain styled movement within time and space. Our body adjusts its own level to the level in the world, and there appears an overall level which is a direction between directions, and a style which joins styles.

The Level as a Constant

A level is a constant. Even though our experiences and the natural appearances are inconstant, this variation has its own constancy. When we perceive along a route, we perceive at a level which is constant relative to the appearances which diverge from that level. A level can shift, but after the shift we perceive at another level. The natural thing is constantly moving in space and time, while our body too is moving. Our moving body experiences the thing, and the moving thing appears for our body. The route along which we perceive, and along which the thing appears, is a constant which does not move. The level is stationary, a flowing stability within the flux. The apparitional and perceptual motion at the level disappears, and the thing appears constant in its various appearances. The motion reappears only when we shift from one level to another. Merleau-Ponty describes the constancy phenomenon, and shows that constancy is a phenomenon of levels.

We could describe constancy by showing how the sensible thing has its apparitional constancy at an intersensory level.[14] But we can more easily understand constancy if we describe more specific sensory levels. Merleau-Ponty first treats constancy in shape, size, and color. Shape and size are sensibles which objective thinkers regard as giving us intellectual access to the material essence of everything located in space, while color they regard as accidental. Merleau-Ponty wants to show that color is just as constant as extension. Thinkers have regarded shape and size as essential, not only because extension seems more invariable, but also because extension is common to more than one sense. Color is a "special sensible," while size and shape are "common sensibles," though much less common than the intersensory thing. Having described those common sensibles which the rationalists deem colorless and odorless, Merleau-Ponty de-

121

scribes color constancy, while also describing constancy in colored light. Light is remarkable as a special visual sensible which becomes invisible when we look along the light at the other visual sensibles. Our author next describes constancy in weight, which is a sensible specific to the tactile sense. And then he describes constancy in bodily motion. Motion is here a sensible which becomes intangible when we touch other tangibles along our bodily rhythms. Although we want mainly to describe light and the sensory media, we should first examine what Merleau-Ponty says about constancy in size and shape, because here he presents and argues against alternative theories about constancy. And here he explains what a real appearance is.

Constancy in shape and size. Although we experience the natural thing as appearing through various appearances, we constantly experience the same thing, and we experience the thing as having a certain constant appearance. The thing does not appear as perfectly itself in every appearance, but there are some appearances which we experience as the thing itself, while the other appearances we experience as intending the perfect appearance. The real appearances are experienced as perfecting our perception.

Consider shape. When the body subject moves around and toward and away from the thing, the thing appears as variously shaped. Nevertheless, some shape appearances we experience as the thing itself, and thus as the "real shape," while the other shape appearances we experience as merely "apparent shapes." Merleau-Ponty considers the theory that originally we experience all the various shape appearances without distinguishing between the apparent shape and the real shape; the distinction arises only in reflective experience, wherein we construct the sensible thing as an intelligible object. Against this view, Merleau-

Ponty argues that the objective distinction between the apparent and the real must be derived from such a distinction within original experience.[15] The object constructed in reflection is a cultural being, and thus the real shape of such an object is a culturally constructed shape. We reflect upon our bodily relation to the perceived thing and perhaps say that the real shape of a thing is "the shape which it assumes when it is in a plane parallel to the frontal elevation."[16] Through such reflection we construct an object which has this shape as its real shape. Merleau-Ponty insists that there is a reality more original than objective reality, from which the objective is derived. More original than the cultural objectively real shape is a natural real shape. Without this natural reality, objectivity would be simply intersubjectivity.[17]

Merleau-Ponty next considers the view that we do not experience through the various appearances a unitary thing, but rather a single relation among the appearances. The real shape then is a constant relation among the appearances and the apparent parts in the phenomenal field where the appearances appear. Thus all the various shape appearances are experienced at a certain distance from the subject, and at a certain angle. The appearances and the distances and the angles vary, but the variation is a constant relationship among the variables. Thus a shape appearance perceived at a certain angle and distance is equivalent to another shape appearance perceived at another angle and distance, when these appearances have their being within that phenomenal system which includes the appearances together with my body. The real shape is the appearance to which the appearances throughout the system are equivalent, and the appearance through which the appearances throughout the system are equivalent to one another. A large elliptical appearance perceived close up and obliquely is systematically equivalent to a small circular appearance perceived frontally and at a distance. The coin or plate thus perceived has its reality in just this systematic interrelationship. The perceived thing is an objective reality whose nature is intellectually known.[18] Against this theory Merleau-Ponty argues that the perceiving subject is not a disembodied mind which thinks the relationships between its body and the appearances. The distances and angles between the body and the apparent shapes and sizes are originally not quantifiable variables whose interrelationships can be thought. An objective thinker cannot distinguish one apparent shape and size from another, since "the object is nothing but the constant product of the distance multiplied by the apparent size."[19] Every apparent shape and size is the same for a thinker. But in original sense perception the appearance perceived at one distance and angle is distinct from the appearance perceived at another angle and distance. Moreover, I originally experience all the apparent sizes and shapes as converging upon an appearance which I experience as the real size and shape. Each perceived thing has a natural focus upon which all our bodily experiences converge. Each thing has a certain angle and distance from which the thing is best perceived. If I perceive a thing from too far away or from too close, I do not experience an objective distance between my body and the size appearance; I simply experience the apparent size as diverging from a real size, and I experience the various distances as diverging from the distance where I perceive the real size. Likewise, I do not experience an objective angle between my body and the shape appearance, but a divergence, or convergence.[20]

How then is constancy in shape and size a phenomenon of levels? When we perceive a thing from various distances and angles, our body moves with a style which establishes a level of operation. We never confront the level at which we operate; we experience our constant perceptual style longitudinally and laterally; we experience our style from within, while we experience frontally the shapes and sizes which appear at the level, and around the level. Though we do not confront the level, we do experience the level, not only internally, but also through the real appearance. While confronting the real appearance, we experience through that apparition the level at which we are operating. The real appearance expresses the overall level, which itself is hidden in our body. The level is an experiential average among the various appearances, and the experienced reality is an average appearance. The real appearance is "typical."[21] The real appearance and the overall level are both "norms."[22] But the level is an unperceived norm, whereas the real appearance is a perceived norm which expresses the unperceived. We experience frontally the real appearance, because we also perceive the merely apparent appearances which vary around the norm. The overall level is a norm which we do not perceive until the level shifts. The real appearance is experienced frontally at the level where we perceive generally.

Color constancy in the light. The intellectualists regard size and shape as the essence of materiality, but special sensibles such as color and weight show us more about the thing than do its "geometrical properties."[23] A colored thing remains the same throughout variations in lighting. This constant color is the real color. However Merleau-Ponty denies that color constancy is an empirically real constancy. The empiricist supposes that the real color is the ordinary color, and that the ordinary color is the sensible which we most often see. We most often confront the colored thing in daylight from a short distance away. When we stand too far away or too close, and when the daylight has shifted to twilight or artificial light, we associate the apparent color with the real color which we remember, so that the association replaces the perception.[24] Against the empiricist, Merleau-Ponty argues that we immediately perceive a constant color, through the various color appearances. We do not remember some apparent color which does not now actually appear, and do not compare the present presentation with a recollected representation. Moreover, the various color appearances are not isolated special sensibles which look the same against every background. Colors which science considers objectively the same look different against various backgrounds, under various lightings.[25] Merleau-Ponty denies empirically real constancy, but he also denies that the constancy is ideal. The intellectualist supposes that we distinguish the real color in a judgment. Since the colored thing is always illuminated, we never sensibly perceive the colored thing, but we can think the real color when we intellectually distinguish the colored lighting. The color which we think has an ideal constancy. Against intellectualism Merleau-Ponty argues that ideal constancy presupposes a color which really remains constant. The intellectualist supposes that in judgment we have access to a color which we never see with our eyes. Against both intellectualism and empiricism Merleau-Ponty argues that colors with objectively real constancy appear in reflective experience, whereas originally the constant is the colored thing; we see the same colored thing through its various colors; originally we do not look at the colors themselves. A colored thing looks the same color under various lightings, because we see the same thing throughout its various appearances, not because we constantly see the same special sensible. The real color is invisible. The real color is a potentiality in the thing, and this invisible potency actualizes itself in the various apparent colors. My fountain pen looks black, whatever the light. "This blackness is less the sensible quality of blackness than a sombre power which radiates from the object, even when it is overlaid with reflected light. . . ."[26] This surface sheen which blocks our gaze is a transparent symbol. Sensible blackness "is visible only in the sense in which moral blackness is visible."[27]

Blackness is the apparitional grade at which the thing appears, a frequency in the route along which we see the thing; at this level the colored thing appears constant through its various apparent colorings. The real blackness remains in the background, where we experience the color laterally rather than frontally.[28] The constant color is a shade within which we see, a shade which becomes visible when an apparent color appears at the overall color level. Through the visible real color, the background color comes to the fore. Merleau-Ponty emphasizes here the constant level, but there is also a real color which is visible, just as there was a real shape and size which expressed the level along which the apparent shapes and sizes appear. The visible real color does not appear constantly. When we see merely apparent colors, we do not remember the real color and then associate the remembered color with the actually seen colors. Rather, we experience the apparent colors as converging upon a real focus which is absent. And we experience the focus as expressing the level along which the apparent colors converge. A black tning does not always look really black, and yet the sombre power is always visible through the variable appearances. Blackness in its depth is seen only through its metaphors, and all the various metaphors converge upon the symbol which best leads our gaze into depth.

We have seen that a constant color is neither a real color which we constantly sense, nor an ideal color which we constantly think. No real color could remain constant, because in the natural world we do not ordinarily see colors without backgrounds. Empiricists and intellectualists presuppose color patches which are constant in themselves apart from the visual field. The world does show us some color patches, but a patch is just one color structure among many. Is the patch before us a color area, or a surface color? There are transparent colors which have volume. There is gloss, glow, and brightness. Especially there is colored lighting which can be distinguished from its light source. This lighting moreover can be distinguished from the colored thing which the lighting illuminates, and we distinguish these in original experience. We do not reflectively distinguish a color on the thing and another color in the lighting, and then judge that one color belongs to the thing while the other belongs to the light. Rather, the whole visual field has a certain color structure. And we sensibly perceive in the structure the distinction between the lighting and the thing lighted.[29]

Suppose that we view something through a small window cut in a screen; the screen frames our view so that we no longer see the field, and no longer see the light source. Through the window we see color sensibles separated from both the light and the thing lighted. The sensibles seen through the screen are indistinguishably lighted colors and colored lights. In reflective experience we likewise can screen out the visual field so that we see just color patches; reflection is critical vision, like the gaze of an artist who scrutinizes the spectacle through half-closed eyes. Suppose that we look through a screen into a box painted black and brightly lighted, and afterwards into a box painted white and dimly lighted, so that the white box and the black box reflect the same light quantity into our eye. In both boxes we see an empty grey space. Now suppose that we place a

128

white paper scrap in the black box and a black scrap in the white box. Then the black box looks black and strongly illuminated, whereas the white box looks white and weakly illuminated. When the paper is put in the boxes, we see a figure against a ground, and thus again see a field, replacing the wider field which the screen hid from view. When we see the world without a screen, we see constant colors within a structured field, under a general lighting. Without the screen we can distinguish a lighted color from a colored light, we see the colors on the things, and we can distinguish a lighted thing from the overall light. We can distinguish the color on the thing from the color in the light.[30]

We want to describe this overall lighting which shines throughout the visual field. Lighting is distinct from the lighted colors and the lighted things which have these colors. And lighting is distinct from light sources and localized colored lights. Lights and colors we experience frontally, whereas the lighting we ordinarily experience longitudinally and laterally. We look along the light which surrounds us on all sides. Colored lights are things at which we look. And lighted colors are things, or else appearances through which appear the things which the lighting illuminates. Lighting is the general mode in which lights and colors appear.[31]

Merleau-Ponty first confronts us with a light which we ordinarily experience as lighting. "Only after centuries of painting did artists perceive that reflection on the eye without which the eye remains dull and sightless as in the paintings of the early masters."[32] This reflected ocular light is ordinarily experienced longitudinally as a lighting along which we see a living facial expression. Merleau-Ponty argues that we do not ordinarily experience this reflection frontally, since artists did not look at the reflection until they had painted a long time. And he argues that we ordinarily experience the reflection at least laterally, "since its mere absence deprives objects and faces of all life and expression."[33] Next Merleau-Ponty mentions the photograph and the cinematograph, which often confront us with lights rather than the things lighted, so that the lighting itself appears as a thing. Suppose we are watching a cinema show, and "a person goes into a cellar holding a lamp."[34] We do not see the light beam as a transparency through which we see things appearing from the darkness. The light becomes opaque and no longer leads our gaze to the thing lighted. "Light moving over a wall produces only pools of dazzling brightness which are localized not on the wall, but on the surface of the screen."[35] Likewise the artist sees the reflected ocular light as a spot which he projects upon his canvas surface. Merleau-Ponty concludes that reflection and lighting are ordinarily experienced laterally or peripherally; they ordinarily remain in the background without figuring as something which we confront; reflection and lighting are backgrounds which surround us; they are "intermediaries"[36] or media through which we look at the thing which figures on the ground. Reflection and lighting ordinarily "*lead* our gaze instead of arresting it."[37]

What does this "leading" mean? In what sense does the lighting "lead our gaze?" Suppose that I am led through an unfamiliar apartment toward the owner who inhabits this dwelling; the person who leads me is familiar with the apartment; the sights which we see while we move toward the owner have a meaning for the leader who knows our goal, "and I entrust or lend myself to this knowledge which I do not possess."[38] Again, suppose that I stand viewing a landscape, and someone points out to me a detail which I could not discern; the person who points has already seen the detail and "already knows where to stand and where to look in order to see it."[39] Merleau-Ponty says that the lighting is like this person who leads me by the hand, and this person who points with his finger. Like a person who "directs my gaze,[40] the lighting "in a sense *knows* and *sees*"[41] the thing toward which I am pointed and led. Suppose that I sit in a theater without an audience; the curtain rises and reveals lighted scenery; "I have the impression that the spectacle *is in itself visible* or ready to be seen."[42] Further, I have the impression that the light, which penetrates into the background and casts shadows behind the things in its path, in a sense "anticipates our vision."[43] I have the impression that our vision merely follows "those paths traced out for it by the lighting." [44] The gaze is a visual ray which prolongs itself into the light beam, and thereby sees the things which the lighting has already looked over.

This sight along the light Merleau-Ponty likens to thought along a speech; speech has in it a track traced by thought, and our thought moves along this track when we hear a sentence spoken. "We perceive in conformity with the light, as we think in conformity with other people in verbal communication."[45] Communication presupposes a "linguistic setting"[46] in which the meaning resides; meaning has its being in words which are spoken within a language sedimented from speech already spoken. Likewise, "perception presupposes in us an apparatus capable of responding to the promptings of light in accordance with their sense."[47] The "sense" is a direction, and the direction is the meaning in the lighting. Our visual apparatus moves along these directional meanings and actualizes the visibility which the light merely anticipates. The "apparatus" about which Merleau-Ponty speaks is animated by the gaze. The gaze is "the natural correlation between appearances and our kinaesthetic unfoldings, something not known through a law, but experienced as the involvement of our body in the typical structures of a world."[48] When we look around us, we employ a bodily potentiality for moving our eyes along the light beams, so that the illuminated externals appear within our vision and actualize there the powers latent in our surroundings. The gaze thus is like thought. The thinking apparatus is the bodily potentiality for moving our speech organs along the tracks already laid down in language; when we actually move our body along these tracks, we activate the meaning lying potential in language. Speech is intellectual vision, and sensual vision is original thought. Moreover, Merleau-Ponty implies that creative vision sees something new beyond the sights already sedimented in the light, just as creative speech speaks the new beyond the speeches already sedimented in language. Light then is a natural language which we speak while gazing. The light leads our gaze, but our gaze also goes where the light has not yet led, and this new vision can be sedimented as further light, just as new speech is sedimented in further language.[49]

Merleau-Ponty now describes the relation between the gaze and the constancy phenomenon. Our gaze activates the vision potential in the light; visual activity actualizes the visual potentialities in our body; bodily vision is situated in the world, and the sights which we see in this world have their being relative to our situation; Merleau-Ponty therefore describes the relation between our bodily situation and the constancy which we experience when we look along the lighting at the thing illuminated. Suppose we stand in a brightly lit room and look at a white card placed in a shady corner. From this standpoint the card does not appear constantly white; the card appears white with better constancy when we move toward the shady corner; and when we situate ourselves in the shade with the card, the color constancy is perfect. When we stood outside the shady corner, the shadow confronted us as something seen; now that we stand in the corner, the shadow "surrounds us"[50] on all sides, and only the white card confronts us. The shadow becomes the "environment in which we establish ourselves."[51] The things visually experienced are not just interrelated objects confronting a disembodied subject; they are not just special sensibles spread out before a worldless vision; the visual sensibles have their being all around a situated subject who experiences laterally the sensibles on the sides, and frontally the sensibles in front. The lighting is not in front with the objects; the lighting is that surrounding medium in which we situate ourselves, and which we experience as "the norm"[52] which we take for granted, "whereas the object lighted stands out before us and confronts us."[53] The lighting is more fundamental than the distinction between lights and colors, and thus is neither color nor even light, but a "neutral"[54] toward which the light tends. The lighting or shading becomes so normal that we no longer experience any shade. Suppose that we are standing outdoors in daylight, and then come into an electrically lighted room. The light looks yellow, but soon loses all determinate color. If some daylight shines into the room this ordinarily neutral light now looks blue. How shall we understand this phenomenon? We should not say that we experience the electric lighting as yellow, and that we reflectively discount this yellowness when we experience colored objects, thereby experiencing objective colors. Nor should we say that we soon experience the surrounding light as daylight so that colored objects remain objectively constant. We should say rather that the yellow light becomes a lighting when we situate ourselves in the light and live at the new lighting level. The lighting tends toward the colorless, and the colors on the lighted objects appear as divergences from the overall color level. Colors, qualities or special sensibles, become determinate in relation to a level which frequently shifts. Because the level shifts, color constancy is inconstant. But this inconstancy becomes a constant, if the levels shift along a level, as happens in the shift from dawn to dusk. A level is laid down when I situate myself within the surrounding light, and the colors which diverge from the lighting level distribute themselves among the lighted objects. When the lighting shifts, I cannot redistribute the colors without *"entering into* the new atmosphere, because my body is my general power of inhabiting all the environments which the world contains, the key to all those transpositions and equivalences which keep it constant."[55] Thus we understand the relation between our gaze and the constancy phenomenon.

We have seen how the overall lighting can become colored light and then become lighting again. The lighting has a certain constancy, but its constancy is inconstant, since the level is constantly shifting so that colorless lighting becomes colored light. The lighting level shifts within a complex structure which includes also the thing lighted and the visual field within which the lighted thing figures. The thing figuring in the visual field has certain lighted colors, but it has these colors only in relation to the organized field and the overall lighting. Thing, field, and lighting each have their constancy in relation to each other, and in relation to the body which structures this complex. Having described lighting and its constancy, Merleau-Ponty describes the field and the figure.[56]

Let us consider first the visual field, and describe how its organization shifts. Suppose that, in a dark room, we project an arc lamp upon a black disk, so that the ray falls exactly upon this surface, and then rapidly rotate the disk so that all surface roughness is eliminated; we see a solid cone with its apex at the projector and its base fused with the invisibly rotating screen.[57] When however we insert a white paper scrap into the light beam, we see that the light is not a solid cone, and the cone suddenly separates from its base, so that we see on the screen a disk projected along a transparent light beam, which casts a shadow behind the paper scrap. We suddenly see the cone as a lighting rather than light; we experience an incompatibility between the illuminated paper and the solid cone; we have inserted a new part which shifts the meaning in the whole visual field.[58] Again, suppose that we experience a visual field within which an overall lighting illuminates colored things. If we divide the field into parts and look at the various parts separately, we cannot distinguish the lighting from the colors; we cannot distinguish a colored light from a lighted color. But when we view the parts all together within the whole, we can distinguish the lightings, and we can see the real color in each thing, quite distinct from the colored light which lights these colors. The lighting is seen only when the parts are no longer seen separately. When the parts are seen together, we see the colors distributed through the field with a certain spread between the colors and a certain divergence from the lighting; we see that the distribution is systematic, and we see that the colors can systematically redistribute themselves when the lighting level shifts. The field can be systematically reorganized or transformed. Suppose that a painter wants to depict something so that it catches our eye when we view his painting; the painter depicts this thing less by putting bright colors on it than by distributing the proper light and shade on the things sur-rounding the most striking thing. Again, suppose that under oblique lighting I gaze at the hollow impression which a signet ring has stamped in sealing wax, and suppose that I momentarily see this hollow as a raised relief; I then see a lighting which comes from inside the wax, because the raised relief is shaded on the side toward the overall light source, and casts no shadows.[59] Suppose finally that a sculptured bust sits upon a pedestal while someone holding a lamp circles around at a constant distance from the central sculpture; even when the lamp is hidden from view, we still see the circling light source, because we see the shifting light and color on the illuminated bust.[60]

Consider now the colors and colored things which figure within the illuminated visual field. Suppose that we stand before a picture in an art gallery, and suppose that the picture is illuminated from a light source outside the picture, somewhere in the gallery. If we view the picture from the proper distance we see another lighting inside the picture itself. This internal lighting gives each pigmented color patch a certain color meaning and also a certain representative meaning. These color patches viewed together within the internally lighted whole represent some scene, such as a landscape. But if we move very close, we see just the lighting which falls from the light source in the gallery. The color patches no longer have a representative meaning, and we see just pigments daubed on canvas. Suppose that the picture represents mountains with a meadow; and suppose that we do not move close, but instead separate one part from the whole through reflective vision: through narrowed eyelids we scrutinize the picture more narrowly. Suppose that within the meadow we isolate a green color patch and view this apart from the mountain; not only does the color patch no longer have a representative meaning, but its color meaning changes; the color patch seen within the whole was a meadow-green with a certain thickness, but viewed separately the patch is another green less thick than the green in the meadow. Color meaning is relative to representative meaning. A color can be seen as just a color, but it nonetheless can always be seen as something colored, or the color which something possesses. "The blue of a

136

carpet would never be the same blue were it not a wooly blue."[61]

We have already understood that the colors within the visual field are distributed around a certain lighting level; we now understand that colors are also interrelated with geometrical forms, whose constancy we have already described. A square rug is not the same color as a round rug, and a large round rug is not the same color as a small round rug. Colors are interrelated with all special sensibles, such as wooliness; and colors are interrelated with common sensibles, or things. A blue rug is not the same color as a blue sky, even when the rug is sky-blue.[62] Lighting has a logic which puts together into a whole the various parts in the visual field. We can reflect upon this systematic lighting and perhaps express its logic in speech, but the system is originally experienced as a sensuous togetherness in the imaginary and the real. The "logic of lighting" or "synthesis of lighting"[63] we originally experience "as the consistency of the picture or the reality of the spectacle."[64] But beyond this interrelationship between the overall lighting and the lighted and colored parts, "there is a total logic of the picture or the spectacle, a felt coherence of the colors, spatial forms and significance of the object."[65] The visual field is experienced within a natural world, which is a relational system whose logic we experience as an overall level; this overall level is more constant than the other levels; the lighting level is inconstant relative to an overall constancy. And the lighting level is interrelated with the color level, the shape level, the size level, the spatial level, the motile level, and so on. The whole relational system distributes determinations among the parts at every level. These interrelated determinations produce the real appearances, and every sensible which diverges from these appearances is "cancelled out"[66] as unreal. Because we experience this overall

137

level, we are certain about the world and experience a reality within this world. Color constancy is founded upon constancy in the things, which in turn is founded upon "the primordial constancy of the world as the horizon of all our experiences."[67] Because we experience this fundamental constancy, Merleau-Ponty argues against the theory that we believe in things just because we experience a certain constancy among special sensibles; the thing is not just the constant color which appears through the various colored lightings, nor is the thing a constant color gathered together with other constant sensibles; on the contrary, only because our perceptual experience is open upon the things and a world do we experience constant colors.[68] Only because we constantly perceive along the worldly level do we perceive things; and only because we perceive along the thingly level do we perceive through the visual sense along the more specifically visual levels such as lighting and color. When a light holds constant, it becomes a level along which we perceive; and conversely, when we constantly perceive along a light, that level becomes a constant lighting.

Tactile constancy along bodily motion. We have described the constancy phenomenon within the visual field, but we also experience this phenomenon within fields specific to other senses, such as touch. Following Merleau-Ponty, we have described color as a special visual sensible which appears within the visual field; we have described color constancy within this field; and we have described light as the medium which leads our gaze through the colored visual field. The special tactile sensible whose constancy Merleau-Ponty first describes is weight, though he also mentions temperature,[69] and hardness.[70] Afterwards, he describes how motion leads our touch in perceiving textures.[71]

Suppose that I pick up a small metal artifact. Whatever

muscles I use in hefting this thing, I always experience it as having the same weight, whether the muscles are extended or already flexed when I pick it up. I experience the same weight, when I lift the thing with my eyes closed, when my lifting hand carries an additional weight, when I lift the thing with my whole hand, when I support my hand and lift with just my fingers, when I lift the thing with one finger or more, when I raise the thing with my head or foot, whether the thing is in air or water.[72] Thus I experience the weight as constant relative to my various bodily organs, and relative to the tangible surroundings in which I use these organs. Moreover I experience the weight as constant through very inconstant tactile sensations.

Weight is a specialized special tactile sensible. This particular weight which I feel when I pick up the metal artifact is a still more specialized sensible. And the particular weights which I feel with my various organs diverge more or less from this particular specialized tactile sensible which I experience as always the same. The pressure on my forehead does not feel the same as the pressure on my hand, and yet I experience these pressures as equivalent. Merleau-Ponty argues that the experienced equivalence is immediate, and not mediated through inductive reasoning. The experimental subject has probably never measured the various pressures and understood these as various subjective appearances of an invariable objective weight. Nor, when underwater, has the subject measured objective weight by gauging the pressure on his hand and then adding to this pressure the weight of his arm in air, after subtracting the buoyancy which his arm has in liquid. Merleau-Ponty admits that the subject experiences an equivalence among the various pressures only after practice lifting weights; the systematic equivalence is learned, and not known innately; only gradually does the subject learn that a certain pressure upon the fingers is equivalent to still another pressure on the head. However the subject learns these equivalences within a system which includes the whole body subject, since the learned equivalences can be used for understanding pressure on body parts which we have never used for lifting weights.[73]

Against the empiricists Merleau-Ponty argues that the weight experienced as always the same is not a "real constancy."[74] The constant weight is not one particular sensible which we experience through the organs most often used, and then associate with the sensibles experienced through the other bodily parts; the constant weight is not one particular sensible which we constantly experience, since the various pressures which we feel are very inconstant. The intellectualist therefore would say that the constant weight is not a sensible but a theoretical invariant; we experience weight through an intellectual judgment, wherein we reflect upon the various sensible pressures, along with our various bodily positions and the various physical surroundings; through reflection upon these variables we see a constant relationship between the sensible pressures and the physical positions.[75] Against the intellectualists Merleau-Ponty argues that we do not know how much our organs weigh, nor do we know what we can do with these organs, in the manner that an engineer knows the weights and capabilities in a machine which he has constructed from separate parts. The "natural physics"[76] through which we originally understand weight is not a science about an objective body. When I compare the pressure on my fingers with the pressure on my palm, I compare these pressures against a background in which are sedimented the pressures which I have already experienced while moving my arm, and hand, and fingers. Indeed, only against this background can I isolate for comparison the pressure on the fingers, and separate this pressure from the pressure on the palm. The various activities in different bodily parts as I lift the same weight and feel various pressures are experienced as equivalent activities only within a unified "I can"[77] which includes the whole body. Likewise, the various pressures which I feel during the various bodily activities are not originally separate and then explicitly compared; the various pressures are immediately experienced as various appearances of the same real weight. This preobjective sameness in the thing experienced through its various appearances is correlative to the preobjective unity in the body. "Thus the weight appears as the identifiable property of a thing against the background of our body as a system of equivalent gestures."[78]

We experience weight through gesture. Weighing is an intentional bodily movement wherein we lift, heft, tug, pull, dangle, swing, suspend, or support the thing whose weight we want to experience. Our description of weight perception lets us understand tactile perception as a whole, because movement in the body subject "is to touch what lighting is to vision."[79] Bodily movement leads our touch toward the special tactile sensibles such as weight and texture. These tactile sensibles have their being in the real world, but our bodily movement is the medium through which we experience the world as tactile. A touched tactile sensible we can localize in the world only when we place that sensible somewhere within our body image.[80] We do indeed have a certain tactile experience when our body is immobile, and does not feel over the thing touched; this experience Merleau-Ponty calls "passive touch."[81] Examples are touch inside the ear and nose, and generally touch inside bodily parts which are ordinarily covered. In passive touch we experience our own body, but experience almost nothing about the thing touching; passive touch even on sensitive

141

uncovered tactile surfaces presents little about the thing which presses upon our body. In passive touch we experience our body as an object touched; when our touch is actively moving, we experience our body as a subject. When I touch one hand with my other hand, the hand which moves is experienced as the subject, while the immobile hand over which I move the touching hand is experienced as the object. Through movement, my tactile experience opens upon a world beyond the active organ. The world beyond may be a passive organ experienced as an object, or may be the world altogether outside my body. When we passively experience pressure upon our body, we do not perceive weight through this pressure, but we do perceive pressure as a tactile sensible which presents vaguely the thing which weighs upon us, though we experience through this pressure mostly our own body. Pressure is a sensible which we can experience when immobile; however there are some special tactile sensibles which disappear altogether when our touch is no longer active. We have seen that weight as distinct from pressure is such a sensible. Further examples are roughness and smoothness. When describing weight perception, we see that movement and time are together "an objective condition of knowing touch;"[82] when describing perception of texture, we can see that the objective condition is also "a phenomenal component of tactile data;"[83] we experience the motility and temporality in texture from within the experience itself.

Smoothness is not just a togetherness among similar pressures, but rather the style with which a surface uses the time during which our hand moves over a smooth surface with exploratory intent. Our hand moves over a smooth surface with a certain style which brings together the various pressures as appearances of the same tactile sensible. Smoothness and roughness are "surface tactile phenomena"[84] wherein a thing with two dimensions is presented for touch and resists penetration more or less firmly while we move along these dimensions. There are also voluminous tactile phenomena, such as the air which flows over our hand, and flowing water. Also there are transparent tactile phenomena. There are phenomena such as dampness, oiliness, and stickiness, which we perceive through still another styled movement.[85] We can distinguish more than one texture in a single thing. For example, when I move my fingers over an artifact carved from wood, I immediately distinguish the natural grain from the artificial convolutions produced with a knife; I feel two distinct textures, and my fingers move simultaneously with two distinct styles. A roughly textured thing presents within a single style various weak and strong pressures; I feel these pressures only within that style; I do not feel various isolated pressures which I afterwards put together. When I touch linen or a brush, between the threads and between the bristles I do not feel "a tactile nothingness, but a tactile space devoid of matter, a tactile background."[86] The threads and bristles I feel as pressures, while the space between these pressures I feel as void; but this void is the background against which the pressures figure; I do not feel the pressures as separated from their background, and thus do not feel the pressures as separate from one another; they are separate only against a background which brings them together as appearances of an overall texture. I can indeed reflectively separate the figures from their ground and afterwards put them together again according to certain laws, but these laws presuppose the felt styles which they reflectively express. Our hand does not feel separate sensibles which we synthesize in reflection; rather, our hand is an "outer brain"[87] which synthesizes in sensation itself. The sensible pressures are synthesized in the style with which I move my hand, and this movement actualizes a potentiality which I already possessed within my body, but a potentiality which the textured things had not yet solicited.[88] Through the various pressures I perceive a constant texture, or a constant weight. When I experience a texture as constant, the various pressures and voids distribute themselves around the stylistic level with which I move my hand; this style, which expresses texture, shifts its level relative to an overall level which is my general bodily movement; therefore my whole body with all its organs is active in every tactile perception; and this overall level along which my body always acts is the most general structure in the special tactile world.[89]

Our hands and eyes manage qualities and things along routes which run through the world in networks. Our bodily behavior modulates a world which presents itself in grades and gradients. The world is always a mode, or way, of being, and perception is a life style. The routes which run through the world are tracks which invite our travel. The tracks come alive in the body which makes its way through the wilderness. In our body, the paths along which we move become ways of moving, routes become styles, spatial directions become temporal rhythms. But the world is dark, and our gaze cannot penetrate into the background without guidance. Our inner light requires an outer light which already dwells in the world, and knows its way around. The light is a melodic line along which we move into the world with natural grace.

THE VISUAL AND TACTILE ROUTES

The active elements in the sensory media establish routes while instituting perceptual levels. Although each sense has its medium, we shall here explore only the tactile and visual media, because touch and sight are the senses which let us construct an objective world. Objectivity becomes sonorous when the things seen and touched are expressed in speech, but we wish to bespeak the prelinguistic realm. Originally, the sounds which enliven the air bring us a background world, indistinct things without definite places. Still less do odors bring us objects, nor do flavors, immersed in moisture. We here describe only the corporeality in which touch is mired, and the fire which bathes our eye, kindling our vision. The auditory, olfactory, and gustatory media surround us and permeate our body, not letting us confront the world as a surface over against our face, or beneath our palm, riveted with the gaze, nailed with the digit. But, preobjectively, visible and tangible things too are atmospheric, ventilated with an ambient which decompresses their positivity.

The sensory media are sensuous materials which prolong our bodily life into the surrounding world, and hence the media are imaginaries. These perceptually penetrated materials are "imaginaries" because they operate here in our living body, on the hither side of the sensibles which we experience frontally. The perceptual imaginaries become nonperceptual when we perceive the world as a merely perceived world no longer opening us toward the unperceived. Each medium, when isolated from the other media, is a specialized imaginary, which lets us experience the intersensory world as a world sensed through a single sense. Light lets us experience the world as merely visible, while bodily motion lets us experience the same world as nothing but tangible. A world sensed through a single sense is less deep than the world perceived through all the senses, and thus relative to the intersensory world is unreal. The special visual world and the special tactile world are imaginary realms which merge in the common world when our special senses converge and focus upon the natural things. My

145

body is "an intertwining of vision and movement,"[90] such that everything which I see is something which I can reach through locomotion, or at least through ocular movement. "The visible world and the world of my motor projects are each total parts of the same Being."[91] Because each part is itself a totality, we can reflectively separate the visual sense from the tactile sense. And the medium which leads the special visual sense into the special visual world, where our body confronts the visual sensibles, we can separate from the medium which leads the special tactile sense into its special world. These reflectively specialized worlds are totalities which remain partial, and refer us back to the original whole.

Mediated Contact Across Distance

When reflectively isolated from the whole, the tactile medium appears as the bodily movement which lets us experience the things which press against our body surface; and the visual medium we describe as the light which lets us experience things at a distance from our body surface: touch is perception without distance, whereas vision is perception across a gap. But prereflectively touch and vision specialize a common sensorium; so, speaking about the senses operating harmoniously within their corporeal commune, we must say that perception generally is contact across distance. Touch best exhibits the contact; sight best exhibits the distance. However, even when isolated from general perception, touch and sight remain perception, and touch exhibits some separation while sight exhibits some contact. If touch is understood as simply perception in contact, we must say that vision is somewhat tactile. And if vision is understood as simply perception across distance, we must say that touch is somewhat visual. Because touch involves some separation, and because sight involves some

146

contact, touch and sight easily harmonize within general perception. The apparent opposites are already harmonies of the opposites which perception harmonizes.

Apparently sight is the opposite of touch, since a visible thing is not seen when it touches our eyeball. Notice however that we do see the thing, though improperly as something which blocks the light and obturates our vision. Suppose that the thing is removed from our eye and properly displayed in the light; again sight seems the opposite of touch. But notice that we see a visible thing at a distance only through a motion in our eyeballs as they converge upon the thing seen. Moreover, we see visible size and shape, and position, only through the style with which our eyes move when the thing moves around our body, and our body moves around the thing. Vision is a gesture, like touch. Further, a visible thing at a distance may press against our body surface through a shining reflection; dazzling light is a visual sensible which is not seen at a distance, a sensible which strikes our eye as something painful. A dazzling light reflected from a distant surface is not a mere light flash; the light is rather the thing itself pressing against our retina through its painful appearance. Admittedly, we experience hardly anything about the thing which blinds us; we experience mostly the pain and bedazzlement in our body. This experience which shows us little about the thing itself is the "passive vision"[92] which Merleau-Ponty compares to the passive touch wherein we experience our body more than we experience the thing which acts upon us. There is a likeness between vision and touch, because there is a passive vision and a passive touch, and because in passive vision the thing seen touches our body surface just as a tangible thing ordinarily does. Having shown this likeness, Merleau-Ponty notes an active touch, comparable to active vision. This touch lets us experience

147

things beyond our body surface; tactile activity ordinarily lets us experience external things at the epidermis, but we can also experience things outside our body, beyond its superficies. We extend our touch into the external world when we prolong our bodily movement into the corporeal movement agitating the things which we touch. In this manner, the blind man touches the pavement with his cane; when he holds the cane rigidly in his moving hand, the blind man feels the pavement at the cane tip, and no longer feels the cane handle against his palm; he felt the handle when he was feeling about for his cane so that he could take a walk; now that he is walking, he no longer feels the handle, except when he shifts the cane to get a better grip. The cane is a perceptual tool, and through tools the sighted too touch things beyond the original body surface. Working with tools requires an active touch. Exhibiting active and passive touch in a single instance, Merleau-Ponty mentions the situation wherein I touch one hand with my other hand. The hand which actively touches does not feel its own surface, but feels the touched surface, located slightly beyond the touching surface. The hand which is touched experiences passive touch, and feels its own surface, but almost nothing beyond.[93]

We have displayed particular instances where vision makes contact and touch crosses distance; we may now generalize the demonstration. Even when we touch things at our epidermal surface, we perceive across a certain distance, since our body is extended. Our hands are animate tools, and our sensitive flesh is an already spiritualized material, mediating the inner and the outer through an internalized exteriority. Our objective body has dimension and holds away from its center the things which press against its superficies. Our soul contacts the externals only when the withdrawn spirit stretches along our limbs toward the periphery. Again, even when we see things at a distance, we perceive in contact; even when our eye is not affronted by a dazzling light, a light is always streaming into our eye. Moreover, when the light is not excessively intense, our gaze exits from the eye and contacts the visible things at their surface. Both visual and tactile feelings take place at the surface separating the animated medium from the matter which spirit has not yet penetrated. The difference then between these two sensory modes is that vision on the average is perception across a greater distance than the distance across which we perceive in average touch. On the average, we touch only the thing which presses against our natural body surface. Light is a highly transparent medium which we penetrate almost instantly. Bodily movement is a much more opaque medium, which allows a much less deep penetration into the world. This relative distinction between vision and touch, and between their media, involves a difference in objectivity. Merleau-Ponty says that visual experience "pushes objectification further than does tactile experience."[94] Objectification is the intentional activity wherein we disengage ourselves from the world. Visual experience "presents us with a spectacle spread out before us at a distance, and gives us the illusion of being immediately present everywhere and being situated nowhere."[95] We have this illusion because our tactile experience is more obviously situated in a body. We feel things pressing against our body surface, and we cannot prolong our touch far enough into the world to hold things successfully at a distance from our denser body surface. The subject who merely sees is circumscribed less narrowly than the subject who merely touches, but both subjects are circumscribed, and both circles have the same center. The central subject is the common sensorium which experiences the world tactilely along bodily movement, and also experi-

149

ences the world visually along the light, which leads us deeper into the world and leaves the body surface farther behind. The visual circle expands and contracts, and so does the tactile circle, but the latter has on the average a much smaller circumference. The gaze prolongs itself into the light much more easily than our bodily motion elongates its energy into the corporeal movements outside our skin.

Perceptual gestures move across distance, through density. Vision, when compared with touch, seems perception across a void; visual distance seems a gap, a gaping distance, an empty longitude. Nonetheless, if we look lightly, we see that perception across visual distance is penetration through an atmosphere, a density whose opacity is nearly imperceptible. Matter has too often been understood as an absolutely opaque being, absolutely distinct from transparent spirit. A sensory medium is a sensuous material, a materiality which is both opaque and transparent, a spiritual matter and a material spirit. The transparency in a medium is intentional, and leads our perception into opaque depths. The sensory media are fleshly; "flesh" is that stuff which is common in our body and in the things. Unless our body and the things had the same being, how could we touch the things? And how could we touch across distance, unless the communicating medium too had fleshly being? The medium is more transparent than the things which we see through the medium, but the things too have their transparency, and thus are media; conversely, the sensuous elements which are most transparent, and which are most properly called "media," have some opacity. Bodily motion is less transparent than light, but light becomes opaque when it strikes our eye and momentarily blinds us. Whenever the lighting shifts its level, the light becomes more dense, and we look at the light, until the light again becomes a transparent lighting. Colored light "cancels out the superficial structure of objects,"[96] and thus is less transparent than the bluish daylight we ordinarily see as neutral. Tactile transparency is less penetrable than all but the densest light, and bodily motion can become absolutely opaque, as happens when our body is shaken with involuntary spasms. Perhaps we suffer epilepsy, or merely tremble from cold or fear, so that we cannot feel delicate textures. Perhaps we are impatient and move our hand hastily over several surfaces which solicit very different movements. Things in the world move with very various styles: some things have a natural motion into which we can easily prolong our bodily movement, while other things move so violently that we feel only a pounding or rending in our own body. And certain things move so gently that we feel only immobility; we feel only a surface as our hand moves haltingly over the thing seeking some answering tremor. Also, in the natural world there are surface movements and movements from the depth, just as there are lights which shimmer on calm lakes, and lights which glow from inside burning embers. The more compacted medium is more opaque, while the less compressed medium is more transparent. Not a void, the perceptual distance is a dimensional density, a density in degrees; the perceptual distance is a graded void, a void which modulates a plenum. Sensory nothingness decompresses positive reality, making matter aetherial, making the opaque transparent. The void in the graded medium is the free space where active elements play, energizing the ambient, making the graded density a graded intensity. The void is invisible, but also invisible is the activity within the void, an activity which animates opacity, making matter a shaded transparency.

151

The Leading and Receiving Elements

Opacity in a sensory medium is a degree of material density, or a degree of energetic intensity, a level of transparency. If, though, we consider the directionality within this graded density, the various opacities and transparencies in the sensory media reveal the operation of leading elements and receiving elements. Things in the tactile world are obscured when bodily movement is too strong, and when the movement is too weak. Things in the visual world also can be obscured, when the light is too intense, and when the light is not intense enough. Light and movement with too much intensity become opaque, and block our access to the things. Human flesh requires a certain weakness in the sensory media. However, if light and movement are too weak, the things are again obscured, though not precisely by light and movement. The things are obscured rather by darkness and immobility. Weak light and weak bodily movement do not obscure the things, but make perceptible their obscurity. Weak light and movement let the things slip into an obscurity which we have not described when we speak just about active directionality; we must also mention the receptive element which our perception penetrates when moving along the leading element. Darkness and inertia are passive opacities through which a sufficiently strong light and movement can lead our perception. We already indicate the passive element in the tactile medium when we call that medium "movement in our body." The body obscures our tactile perception when the body is immobile; our immobile body blocks tactility, as when a limb is paralyzed. We should say that the tactile medium is motion and rest within our own body, and motion and rest in those corporeal things into which our body prolongs itself; bodily motion is that element in the tactile medium which leads our perception through the motionless depths. Let us speak now about the passive opacity in the visual medium. Clearly, darkness is the element which obscures our gaze, and the light clears through this element a path along which our gaze travels. Without darkness, the light could not lead our gaze, but would blaze into our eyes like the sun; light must have in it some darkness so that we can see. Even noonday illumination has some darkness, which we can see if we glance at the sun and then look back at the things which the sun illuminates. Everywhere we see light shading into darkness, and without this shading the light would have no direction; light directs our gaze along the shading, and also along the shadows which the things cast behind them; the light drives back the darkness, but the darkness hides behind the things, and lurks in the twilight zones. Hence we say that the visual medium is light together with darkness, and that within this medium, light is the leading element while darkness is the receptive element. The light clarifies the visual medium so that our look can orient us in our surroundings. The leading element and the receptive element each have their opacity. Too much light can obscure the things, and so can too much darkness; but when the light and darkness intermingle, both become transparent, and let us see the things in chiaroscuro.

Active and passive transparency. When the leading elements penetrate the receiving elements, the sensory media are transparent, leading our sight and touch into receptive depths. This elemental transparency is both active and passive. Darkness and inertia make transparency passive, while light and motion make it active. Passive transparency requires activity, since pure darkness and inertia are opaque. And active transparency requires passivity, since pure light and motion are active opacities. Light is only potentially transparent, until darkness shades the light; darkness too is only potentially transparent, until light illumines the shadows. Thus light and darkness are quite unlike a lighted or shadowed thing which blocks our gaze, since the material thing has no potential transparency, until it decompresses into the ambient and becomes atmospheric. The potentially transparent active element is the light at which we look, while the actually transparent activity is the light which we look along, the light which we see within. We can look into the light, and live within the lighted world, because we look into the dark and along the light. Without the yielding element, the light would be powerless to lead. The potentially transparent passive element cannot activate, and thus is not an actuality, if actuality is understood as activity and activation. Darkness is, however, real, a passive actuality. Light is the active power while darkness has its power in its passivity. Without the passive power, light could not yield before our gaze, but would block our prospection, like a lighted surface. Because darkness shades the overpowering light, lights always tend toward lighting, when we look along the light.

The ubiquitous darkness which lets the light lead is not a mere privation, an absence of light. When we are deprived of light, we see a positive darkness, a positivity which our hands cannot see. The passive positivity in our hands is inertia and numbness. Admittedly, we cannot see darkness unless light is lacking, but darkness is not the mere lack. Unless light is lacking, the dark cannot make itself seen, because all activity resides in the light. Darkness is an overpowering passivity in which there is nothing visible. Darkness cannot surge forth and extinguish the light, like a storm cloud; only a thing can block the light; darkness is not something dark. The darkness which struggles against the light is a fallen angel, which actively obstructs the overpowering light with opaque densities, tangible things which cast

154

the world into shadow. The light, with a burst, can cast down the blockade and vanquish the lesser light, but never the darkness, the dark is more powerful than the powers of darkness, because absolutely passive.

Active and passive opacity. When the active and passive elements are not actually transparent, they are opaque. Light and motion block our perception with their excessive intensity, while darkness and inertia block our perception with their passivity. Active and passive opacity are quite different. Light blocks our gaze, and blanks out the lighted things, when the light itself is blindingly clear. Suppose that, on a sunny day, I look outdoors and see a moving vehicle; my gaze reaches across the intervening distance and contacts the window shielding the driver; beyond this reflective surface the lighting shifts to a lower level, but my gaze adjusts to the relative darkness, and I penetrate through the window into the cab, where I see the driver manipulating the controls. Suddenly the sunlight bursts off the glass and obscures the vehicle along with its driver; the sunburst stabs into my eyeball, leaving behind a dark wound floating over the cab which has come back into view. The light does not stab without warning; I glimpse the blade coming; and before I glimpse the blade, I see the sun burst into shivers on the glass; and before I see the burst, I see the sun strike the glass; and before the strike, I see the sun streaming down upon the earth, casting shadows behind the trees. Suddenly, the sun invisibly hurls a fireball, which becomes visible when it strikes the glass. I see the direction from which the bolide has come, because I see peripherally the shadows running away behind the trees. Before the sun strikes the glazing, I am looking through the window into the cab; the sun strikes, and suddenly I see the window glass again, but only for an instant; the fireball

155

bursts into blades, which thrust to the horizons along the radii of a slab-sided sphere; the bursting fireball has a central hot spot from which blades radiate in my direction, and thrust directly into my eyes, or whiz inaudibly past my ears. The sunburst blocks my gaze with its fiery directionality. The sun cuts my gaze short at the window glass, and thrusts this truncated glance back into my head, where the retinas are burnt. When the sunburst has done its violence and vanished, my gaze again beams from my eyes and penetrates into depth, but my vision has darkened, and momentarily beams less strongly than it did. My weakened eyesight pushes before it the dark after-image, which no longer rests upon my retina. I see the image in the world, but it floats on the hither side of the things, and never quite merges upon the things themselves. Somewhere yonder in the world the image fades and disappears, though the image will fade over here in my body, if I shut my eyes. Sometimes an energetic gaze can block the sensational light which obstructs our vision; we can direct our gaze against the rays, and thrust the light back into the source from which it radiates, so that we see the light yonder. In a vivid scene which exhibits strong darks and lights, there is a continual struggle between the gaze and the light, the light pushing the gaze and the gaze pushing the light until the power which has least strength is pushed back to its source. Again, we can direct our gaze against the light, if we block the light with something opaque, and then stand in the darkness behind the thing and look at the back side. However in this perceptual situation the gaze does not itself block the light; and thus we do not see the light source, but only the rays which spread around the obstruction. The back side can actually be seen only if the light has turned against itself; unless a few rays are reflected back into the shadow, we look without seeing anything, except receptivity.

Darkness is a passive opacity, which frustrates prospection without struggle. A blinding light actively directs itself against our gaze; darkness passively withdraws before us. Though our gaze penetrates into the darkness without meeting any resistance, we cannot see, simply because in the darkness there appears nothing upon which our gaze can strike, nothing lit upon which the eye can light. Darkness receives our gaze without direction, and hence our gaze must direct itself. Without light, looking becomes seeing, a nonperceptual imagination which spies figments in the abyss; we cannot really see unless the light shines. When our eyes are shut, the light which directs itself through the darkness does not see, nor do we see when our gaze directs itself without light. When the light shines and we look, then we see. When the light disappears, we see darkness, into which we look without seeing, until we are exhausted, our eyes no longer having the strength to look. The dark smothers our gaze in its trackless depths. Black obscurity pains the eye which wants to look, but also rests the eye from its activity in the light. When the sun drops and night descends, we see that nothing is visible, and no longer look. Our gaze flickers out and withdraws into its source, and there the gaze rests, awaiting a call from the light. We no longer look even at our eyelids, for no light filters through. The dark obscures our bodily surfaces, and the shadows outside our body merge with the darkness hidden within our brain, an inner darkness we can glimpse even in the light if we shield our eyes.[97] When we can no longer see even darkness, we experience that veritable blindness wherein we cannot even look; in this sense our hands are blind. The look is an inner light which beams forth from inside our

157

body, and sightless eyes shut the inner light inside without an exit, except through other organs.

If we soar into the sun, we see light without darkness. If we plunge into the earth, we see darkness without light. But man lives above the underground and below the sky, in a terrestrial habitat where lights shine in the darkness and darks shade the light. The light penetrates the surrounding obscurity, and strikes against something perceptible which blocks our gaze, and casts a shadow behind its bulk. The light shapes the thing before us, moving around the contours, moving around the sides, shading into the darkness behind, into the darkness beneath, into the darkness in surface hollows. Dusky light surrounds our body, immersing us in the medium which lets us see. Inside the body and the thing hides additional darkness, except where the materials are translucent or transparent. When passive opacity is present alone, the darkness inside the body subject merges with the darkness in the thing, through the outer darkness in which they are immersed. When the active element is present, there is a clearing between the body and the thing, where the light plays and the gaze disports itself. In this clearing the things stand forth from the darkness and face the light, but beneath the surface hides the darkness within. Our gaze strikes the surface from across the clearing where we stand looking out from the darkness inside our own body. If we open the thing before us and turn it inside out, we see just more lighted surfaces. The light outside penetrates into the inside darkness, and we see the darkness move around behind the things inside, as we bring the insides outside. Once we have seen the inside, we project on the outside an imaginary inside, through which we see the inside without turning the thing inside out. The projected view presents the inside as a lighted outside, and thus conceals the inner darkness, seals away the dark more deceptively than does the shining surface which confronts our face before we project the view we have already seen.

The Media and the Things Mediated

The light waxes and wanes, swells and fades. The lighting, with its shading, is a degree of energy, present all at once, not arriving in slices like the things. The circumambient atmosphere is pure presence, not an apparitional process always on the way toward completion; but into the medium, from across the clearing, the things come forth from the background, in layers. The things are a perpetual oncoming, with a depth farther on beyond the surfaces which have appeared so far.[98] The things appear along earthly routes which let our gaze penetrate into the background, if the light leads. The atmosphere has its leading element which traces trajectories through the air, drawing our eye into depth, where the earth begins to breathe. Light and motion lace our surroundings with routes, which solicit our activity, exhausting our perceptual energies. But also, the sensory media let us rest, because the leading elements pierce yielding elements, whose passivity receives our body, without projecting us toward absence, arousing our anticipation. We rest in the darkness which shades the light; and we also rest in the light, because we rest in our activity, enjoying our life along the light beams. As we move along the atmospheric routes, we live at a certain level; our gaze vibrates at a certain level, while the light draws us along its routes into depth. The medium then is pure presence, but a directional presence, which brings our body into the presence of the things, things which present themselves across the clearing. This directional presence lets our phenomenal body contact distant surfaces; all the surfaces appear across the clearing, stopping our gaze where the light strikes the things. The things yonder appear in layers along a style

159

which delves into hidden depth; from the yonder depth, the things radiate their surfaces into the atmospheric depth over here, where the light plays; but the apparitions which come forth into the air become imperceptible. These ghosts and intercalated gauzes become operative invisibles, visible only as an atmosphere which haunts us without confronting us, so long as we live in a light whose level remains constant.

NOTES

[1] *PP*, pp. 243-67.
[2] *PP*, pp. 267-80.
[3] *PP*, pp. 280-298.
[4] *PP*, p. 246.
[5] *PP*, p. 253.
[6] See *PP*, p. 252.
[7] *PP*, p. 249.
[8] *PP*, pp. 244-48.
[9] *PP*, pp. 248-51.
[10] *PP*, pp. 254-67.
[11] *PP*, p. 279.
[12] *PP*, p. 279.
[13] *PP*, p. 275.
[14] See *PP*, p. 317 ff.
[15] *PP*, pp. 299-300.
[16] *PP*, p. 299.
[17] *PP*, pp. 299-300.
[18] *PP*, pp. 300-1.
[19] *PP*, p. 302.
[20] *PP*, pp. 301-3.
[21] *PP*, p.302.
[22] *PP*, pp. 302-3.

[23] *PP*, p. 304.
[24] *PP*. p. 304.
[25] *PP*, p. 305.
[26] *PP*, p. 305.
[27] *PP*, p. 305.
[28] *PP*, p. 305.
[29] *PP*, pp. 306-7.
[30] *PP*, pp. 307-8.
[31] *PP*, p. 309.
[32] *PP*, p. 309.
[33] *PP*, p. 309.
[34] *PP*, p. 309.
[35] *PP*, 309-10.
[36] *PP*. p. 310.
[37] *PP*. p. 310.
[38] *PP*, p. 310.
[39] *PP*. p. 310.
[40] *PP*, p. 310.
[41] *PP*, p. 310.
[42] *PP*, p. 310.
[43] *PP*, p. 310.
[44] *PP*, p. 310.
[45] *PP*, p. 310.
[46] *PP*, p. 310.
[47] *PP*, p. 310.
[48] *PP*, p. 310.
[49] See *PP*, p. 310.
[50] *PP*, p. 311.
[51] *PP*, p. 311.
[52] *PP*, p. 311.
[53] *PP*, p. 311.
[54] *PP*, p. 311.
[55] *PP*, p. 311.
[56] *PP*, pp. 311-12.
[57] *PP*, pp. 317-18.
[58] *PP*, p. 312.
[59] *PP*, p. 312.

[60] *PP*, p. 312.
[61] *PP*, p. 313.
[62] *PP*, p. 313.
[63] *PP*, p. 312.
[64] *PP*, p. 312.
[65] *PP*, p. 313.
[66] Compare *PP*, p. 313.
[67] *PP*, p. 313.
[68] *PP*, p. 313.
[69] *PP*, p. 313.
[70] *PP*, p. 304.
[71] *PP*, p. 315.
[72] *PP*, p. 313-14.
[73] *PP*, p.314.
[74] *PP*, p. 314.
[75] *PP*, p. 314.
[76] *PP*, p. 314.
[77] *PP*, p. 314.
[78] *PP*, p. 315.
[79] *PP*, p. 315.
[80] *PP*, p. 315.
[81] *PP*, p. 315.
[82] *PP*, p. 315.
[83] *PP*, p. 315.
[84] *PP*, p. 315.
[85] *PP*, pp. 315-16.
[86] *PP*, p. 316.
[87] *PP*, p. 316.
[88] *PP*, p. 316.
[89] *PP*, p. 317.
[90] *PrP*, p. 162.
[91] *PrP*, p. 162.
[92] *PP*, p. 315.
[93] *PP*, p. 315.
[94] *PP*, p. 316.
[95] *PP*, p. 316.

162

[96] *PP*, p. 308.

[97] Compare *PP*, pp. 283-84.

[98] See Alphonso F. Lingis, "The Elemental Background," *New Essays in Phenomenology*, ed. James M. Edie (Chicago: Quadrangle Books, 1969), pp. 35-36.

Chapter IV

THE SENSUOUS INTERMEDIARIES

The sensory medium is an ambient which bathes our body, and soaks the things which surround us. The encircling materials dissolve in the medium, and permeate our corporeal sphere. We swim in an air which ventilates the material externals; we bask in a breeze which vaporizes corporeal density. The earth populates the aether with apparitions, lending each thing an aura, lending our body a living aureola. Along our luminous look, phantoms invade the phenomenal body. Shining surfaces advance in layers. The encroaching slices vanish in thin air, leaving a crepuscular mist, a shimmering cloud. The vaporous intermediaries are luminaries which lurk in the light; secretly they refract our look, focusing the gaze, and diffusing it. Submerged in light, immersed in twilight, we embrace the swarming wraiths with our phantom limbs. Our phenomenal body breathes illusion, and renders the world auroral.

The enveloping cloud, on the inside, has routes without

surfaces. The ambient appears as flat opacity only when we shift from one level to another, moving from light to dark, or from one colored lighting to another. We glimpse the medium when we shift levels, but the mediated things are less elusive. Through the atmosphere, along the light, we plainly see lighted surfaces across the clearing, impenetrable planes surfacing solid matter. But these outer sidings, like the light, can become media, or intermediaries. A lighted surface, or a lighted color, is a colored light which can become a lighting. A lighted and shaded contour is a patterned light which can become a level of illumination. Reflective surfaces become refractive, leading our gaze through transparency, into depth, not rebounding light beams into our dazzled eyes. Shining skin becomes insightful flesh; surfaces become fathomless faces. Through their facets, the things yonder exhale themselves into the atmosphere, exfoliating inspirational splendor. Material halation inflames our senses, generating the internal pressure which demands expression.

Our body is a living symbol in which the earth becomes significant. In the place where we live, earth becomes world. We prolong our body into the things yonder, as we penetrate into the background. Indwelling the externals, we employ things as perceptual instruments for probing the thickets, and making our way inside. The things become expressive as we press them into our service. We too become expressive, when a spectacular view, an impressive panorama, enlists our energies, and utilizes human eyesight for impersonal reflection. Freely expressive, the things unfold into their surroundings, appearing as shadows, impressions, speculations. We prolong our sensitive body into the world through instruments, and the tools reflect the things upon which we operate. Through our bodily organs and artificial limbs, sensation becomes teleperception, making present the hidden, through images. Exercising imaginal perception, we experience the real through apparitions which fill inner emptiness, making our mind a phantom body, our body a body image.[1]

VISUAL EXPRESSION

The visual artist ossifies the intermediaries, makes the apparitions visible as a painted product. But the paint disappears while we look; the pigment beguiles our gaze into forgetfulness. Bedribbled cloth, scribbled paper, is an external sensible through which we witness the externals which first inspired our production. Face to face with the things, and confronting paper with marking tools, our view becomes a visage, a paper vision, which lets us view again the thing which caught our eye, and made our face light up. There is a "system of exchanges"[2] between the body subject and the things. The style which stirs in our flesh joins with the style along which the thing appears. Across this jointure, the thing is changed into my body, and my body into a thing, as my bodily style prolongs itself into the world. The exchange is systematic, and therefore meaningful. The "things have an internal equivalent in me," a "carnal formula" which becomes externally visible when I labor in the world.[3] My private image is the "inside of the outside," and the public painting is the "outside of the inside."[4] In my habitation, each furnishing is a "carnal essence or icon"[5] of the things perceived in the untamed outdoors. The effigy which lets us grip the soil is not a "faded copy" or a "trompe-l'oeil,"[6] not a thing set beside other things, not an isolated object which can be set aside without altering the original. A flat representation does not possess that depth which I experience with my nerve endings, when I take drawing tools in hand. My instruments become "detachable organs."[7] The artist and his tools grow together; we cannot remove his artificial limbs without maiming the man. Where the musician uses tongue and stringed instruments, the visual artist uses brushes and chisels. The draftsman may unclasp his pencil, but he never lays down his eyes, which have been wedded with his tools. When he looks about him, empty-handed, phantom brushes are at work, predelineating the scene which the real brushes could paint. Wedded for life, the painter is immured in his studio, so that his eyes can no longer see the world, without seeing a painting. The imaginal eyes and phantom brushes gesture toward a ghostly intermediary always hanging between the body and the world. But through this veil the painter sees his native habitat better than he saw it when suckling there. The painted canvas is a manufactured tool, meant for perceptual employment, a hand-tooled surface where we see a world that looks strangely familiar.

The eye works together with the hand, which manipulates the brushes. The eye operates in the head, which confronts the world through its front surface. We cannot use our eyes without facial expression, and therefore the artist has a physiognomy, and a physique. His facial expression permeates his body, and spreads across the canvas. Upon the linen support he magically exhales his own face, whose lineaments shadow forth the things which he inspects with his eyes. The painter through manual play brings within his grasp the things which originally confronted him from across the clearing, making an expression flicker across his features, and igniting his vision. The painter, his body sprouting tentacles and tenterhooks, stands mesmerized before the thing, whose luminous body flashes forth its message, in layers. Layer upon layer, bodily reality puts on its glorified body, clothing itself with our face, in facets.

167

The visage shining from across the clearing is an image which makes the thing imaginal. The body subject and the thing have their being in a surrounding sensory medium, through which the subject probes with his organs. The subject experiences the medium laterally and longitudinally while experiencing the thing frontally, at its surface. We explore the sensory routes in foreshortened perspective; we look along the light, through the darkness, to the thing at which we look. We look along the leading element, which guides our gaze through the yielding element, until our look strikes the more resistant earth, and embraces the thing, spreading over its surface. We look at the light, and then along the light, as the light becomes lighting. The light strikes the eye with its outside, and then lets us inside, as it leads us into the world. Inside the light, our sunken gaze strikes upon an illuminated outside. Looking at the thing from the outside, we slowly see that the thing too is a medium, a matrix in which its shining surfaces are enmeshed. The thing is a flowing continuum which presents itself in slices, with darks and lights. Each surface is a patterned and figured light, and thus is like the overall light, which assumes the patterns appearing in the world that it illuminates. As the light falls upon textured surfaces and falls between the things casting shadows, the light is pressed into shape against the things which block its progress or let it pass. The light is an ambient which surrounds our body and the things, taking on the shape of its containers and strainers. The light flows through an obstacle course, which sets up cross currents and backwaters. A lighted surface is a figured light; our gaze swims around the contours, looking for its element. Gradually, this light becomes subterranean, leading our gaze farther than we see. From some place underground, our eyes receive buried signification. The thing is a medium for transmitting its own message, through its appearances, along its style. Simultaneously, the thing conveys meaning from the other things knotted into the same network. Looking at the thing from the outside, I suddenly have an insight, an inspiration. The thing which obturates my gaze suddenly opens, becomes translucent for my vision, and leads me into receptive depths beyond the impermeable surface which I first saw. The thing has become an image; the real has become something imaginal which shows forth more than itself. The lighted thing, which we see in the light, becomes itself a light which illuminates something obscure. The image is a surface with a certain depth that lights our way, until something farther on stops our gaze, and closes our world. The image is a light and a lighting, a surface which delves into a depth beyond its reach.

We wish to witness natural expression. We shall interrogate vision, the most theoretical sense. We want to see how reality decompresses its density, how the earth exhales its compacted positivity. We want to see how solidity becomes insubstantial, how depth becomes superficial, as the surfaces of polyhedrons flash light in layers. Facing solid reality, we shall describe the shining visage which greets us from across the clearing; we shall see how the cube draws us within its sphere, where we inhale its aura. We shall next describe how we visionaries assume the face which we envisage, and project the envisagement into the world, as an engraved surface; we shall see how we exhale the visage within our projected atmosphere. Having described the graven image which emerges in the world among the things, we shall finally describe the specular reflection in which the natural things already admire themselves, anticipating the human looking glass, whose eye reflects, and sees.

The Shining Visage

A thing with depth exhibits solidity through lighted surfaces. A cube or die, when seen from one viewpoint, leads our gaze along its visible side toward the sides not actually seen, and solidifies in our sight.[8] But also, the visible side holds our gaze; the cube becomes flat before our face. On a cube, each side holds our gaze equally, though not every perspective upon these sides is equivalent. Each side has an equilibrium between effrontery and modesty, and each side has equal equilibrium, so that no one side is the front, because all six sides have equal claim. But not every solid faces front on all sides. In nature, most polyhedrons are irregular, and may have one front side which holds our gaze, while the back side directs us around to the opposite side for a better view. In culture we find sculptured solids which are frontal, and we discover others which lead us around to the other side, so that we get an equally good view from every angle. Paintings are frontal; the more we look at a depicted landscape, the less we feel drawn to inspect the stretcher on the back. Nonetheless, everything with more than one side leads our gaze toward the other sides, even if weakly. Even a thing which has a facade on the front side weakly leads our gaze around the corner, so that the facade gradually reveals itself as a false face. A true face is a surface which has become sensuous, holding our gaze while directing us into depth, so that we see the thing itself through a single aspect. A face is a surface which effaces itself without stepping aside. During the apparitional process, sides step aside, making way for hidden sides, until the shining surfaces assemble a radiant face in which the thing itself stands forth. In a face, effrontery is modesty.

Surface and face. A cube has no single front side, but one becomes temporarily the front for us, just because our body

170

has a front side through which we confront the cube. We look for the front, confronting one side after another, until we see that each side faces us, and also faces away from us. But we turn the cube back and forth, toward and froward, until a back side appears on the back; we position the sides at the side, or turn them slightly toward our face. Each shining facet is a sensation which attracts our eye; the front side is the most vivid aspect, holding our gaze the longest, before we are drawn toward the other sides. The front side is the most striking surface, but is not yet a face. A face is a shining surface whose radiance has become a phosphorescence from depth; a face lets us see all the sides from the front, without leading us around the side. The back side leads us toward the hidden sides by standing aside, by leading us around the corner; but the face leads us toward the hidden sides through a surface which has become sensuous. A facade is a sensational side which promises revelation through its surface, but which disappoints us when we investigate, when we check around back. From behind we see that the front side does not express the reality which it hides. We therefore push aside the facade and look for the face, or settle around back, if the front side has become impermeable.

Let us describe the cube as it unfolds and assembles itself in original visual experience. A regular solid is not initially seen as regular; we can see the cube from various distances and various angles. But let us hold the cube at a more or less constant distance from our eye, so that the sides remain fairly constant in their apparent size; let us then attend to the various apparent shapes as we turn the cube and view its sides from various angles. We rotate the cube until we confront a side which we experience as the face. We look for the face, because we want to see the cube itself, and the cube in its bodily reality shines forth fully only from the face. The face is a surface which opens into depth, and a place where the depth comes to the surface. The back side is the place where the cube faces away from us and leads our gaze around to the side where the cube faces outward, letting us inside. The back side is a surface which obscures the cube itself, if we stare at this surface without turning the cube as directed. When we confront a side, we turn the cube until that side is parallel with our face so that our gaze meets the surface at a right angle. We align our face with each side, and then turn the cube again, looking for the front side. Each side directs our gaze onward to the side around the corner. Just around the edge we see from an oblique angle an apparently tapered side, which directs our gaze toward that right-angled viewpoint from which we can see an apparently square side: the real shape. Each square side directs our gaze around to the next side. And each side seen just around the corner directs our gaze toward a viewpoint from which we see the side as square, and see nothing around the corner. As we turn the cube looking for the front side, we slowly see that each side is equally the face; and we stop turning the cube. We come to a stand, and stand looking at a single side which invisibly directs our gaze toward all the other sides and toward the cube itself. The front side which directs our gaze around the corner to all the other sides directs our gaze back to the front side which we confront. Our gaze comes full circle, and all the sides around the corner which directed our gaze back to this side come themselves around the corner with our gaze and invisibly overlap on the front side, where the cube itself shines forth with more radiance than ever. While turning the cube, we have incorporated into our body the sensuous ray along which the cube presents its sides and apparent shapes; all the seen sides have come around to the one side at which we stop. Through that motionless side, we look at all the other sides, and through all the sides we look at the cube itself which is further on beyond. The sensuous ray, which originates outside my body in the thing, penetrates inside my body as I turn the cube. As the cube revolves, each side flashes into view, and then disappears into my body as an invisible lens through which I see the next side when it appears. Simultaneously my visual body penetrates along the ray into the cube; as each side flashes into view, my gaze penetrates through its surface, along the ray, toward the next apparition.[9] The visible cube and my visual body interpenetrate, so that the stuff which shines forth in the radiant face is my body seen from the inside and the cube seen from the outside.

If we remain for a while face to face with the cube, the radiance dims, and the elemental ray in our body fades. The cube withdraws into itself and turns away its face. Likewise, our gaze draws back to the surface and withdraws into our body. Our visual body now contacts the cube at the surface, without interpenetration. We look at the visible side, without looking along that side toward the other sides, and without looking through that side at the cube itself. The face becomes again a surface, and the cube seen from one side at a right angle becomes just a flat square. The side which we confront becomes an objectively real surface with no imaginal depth. If we turn the cube slightly, we see another side around the corner, and the square suddenly appears again as the side of a solid; again we rotate the cube, looking for its face. Thus a cube is best seen from a viewpoint which lets us see around a corner or two; we see the cube best if we do not quite confront any single side. The front should be seen from a slightly oblique angle, so that the front appears as almost square, while one side and the top are seen from a very oblique angle. These apparently tapering shapes draw our gaze toward a lateral viewpoint, which would show us the partially hidden side as a square shape, like the side which now confronts us. This view, which lets us see around the corner, lends the cube an imaginary turning motion; when seen rotating, the cube less easily becomes flat. Since we have two eyes, we often see around a corner with one eye, when we look with the other eye from a right angle. Yet the cube, even when seen in the best perspective, can be seen as flat, if we look awry.

Why does the cube become flat when we stare? Why does the face become a surface, and then a plane? The spatial depth is also a temporal depth, and the turning cube propels our experience through time. The actually present surface at which we look is a visible appearance standing between the appearances hidden in the spatiotemporal depth on our side and the appearances hidden in the depth on the yonder side, in the world. We turn the cube around, or move bodily around the cube, and the real surface gradually takes on imaginal thickness. We imaginally perceive the front side as the cube itself. The imaginally perceived cube is a depth which stands between the depth on the hither side and the depth on the yonder side, where the hither and yonder spatiotemporal depths interpenetrate. When we no longer turn the cube around its own axis, and no longer circle bodily around the cube, the depth on the yonder side no longer interpenetrates with the depth on the hither side. The already achieved interpenetration fades into the past, and our gaze is impressed with the present sensation. We gaze at the cube from a single side, and the cube hides behind its visible skin. The solid thing disappears, and we see a planar thing. The surface becomes a plane, because the surface itself takes on spatiotemporal depth. We do not turn the cube, nor does our body circle; the cube and our body rest in place, while body and cube move through time together. The single side radiates a square shape into my eye, and my eye beams upon the single side. This side moving through time becomes an imaginally perceived thing whose spatiotemporal thickness obscures the imaginally perceived polyhedron. The single side is never quite a planar thing, but remains ambiguously the side of a solid, unless I can imagine the side as a sheet, or a slice. From the spatiotemporal depth on the hither side, I can project an image of the actually seen side as this surface would be seen in profile. I imagine that from a lateral viewpoint I would see only a thin edge, or nothing at all. Through such imaginative variation, I can construct a slab located where I see a surface parallel with my face. However, the visible side is never quite seen as a planar thing, unless I see some real variation in the thing before me. But, if I really turn the thing, I suddenly see a cube again, because the cube projects from the spatiotemporal depth on the yonder side a tapering surface seen around a corner. This obliquely seen side draws my gaze around to the hidden sides. The planar thing seen sideways, which I imaginatively projected from the hither side, diverges from the cube which I now imaginally perceive, and vanishes as an artificialism. During the imaginative variation, the single visible surface appeared as the face of a planar thing; but during the real variation, this face appeared as a mere facade, and disappeared. The front surface becomes, once again, the face of a cube.

We pose the stereometric figure in the way we portray the human body. We experience the body as projecting itself outward, not as turned inside out; and the back side projects outward just enough to show a body which faces away from us. We best experience the embodied subject from the front or side, so that we can see the eyes, and the other organs whose gestures are most expressive. In a portrait, the head is shown full face or in profile, or in some aspect

175

between these views. The back has less transparency than the front, and strongly directs our prospection around the side. When the human body is depicted from the back in a painting, we envisage the hidden face. But also, the back side tends to appear as the front, since the back is the only side we can actually see. The human body is a solid which does not face outward equally on all sides. Unlike the cube, our body has a distinct forward surface. But the front side, when first seen, is not yet a face. The face is the side upon which the other sides assemble during perception; the front is the side that gradually becomes the face; the imaginal solid emerges most readily on the dominant surface. The front side acquires depth, and becomes a face, when we rotate the solid, generating atmospheric layers which haunt the forward surface. If we cannot find a front, the face emerges on the side toward us.

Face and depth. A surface is not initially seen as the side on a solid thing. Nor is this surface seen as a planar thing, since a slab is just a solid without much thickness. A surface has no thickness at all, and is strictly two-dimensional, like the surfaces studied in plane geometry. A surface is a forward side without sides or a back. This one-sided sensible initially stands between the mental depth on the hither side and the real depth on the yonder side. An actually seen surface is instantaneous. It disappears as soon as it appears, leaving behind a fading after-image. Anything which remains in view takes on during that time a certain thickness into which our gaze penetrates. A surface thickens and leads our gaze into depth, or else diverges from the leading element and disappears. Sometimes a surface appears as a facade, which suddenly stops our gaze, and thickens only as something thin; a mere facade is a planar thing through which we can see something more solid behind, or see nothing but vacant

176

depth. A surface which endures without appearing as a facade is experienced as a face which directs our gaze toward other surfaces, and leads our gaze into the background. A face is a surface through which we see something in depth which comes to the surface in facial expression.

The depth suspended in a face is fundamentally temporal. Empirical spatial depth unfolds from a temporal depth, and this is why something spatially thin can be ontologically real. We cannot empirically see the cube in depth unless the ontological depth on the yonder side penetrates along the elemental ray into our body, and unless the ontological depth on the hither side intentionally penetrates along that ray into the world. Empirically, I confront the cube from one side, and the confronted side leads my gaze around to the laterally seen side, and then around to the back. The empirically seen side which I initially confront is the actually visible separation between the hither depth in my visual body and the yonder depth in the potentially visible world. When the confronted side leads my gaze around back, the cube thickens as the front side overlaps the back side. The front side converges upon the cube and disappears on the back, where the initial front becomes an invisible medium through which I see the back side and the cube itself, which faces toward us and away from us. The front side crosses over from the yonder side and enters inside the depth on the hither side, while the back side emerges from the depth on the yonder side and separates anew the yonder side from the hither side. The back side is now the yonder separation between the yonder side and the hither side, while the initial front side, which is no longer actually seen, is the hither separation between the yonder and hither sides. Between the hither and yonder separations is the ontological thickness which we experience as empirical spatiality. Between the hither and yonder separations, the

177

depth on the hither side and the depth on the yonder side interpenetrate. The depth over here penetrates through the depth on the yonder side up to the yonder separation, while the depth on the yonder side penetrates through the depth on the hither side up to the hither separation. The hither and yonder sided cube caught between the hither and yonder separations is the imaginally perceived cube. The hither and yonder separations carve out an inseparably imaginary and real place between the merely imaginary depth on the hither side and the merely real depth on the yonder side. This cubical carving leads our gaze through the yonder separation toward unperceived depths beyond, and leads the elemental ray through the hither separation toward unimagined depths in our body. The depth on the hither side of this hither separation is the merely imaginary, whereas the depth on the yonder side of the yonder separation is the merely real. Between the merely imaginary and the merely real we experience the imaginally perceived cube, which becomes more perceptual as our gaze penetrates toward the nonimaginally perceived, and more imaginary as our gaze withdraws toward the nonperceptually imagined. Once we have rotated the cube, so that we confront the side around behind the side which we initially confronted, the back side leads our gaze back around to the initial front. This front side now appears as the yonder separation, while the back side enters inside somewhere between the new yonder separation and the old hither separation. The hither separation is the initial front side as seen the first time, while the new yonder separation is the front side seen the second time. The shining surfaces pile up on the front side, and make the front a face. The face, with its compressed layers, is the carnal essence of the thing itself. The thing seen from behind is more carnal, but less essential.

Rationalism adores frontal sculpture and regular solids. Objective thought wants to experience everything frontally, and dead center. Thus objective thought posits as real just the side which we actually confront, or confronts the real front side and ignores the hidden sides. Or else, objective thought brings all the sides around front and spreads them out in breadth, so that we see the thing as a flat projection. The really real thing then appears as the ideal relationship among all these sides, and among all these as seen from every viewpoint. But objectivism is just an uprooted reflection upon our original experience. Situated within our body, we experience the real thing through the side which we actually confront; from the front we see the back without bringing the back around front; likewise we see the front when confronting the back; each side leads our gaze more or less strongly toward the unseen sides so that we always see farther than we actually see; each side lets us see that we could see the other sides; the side seen in breadth leads our gaze toward sides hidden in depth; the seen images forth the unseen. When objective thought brings all the sides around front and spreads them out side by side, the sides no longer have imaginal power. Each side is positioned so that we confront its breadth, and we see nothing which is not altogether real; each real side is a signal which lets us think about the other real sides; imagination is replaced with intellection. The intellectual process which flattens the thing is also a process which disembodies the thinker. We said that a thinker who confronts the front side brings the back side around front so that he can confront the back side alongside the front side; but we can also say that the thinker, while confronting the front, goes around back and confronts the back side. A thinker who simultaneously confronts each side from that side has abandoned his bodily situation; he is located everywhere, and hence nowhere; he is spread out through space, so that he sees the thing from all sides and from every viewpoint. Each side is immaterial, because it is a front without a back, a surface without thickness; the thing itself is an immaterial interrelationship among these phantasms. Objective thought is essentially this process which dematerializes the thing and disembodies the subject. The thinker has no lateral vision, and has nothing behind him; he is pure confrontation; he has no thickness, except in language. Language is the aetherial medium which lets us confront the sides which are perceptually hidden. Through verbal formulae, objective thought sees the most irregular solid as regular. All the various sides are spread out in breadth and positioned so that we see a lawful relationship among all the visible surfaces; variation among the sides is seen as regular variation. The cube is a paradigm through which the intellectualist imagines all the spatial realities which objective thought regularizes. Depth is demoted to third place, and finally eliminated.

Empirical depth is a third dimension which appears beyond width and height, the first and second dimensions. These first two dimensions form a surface whose dimension we can call simply "breadth." Ontological depth Merleau-Ponty calls the "first dimension," because there are "forms and definite planes only if it is stipulated how far from me their different parts are."[10] Empirically perceived breadth requires perceived depth: we do not perceive a broad thing with an apparent size and shape, unless we perceive it at some depth; and we do not perceive the thing as having a determinate breadth, unless we perceive that thing at a determinate depth, and the various parts of that thing at determinate distances from our face. Empirically, the reverse is just as true: there are distances and definite solids only if it is stipulated what their size and shape is; we do not perceive a thing and the various parts of that thing at determinate distances from our face, unless we perceive that thing as having a determinate breadth; the various parts of the thing have various distances from our face, and these distances determine the angle from which we view the surface; we cannot determine this angle without determining the shape of the plane we see. True, the empirical argument for the primacy of depth can be reversed, but fundamentally we are not arguing "that height and [width] *presuppose* depth because a spectacle on a single plane supposes the equidistance of all its parts from the plane of my face."[11] Such an argument has already objectified the three dimensions, and does not describe "the experience which opens these dimensions to us."[12] The "vertical" and the "horizontal" along with the "near" and the "far" are abstractions which reflectively separate the various dimensions from that original situation wherein our body faces the world.

Height and width "appear, at first sight, to be concerned with the relationships of things among themselves, whereas depth immediately reveals the link between the subject and space."[13] However, at second glance, we see that "the vertical and the horizontal too are ultimately to be defined as the best hold our body can take upon the world."[14] The objective spatial dimensions are derived from the preobjective. When "viewed in their primary significance," height and width "are 'existential' dimensions," like depth.[15] Empirical depth is the model for an ontological depth which includes height and width; empirical height and width are the dimensions which objective thought uses for imagining an ontological breadth. Objective thought often argues that we do not see depth; in such arguments "depth is tacitly equated with *breadth seen from the side*, and this is what makes it invisible."[16] Moreover, these arguments insinuate a fun-

181

damental ontology which denies the embodied subject a view into the natural world. When Merleau-Ponty calls depth a "first" dimension, he is engaged in ontology. He admits that "a first dimension that contains all the others is no longer a dimension, at least in the ordinary sense of a *certain relationship* according to which we make measurements."[17] When we measure depth, we view it from a lateral perspective; we spread depth out in breadth so that we can lay the measuring instrument alongside. Fundamental depth is "the experience of the reversibility of dimensions, of a global 'locality'—everything in the same place at the same time, a locality from which height, width, and depth are abstracted."[18] The reversibility among the various spatial dimensions is experienced through time; ontological depth is essentially temporal. The "first" dimension is fundamentally the fourth dimension into which we look when we see the first and second dimensions opening upon the third dimension.

We are always running headlong along the temporal vector, and thus are always in the midst of things before we can array them before our face. The things therefore must present themselves in layers along our path, and not all at once. The things have a background whose depth receives our forward thrust. In two ways the thing leads us into distance: first, each side on the thing leads our gaze around toward the other sides, stepping aside so that we can see the hidden aspects; secondly, one side holds our gaze more than the others, and the other sides direct our gaze toward the most striking, so that the sensation becomes sensuous, showing forth the other sides without stepping aside. The strength in the sensuous image is a radiation from depth, while the strength in the single sensation is a shining from the surface. The shining surface catches our eye, but the prospecting gaze glances off, toward the surfaces not yet seen. In both these ways we follow our lead: our gaze moves laterally along the front and around the sides to the back, and also penetrates longitudinally through the front into the cube itself which radiates all these sides. In original experience, a single shining surface positions itself before our face and leads our gaze around the corner toward the hidden sides; the shining surface becomes a light along which we laterally experience the other sides, and a light along which we longitudinally experience the cube itself, with all its sides. The shining surface becomes a radiant face which leads our gaze into ontological depth to the global place where the cube invisibly creates and conserves itself. We see along an elemental ray which shines forth from the face and leads our gaze back toward that source whose radial fulgurations make the front so refulgent. Whether the front surface leads us longitudinally or laterally, the world as a whole leads us always longitudinally, yielding before our gaze, and guiding us.

Abysmal radiance and surface sheen are quite distinct. Our gaze glances off the surface, or penetrates. A sensational surface is potentially sensuous; the front side is the most sensational, and also becomes the most sensuous while we look, unless the front is a facade. The distinction between a shining surface which will become a face and a surface which will become a facade is a difference proverbially difficult to mark in advance; not everything that glistens is gold. We cannot tell beforehand; we must take the shining thing in hand and turn it on all sides, working it over in perception. An image is a sensational surface which has become sensuous, a surface which has been perceptually cultivated. An image is a face, a surface which has aged through our labor. With the empiricists, we can say that an image is a faded sensation. When we look at the imaginal surface, we see that the pellicle shines much less strongly than it did when it first flashed into view. However, an image seen as a weak sensation is not yet seen as an image, since the image tends toward operative invisibility. The image is properly imaginal only when we no longer look at its surface, but see through it. Moreover, an image, especially a painted image, is rarely a single surface. When we look into a painting, or a face, we see through innumerable surfaces, which overlap on something far beyond; the overlapping layers are compressed into a single image which merges upon something absent. The absent thing may shine more strongly than the things present at hand which we see without so many intermediaries. Indeed, the things which we confront nearby may merge with the imaginatively seen thing and strengthen its radiance. Thus the empiricists see the image as a weak sensation, not only because they see it superficially, but because they skim off the surface layer; they isolate a single surface from the innumerable overlapping surfaces which together give an imaginally perceived thing its atmospheric radiance. Weak sensations shine more strongly when they pile up, but this strength should not be confused with sensational strength; repeated impressions can overlap one another and merge as a stronger impression, but the luminosity in an image is not just this sensational strength which we achieve with several coats of paint. A deep image may indeed make a strong impression, but the empiricist looks at this sensation and describes it, without looking below the surface. When the impression begins drawing the gaze inside, the empiricist lets the impression disappear and looks around for another sensation which is similar, or else he resurfaces the impression with his objectifying gaze. Avoiding both the roving and the riveting eye, we can see that a face has a surface more resplendent than a surface which has no depth. When we look at a face and see its surface, this skin looks different from a surface into which we cannot look; we cannot fully understand the different look which a facial surface has, unless we let this sensation become sensuous; but some things look deeper than other things, even when we do not enjoy their depth. The vividness in a surface which appears deep is a quality different from the vivacity in a surface which is merely striking. Depth is striking, when it comes to the surface in an image, but the sensuous does not thereby become a superficial sensation. The image, at its surface, is weak enough that our gaze can pierce through into the layered depth behind. An image with depth is an element where uncounted weak sensations overlap in layers; these worn surfaces merge as a strong image in which our gaze can become immersed; the fading sensations overlap along an elemental ray which runs from the yonder side into our body over here. Along this ray our gaze can run hither and yon, stopping along the way to look at the various sensations which become visible when we pause. But each surface has a quality which again draws our gaze into depth along the beam which transfixes us.

The front side, which becomes a face, is more essential than the other sides, because all the other surfaces converge upon the front side, while the front directs our gaze full circle back to itself, overlapping itself in various views. Our vision, when we see something from the front, is one-sided, but our one-sidedness is not partiality, once we have seen the face. The face is a total part, through which we see the totality. Our own body is one-sided, because we must envisage the world through our face. We turn the thing around, and ourselves circle around the thing, looking for the face, because we ourselves have a face with which we confront the thing. Furthermore, our leading side is usually lopsided; in binocular vision we do not confront the world equally through both eyes; we are right-eyed or left-eyed, just as we are right- or left-handed. In right-eyed binocular vision, the eye on the right-hand side leads the gaze more strongly than does the other eye; the monocular image we see through the left eye directs our gaze toward the monocular image seen through the right; the right monocular image also directs our gaze toward the left, but less strongly; hence our visual body faces the thing itself more directly through the right eye, if our face leads from the right-hand side. Nature squints, and gives the artist a gimlet eye.

The Graven Image

The shining visage of solid reality lights our features, ignites our vision; inanimate refulgence generates human radiance. Our subjective impression builds internal pressure, activates our manual technique, and achieves external expression. Under my hand, at my fingertips, grows a graven image, a material object which my idolatry makes aetherial. Manipulated matter shows me a living nature whose anima is mine projected.

The graven image is engraved, inscribed, or carved, with stylus, pencil, or chisel. Let us concentrate upon line drawings and engravings. Areas are the light and dark spaces between lines; volumes are the spaces between carved contours. Painting can be understood as drawing in darks and lights, sculpture as delineation in plane and volume. Drawing and painting we may distinguish from sculpture, differentiating between the visual image engraved on a tactile plane and the visual image gouged out in tactile depth. The polyhedron, whose visage we have described, is a natural growth, or something crafted from natural materials. Rather than considering how this volumetric figure is reflected in a carved cube, we shall consider the image engraved on a plane surface; we shall consider an inscription

186

which expresses the cube we have already described in the round. How do we see the engraved image as a graven image? How do we see flat incisions as stereometric?

Solidity seen through surface. Merleau-Ponty presents us with three line drawings.[19] All three can be seen as cubes, but they are drawn so that they remain somewhat ambiguous; the cubes have transparent sides, so that we can see all six sides through the three forward sides; consequently, there is an ambiguity about which three sides are forward and which three are behind. One of the three forward sides is seen as the front side, but this is drawn as the square which we would see with our eye at a right angle with the surface; at such an angle we cannot see around the corners of a real cube. Nevertheless, the drawing shows two sides around the corner; these are the top side and the side on our right, or the bottom side and the side on our left, depending on which three sides we see come forward. Moreover, the two sides which we see obliquely around the corner are drawn skewed, but they are not tapered toward a vanishing point. If the draftsman had tapered the sides, slightly tapered the front, and drawn the forward sides opaque, hiding the three sides behind, the drawing would be an unambiguous figure, which we could still manage to see as a flattened plane, if we were looking awry. Merleau-Ponty draws the basic figure untapered and transparent so that the figure is unambiguously a cube, but ambiguous regarding the kind of cube; the cube is indeterminately a cube seen from slightly above and a cube seen from slightly below. This basic figure Merleau-Ponty presents three times; one figure he disorganizes with wavy lines which do not destroy the apparent depth; a second figure he disorganizes with destructive lines which let us easily see the cube as a mosaic pattern with ten triangles and a square. The destructive lines are those which divide single sides, and bring together sides which in a cube are separate.[20]

His three drawings Merleau-Ponty presents in a row, and asks how we see a cube through an image drawn on a plane. How do we see depth? Our author argues that we see by looking, and not by thinking. We do not initially look at the lines as spread out in breadth, and then think of a cube somewhere beyond this flat projection. We simply focus our gaze upon something beyond the surface. "The lines which sweep towards the horizon are not first given as oblique, and then thought of as horizontal. The whole of the drawing strives towards its equilibrium by delving in depth."[21] The lines draw our gaze into the distance; we do not push them. However, the lines can lead our gaze only because our gaze is looking for a lead. We see depth because our gaze always wants to see something, a thing beyond the immediate surface. With certain disorganizing lines we can destroy the depth in the figure which we saw as a cube; but this destruction is not a real causation whose effect we passively see; we must separate the destructive lines from the others and actively trace out these lines so that the depth disappears. Still, the destructive lines really solicit our activity. We can ignore this solicitation, because the drawn figure is ambiguous. In a normal visual field the solicitations become more imperative; normally I cannot ignore the natural separations among the planes and outlines. "When I walk along an avenue, I cannot bring myself to see the spaces between the trees as things and the trees themselves as a background."[22] We do not deny that while walking we can assume a forced theoretical posture from which we can look awry; but this posture and visual gesture presuppose the practical activity which our author is describing. The theoretical posture is a selfconsciousness which is conscious that my experiences are my own. Even though practical perceptual activity is not selfconscious, Merleau-Ponty allows that I am indeed the one who experiences these trees and the spaces between them. "But in this experience I am conscious of taking up a factual situation, of bringing together a significance dispersed among phenomena, and of saying what they of their own accord mean."[23] The normal visual field has in it many figures which are unambiguous. Even veritably ambiguous figures I cannot disorganize and reorganize without letting the figure guide my active gaze as much as possible: the transparent cube which is ambiguously a cube seen from slightly above and a cube seen from slightly below has two squares which are ambiguously fronts and backs; one square comes forward when I see the cube from below, the other comes forward when I see it from above; I can see one square side rather than the other as the front, only if I first look at this one side and see it as a starting point from which the oblique lines lead my gaze toward the other square side, which now appears as an indeterminate background. The figure with the destructive lines I can see as a mosaic pattern only if I first look at the square in the center, and then move my gaze "equally and simultaneously over the whole figure."[24] When I have disorganized a figure, I often must wait for the reorganization. I do not reflectively construct an organized figure from lines sensed separately; my organizing gaze is motivated by the sensible situation in which I am already looking; my gaze "takes things as they need to be taken in order to become a spectacle," and "divides them in accordance with their natural articulations."[25] My gaze always has a focus, or looks for one. "Every focus is always a focus on something which presents itself as to be focused upon."[26] I organize the drawn figure into a cube, not by calculating, but by looking. "The gaze is that perceptual genius underlying the thinking subject which can give to things the precise reply that they are awaiting in order to exist before us."[27]

We have described how we see the drawn figure as a cube in depth, and how we see the same drawn figure as a mosaic in breadth. We should notice further that the mosaic is ontologically just as deep as the cube. Empirically, the cube is a volume in depth, whereas the mosaic is a plane; but ontological depth includes time along with space; when I see the drawn figure as a mosaic, my gaze moves over its spatial breadth into temporal depth; looking requires time; whether the figure is seen as a cube or a mosaic, my gaze penetrates beyond the spatiotemporal present. The drawn figure is first seen as present in the present; it is seen here and now as an indeterminate something which is so far neither a volume nor a plane. The drawn figure has an ontological depth beyond the sensible presentation. As soon as I see the presentation as a drawn figure, I have already seen into depth; a drawing is a planar thing; lampblack or graphite are distributed on paper; even a planar thing has some spatial depth along with its temporal depth; paper is seen as having a certain spatial thickness. And when we see the drawn figure as a mosaic, we see the lines as cracks between tiny tiles sunk in cement. A determinate spatial surface must have enough visible spatial thickness to block the gaze which wants to penetrate into depth. A blank paper upon which nothing is yet drawn is neither flat nor deep; the drawn line itself shows forth the paper as flat, or else denies the paper and shows us something in depth. Drawing is a "process of gouging"[28] in the indeterminate.

The pencil is a chisel, and the drawing is a sculpture; the drawn cube is carved out in space like the sawn and chiseled cube. There remains indeed a distinction between a drawing and something carved in the round: a drawing is a merely visual sculpture, whereas a statue is tactile too. We can, of course, touch a drawing; but we touch only the paper, and not the thing drawn thereupon; when we touch a sculpture, we touch the same thing that we see. There is the further difference that the sculptured thing can be seen from more angles than can the drawn thing; the drawn thing becomes flat when seen from a very oblique angle, and disappears altogether when seen from the side. Furthermore, there is the difference that a sculpture seen from various angles lets us see the background which is hidden behind the sculpture when seen from a single angle; we can never actually see behind something drawn on paper. Moreover, a sculptured thing seen through two eyes is seen from two angles, whereas a thing drawn is seen at the same angle from any angle. All these differences show that sculptured depth is more real than drawn depth, but we should not conclude that drawn depth is sheer illusion; drawn depth is depth itself, but depth as merely seen. Drawn depth can even be seen as merely seen, since we can see the tactilely flat surface upon which the drawing is scratched; with our bodily eyes we can look at the grainy drawing surface and see the paper which our hand will touch.

The penetrative movement into spatial depth is also a penetration into temporal depth, and we still move into time even when our gaze has struck a surface that lets us stare. All vision involves some spatial motion, but the movement is not always straightforward. Light zigzags between reflective surfaces, and so does the gaze. When I stare at a motionless object, there is a vibratory movement in my gaze, and also an invisible fulguration from my eye toward the reflective surface. These phenomena are movements within depth, and not continuous rectilinear movement into depth. Movement "within depth" is a rectilinear movement "into depth" which hits bottom and takes a turn. But movement into time is continuous while life remains, even if this movement should prove circular rather than rectilinear; time in this sense has the most fundamental depth. Merleau-Ponty explains this fundamentality as follows. Arguing against objective thought, which brings all the sides around front and spreads out the views in breadth, Merleau-Ponty says that we do not originally posit all these views as separate entities and then synthesize them. Rather we see all the various views against a background; the background is the thing itself whose appearances we are viewing. The perceptual process is a "quasi-synthesis"[29] which can be understood only as temporal. When I see something in depth, I already see it or still see it; the thing in spatial depth I see at a temporal distance in the future, or I see at a temporal distance in the past. Suppose that I see a cube across the room: in anticipation I already see the cube which I shall see, and in recollection I still see the cube which I did see. Perhaps someone will say that the cube has its being in the future or past only for me; in itself the perceived cube has its being at the same time I have mine; depth is always a distance between things which are simultaneous, and perception means simultaneity; a thing which I now perceive must be a thing which now exists, otherwise I do not perceive it. Merleau-Ponty replies that coexistence in space is not existence outside time; spatial coexistence "is the fact of two phenomena belonging to the same temporal wave."[30] A temporal wave is a present which spreads a certain distance between past and future. Thus a cube which has for me a recollected or anticipated existence can still have an existence with me in the present, because the present has temporal thickness. The perceptual relationship between my perceiving body and the thing perceived is not a relationship outside lived time; my body and the thing are "contemporary."[31] Coexistence is inseparable from sequence, "or rather time is not only the consciousness of a sequence."[32] We can experience the perceived thing as moving through temporal depth, without necessarily experiencing one appearance after another. "Perception provides me with a 'field of presence' in the broad sense, extending in two dimensions: the here-there dimension and the past-present-future dimension. The second elucidates the first."[33] The various views which appear when we see depth are not experienced as separate sequential appearances which we intellectually synthesize after spreading them out in breadth; rather we experience a "passage"[34] from one view to another as we bodily move into temporal depth; this mobile experience Merleau-Ponty calls a "transitional synthesis."[35] Time is a pure passage in which we carve without ever achieving a "synopsis"[36] of the world which passes.

Temporal depth then is more fundamental than spatial depth. Perceived spatial depth is always perceived through time, though the time may be a continuous movement without sequence. Perceived temporal depth always involves movement within spatial depth, but is not always movement further into space: we penetrate into space until our gaze alights on an illuminated surface; moving no farther into spatial depth, our gaze moves back and forth in breadth across the surface; or we simply stare, and the light vibrates back and forth within our gaze. This discontinuous rectilinear movement back and forth in space is a continuous movement into temporal depth. The thing located in spatial depth I see without looking at the apparent size and shape, these appearances become invisibles through which I see the thing itself. Likewise, I see the thing in temporal depth without looking at any present anticipations or recollections which would separate me from the thing itself; I recollect the thing without looking at my recollection, and this nonpositional recollection is present in perception. The field of presence is "presence" in the broad sense: things located in this field are "present" in the "present"; they are spatially and temporally present. The spatial present is a certain spread between my body here and the thing over there, while the temporal present is a certain spread between the past and the future; my body here and the thing there are contemporaries which coexist within the moment. The sculptured cube and the drawn cube are viewed within an indeterminate field of presence; this presence is a spatiotemporal surface which is not yet a planar thing, since every "thing" has some temporal depth. While we look, the present gradually spreads between a past and a future. The visual process whereby we look into spatial depth is also a process whereby we look into temporal depth; even if we gradually see the spatiotemporal surface as a planar thing, we still travel through time.

Looking once again at the figure drawn on white paper, let us summarize how we see a cube in this visual field. The empiricists would say that I look at the drawing as presented, and then associate with this presentation the various appearances which I would see from other angles and other distances. Against the empiricists, Merleau-Ponty argues that "when I see a cube, I do not find any of these images in myself."[37] Once I have looked into depth, I can indeed look within myself and confront there the various images; but these images require depth perception, and not the reverse. There must be a single visual act in which I see that various appearances are possible. What is this active gaze? The intellectualist would say that the gaze is an intellectual activity wherein we think the cube as a solid with six equal sides and twelve equal lines at right angles to one another. Depth then is a coexistence among these equal sides and equal lines. Against the intellectualist, Merleau-Ponty argues that such a cube is a construction which is derived from original-

194

ly experienced depth, but which does not fully express that depth; the six equal sides and twelve equal lines are not the full meaning of depth, "and yet this definition has no meaning without depth."[38] The six sides and the twelve lines coexist and remain equal for me only if I see them in depth; my gaze sees the acute or obtuse angles as right angles, and sees the skewed sides as squares. While looking, I do not think about an ideal geometry; my gaze "animates" the drawing so that the lateral sides are immediately visible as "squares seen askew."[39] Strictly, we do not even see the skewed sides; we look at the square sides along the skewed sides, which we never quite confront. "This being simultaneously present in experiences which are nevertheless mutually exclusive, this implication of one in the other, this contraction into one perceptual act of a whole possible process, constitute the originality of depth."[40] Depth is the dimension in which the things and their sides as seen from various perspectives have being inside one another; breadth is the dimension in which all these views are outside one another side by side.[41] The particular sensation which appears here and now is a surface phenomenon which opens along primordial time into the spatial depth over there, and into the temporal depth back in the past and forward in the future, or else disappears into nothingness.

Depth presentation and flat representation. The flat sides on a solid cube become images through which we see the cube itself, when the surfaces assemble a face on the front side. The artistic product is a thin frontal solid, and the figure drawn on the surface becomes a facial inscription exhibiting a solid thicker than the paper. Does the drawn cube represent a sculptured cube? Nothing prevents us from seeing the engraved image as representing something located somewhere else, and indeed the drawing is sometimes meant to be seen as a representation. However the drawing can also be seen as presentative: the drawing lets us see in depth a cube which is located just where we see it; the depth into which the drawn lines lead our gaze is a real depth, though less real than the depth which is tactilely sensible. With the pencil we sculpture a merely visible space; with the chisel we draw in a visual and tactile space which lets us move around the thing drawn and see an outline from every angle; we cannot move around the thing drawn on paper. However the depth seen in the drawing makes our body anticipate feeling a tactile depth; our body gets ready to perceive the thing tactilely; our anticipatory posture makes the visual depth more real than would be a depth seen by a person with no tactile sense. But our posture also makes the visual depth seem less real than a depth which would fulfill our tactile anticipations. Because the cube drawn on a flat surface motivates a posture in which our body is ready to touch a cube, the merely visual depth directs our intentionality toward an intersensory depth; thus the merely visual cube appears as an anticipatory presentation of something farther on. The drawing can appear as either a pre-presentation or a re-presentation, because the merely visual presentation motivates the common sense toward tactile experience. The visual presentation sometimes looks tactile, because the body is a common sensorium; our bodily tactile anticipation lets us see a merely visual cube as representing an intersensory cube somewhere else. Original experience thus has a foundation for the representations about which objective thought speaks; however we do not always experience the drawn cube as representing a sculptured or naturally formed cube. The drawn cube has spatial depth, and we experience the visual depth and the tactile depth as both depth itself; the drawn cube and the sculptured cube are both the cube itself. If we place a drawn cube beside a sculptured cube, we sometimes see the cube itself in the sculpture, so that we see the drawing as representing the sculpture; sometimes we see the cube itself in the drawing, so that the sculpture is seen as representing the drawn cube; and sometimes we see the cube itself somewhere between the drawing and the sculpture, so that both are seen as representations. But representation presupposes that somewhere we see the cube itself. Every graven image can be seen as a representation, if we look at the image and compare this objectified item with something seen elsewhere; but a graven, or engraved, image can also be seen as a presentation, if we let the image become an operative invisible. When I see something drawn on a wall, I cannot say exactly where the drawn thing is located; it is not here on the wall, but neither is it elsewhere; the drawn thing is exactly where I see it, wherever that is; the drawn thing is somewhere out there in the world, located so that I can see it from here. When I look at a drawing, and see the thing drawn, I do not look at the drawing "as I do at a thing; I do not fix it in its place. My gaze wanders in it as in the halos of Being. It is more accurate to say that I see according to it, or with it, than that I *see it*."[42]

Fundamentally there is no distinction between representative and nonrepresentative art. Even the most figurative painting presents visions we have never seen before, while the most abstract painting remains within the familiar world.[43] A polyhedron painted on a flat canvas is a new presentation in which we, perhaps for the first time, see face to face the cube which we had already seen in the intersensory world. Perhaps we believe that during daily life we have already looked the cube in the face; if so, the painted cube appears as the cube itself seen from another side; if we look at the painted cube as a surface presenta-

197

tion, we can see the paint as a similacrum which represents the cube in the world. But, we can also look at nonrepresentative art and see similarities between the painted image and things in nature: blotches on the canvas represent blotches on seaside cliffs; freely drawn forms unconsciously represent microscopic landscapes; dribbled pigment represents galactic dust. Merleau-Ponty however is not viewing abstract painting as representative when he argues that no painting can get away from the enveloping world; he is viewing figurative painting as abstract, and expressive. The painted cube prolongs the cube into paint; but mere paint also is a prolongation. Abstract painting at least prolongs the most general contours in the natural world where the polyhedron too has its being; and the world prolongs the contours in the paint. The distinction between representative and nonrepresentative art disappears, because the world is fundamentally a sensuous element in which our visual body bathes without experiencing any separation between the things in the world. The elemental world has depth with only enough breadth to make the depth visible. We penetrate into the world various distances along various elemental rays, but the elements are never quite spread out so that we can confront the various sensibles and compare one with another. We cannot deny that the world also has a breadth which we confront; across this breadth we see things which look like other things, and we see that the resemblance is sometimes greater and sometimes less; and sometimes things look altogether unlike one another; thus the abstract painting looks utterly unlike the polyhedrons we see in the world. Merleau-Ponty does not deny that we can see similarities and dissimilarities; he insists only that the breadth across which we make comparisons is a temporary slice in a fluid continuum; each slice is an artificial

198

division, which becomes an artificialism if we regard this surface as the world itself.

Suppose the image were merely a flat projection; suppose the perceived world were a superficial apparition. Suppose drawings and natural images were flat representations of a solid reality hidden behind the scenes. The empiricists live in this flat world, this panorama where similar images associate, and unlike images separate. Descartes too describes this depthless world, but he is an intellectualist who correctly understands vision as an active process, and not merely as a mechanism operating in a passive consciousness. When considering the image, Descartes likes to speak about linear inscription; he does not consider color; he regards color as a "coloring"[44] which decorates things drawn with darks and lights. Painting is essentially "design;"[45] we can paint only things which already exist; things are essentially extended, and design lets us represent extension. If Descartes had considered color, he would have seen that we can see into depth without forms or concepts; because colors are formless, there cannot be a representative relationship between a color painting and the extended things; and yet, in a color painting we see depth.[46] Line too lets us see depth without representing things; the line carves itself a place within an indeterminate space.[47] If Descartes had more carefully considered line, he would have seen that line, like color, can present depth without representing. Moreover, when the depth presented with line does represent a depth already perceived in nature, this representation is an expression, for there are no lines in nature. Extended things are seen without visible lines; only the draftsman sees lines. The outline around the apple appears "on the near or the far side of the point we look at."[48] The borderline between the apple and the table appears somewhere between the point on the apple where our gaze settles and the visual resting place on the table; lines "are always between or behind whatever we fix our eyes upon."[49] Nonetheless, the draftsman does not artificially impress his lines upon nature; lines express nature and actualize a natural potency; lines are "indicated, implicated, and even very imperiously demanded by the things, but they themselves are not things."[50]

Descartes supposes that there exist in the natural world extended things with real outlines, or at least real edges which can be outlined. Drawn lines represent the superficies which surrounds the thing. "They present the object by its outside, or its envelope."[51] The things are really extended, but this extension has nothing visible spread across its surface; the things look colored, but they are not really. The draftsman engraves upon copper, or inscribes upon paper, the outlines which represent real extension. These line drawings can represent, because the draftsman sees from a certain viewpoint and projects upon his drawing surface the things which he sees from that perspective. Between his viewpoint and the things positioned in real space there is a plane projection. The image which the draftsman projects upon his drawing surface is a thing similar to the image which the things themselves project onto his retina along the natural light. Thus a drawing "is only an artifice which presents to our eyes a projection similar to that which the things themselves in ordinary perception would and do inscribe in our eyes."[52] The natural light which projects these things into our eyeball also projects into our eye the drawing which we draw from these things. Thus, the light projects a projection; the light projects the drawing as a retinal image; this image is a projection similar to the drawn projection, which is similar to the natural projection on the draftsman's retina. The drawn projection already projects a projection, and the retinal projection is similar to the thing extended in real space; thus, upon the eye which views a drawing is projected the projection of a projection. Along this zigzagging projective route a drawing "makes us see in the same way in which we actually see the thing itself, even though the thing is absent."[53] The draftsman views his own work while he is drawing; when his drawing is representative, he looks back and forth between the drawing and the thing represented; we can say that he compares the thing itself and the drawn projection. But since the thing is already projected into the eye along the natural light, and since the drawing itself is projected into the eye along that same light, we can say that the draftsman, when looking back and forth between the thing and his drawing, looks back and forth between the image projected from the thing and the image projected from his drawing. The draftsman compares two images upon his retina; if the second image is unlike the first, he redraws the drawing, until the natural light projects from his drawing an image more like the first image. We therefore can say that the draftsman looks at a natural projection and compares this first image with the natural projection of an artificial projection of this projection. We wonder how the artist projects his drawing upon the paper or the copper plate. Can the artist look at his drawing and compare this projection of a projection with the first projection? Or does he blindly project his drawing through a bodily mechanism, as the natural light blindly inscribes the thing itself upon the eye? Perhaps the artist draws blindly but not numbly; through his hand he feels himself drawing something out there which the natural light projects back in here; the hand feels, but draws blindly. Of course, the light projects into the eye an image of a hand out there drawing; but why should the artist looking at this image suppose that he sees

201

the outside of something he feels from the inside, since the inside he feels out there, while the outside he sees in here?

Whether we say that the artist looks at his drawing surface, or say that he looks at his retinas, still the projected image "makes us see a *space* where there is none."[54] The image which "the light designs upon our eyes"[55] and the image which the hand designs upon the paper are both inscribed upon a flat surface which has no transparency. The projected image is flat and thus does not resemble the depth in the things themselves; the flat image can resemble the things, insofar as the things are extended in breadth; but "a figure flattened down into a plane surface scarcely retains the forms of things."[56] The flat figure has a shape which resembles those sides on the things which we confront; when we look at a side from a right angle, we see its real shape; and a figure which depicts a thing seen from that side at a right angle resembles that thing. But the flat figure deforms the sides which we see from an oblique angle, around the corner from the side which we face. "The square becomes a lozenge, the circle an oval...."[57] However, a side seen from that perspective and flattened into a drawn figure "*ought* to be deformed."[58] Only a deformed figure can represent the thing itself; the figure "is an image only as long as it does not resemble its object."[59] Descartes understands the image as a "representation" which scarcely ever "resembles" the thing which it represents. And, if we consider that the image represents "forests, towns, men, battles, storms" and yet "is only a bit of ink put down here and there on paper," we can say that the image does not at all resemble the things.[60]

Images can represent without resemblance, because the deformation is systematic. We understand the relational system in which deformed images are projected along the light. The image is a sign which signals us to think along

202

these intelligible rays until we form an idea of the thing represented; the deformed image "occasions" the correctly formed intellectual image.[61] If we ourselves do not understand the relational system along which we think, then god does, and we see all things in god; the only light is intellectual, and the only intelligibility is superhuman; the image is a sensible occasion upon which we let our thought move along the divine light to the intellectual image whose form resembles the things.[62] The image leads our thought to the true idea, just as written words lead our thought to ideas outside the text; a drawing or painting is a "text to be read, a text totally free of promiscuity between the seeing and the seen."[63] The image does not prolong our body into the thing represented; the thing is located outside our body, and the image is located somewhere else, finally in the eye and brain; the intellectual idea is not in the body, but somewhere in the soul, shut off from the things behind the body and its opaque images. Descartes cannot say how these images resemble the things outside the body, because we would require "other eyes in our head"[64] for viewing this resemblance; the images inscribed in our bodily eyes we could compare with the things themselves only through additional eyes which would look at our eyes alongside the things seen. The images on our retinas would be discovered not to resemble the visible things any more than etchings do.[65]

In sum, objective thought imagines that images are flat and opaque things which the light inscribes in our body, and which our body manually inscribes on other things outside the body. The manual inscriptions are then inscribed back upon our body through the natural light. The various inscriptions within our body are signs which the intellect deciphers; these sensible ciphers signal the intellect to form a "mental image"[66] which presents us with the absent thing. But the intellect even through this image does not have insight into the natural world, because the mental image was formed while looking at "bodily indices"[67] which are interpreted as saying more than they actually mean. Drawing is a mode of thought, and thought is a reflection which is certain about its object. "A Cartesian can believe that the existing world is not visible, that the only light is that of the mind, and that all vision takes place in God."[68] But a painter cannot believe that original depth is intellectual, or that sensible depth is illusory, since he lives in the light, and sees the illuminated world with his own eyes, looking through elemental lenses. "Icons"[69] have power. There is an "oneiric world of analogy."[70] The painter cannot believe that the sensible world is flat, because his own body is a natural image whose operations carry him beyond sense presentation. His stylus is a scalpel which in a single stroke pierces through the panorama.

The Specular Reflection

The engraving is a mirror, and the mirror image is an inscription, a cicatrix which nature tatoos in its flesh, long before the artist grips a pencil, or unshutters his eyes. Like the graven image, the specular reflection manifests a merely visible world. When working with his tools, the artist sees the world as a visual realm; and he sees, in the mirror, a prehuman world already reduced to visibility. Nature is an intersensory world, but we discover things which reflect the surroundings as they would be perceived through a solitary sense organ. "More completely than lights, shadows, and reflections, the mirror anticipates, within things, the labor of vision."[71] The mirror is a device more reflective than the woodland pool where the narcissus droops its head, casting an image in unruffled water. Liquid placidity invites vision-

merge into the background, and shift with the background, behind things seen close up; the natural background is like a painted backdrop. At long range, the mirrored world and the unreflected world both lose their apparent depth. However, at close range the depth seen in the mirror looks more real than the depth seen in a drawing depicting the same view, but less real than the depth seen in a sculpture, or the depth seen in the intersensory world which the mirror reflects.

Originally we see depth in the mirror; but we can shift our stance, and reflect upon naive experience, from outside; we can see that the mirror is really flat; original depth is illusory. Empiricism and intellectualism live in this flat world where mirrors resist our gaze and insist upon their surface. How does objective thought explain the specular reflection? The light from the light source strikes the thing, rebounds from the thing and strikes through the glass to the silver backing, from which the light rebounds into our eyes, striking the retina at the back. The mirror image is a real effect produced by the light. The beam, along which the bouncing ball bounds, is a mechanical arm which inscribes the illuminated things upon the mirror surface, and thence upon our retina. "In the world there is the thing itself, and outside this thing itself there is that other thing which is only reflected light rays and which happens to have an ordered correspondence with the real thing. . . ."[72] Between the thing in the world and the thing on the mirror surface there is an external causal relationship. The resemblance between these two things is seen intellectually, and we see that the resemblance is "cross-eyed,"[73] but the causal relationship along which the light projects the mirror image is altogether clear. The mirror reverses the things, crossing the right side over to the left, and vice versa. This crossing fools the eye, but not the mind, for we mentally see

207

the reversal, and thus understand the things as they are in themselves.[74]

Originally we see depth, but also flatness. We can see the mirror as flat, within untutored experience. Avoiding objectification, we simply look at the mirror from the side. Perhaps we see another person standing before the mirror, apparently looking at this flat surface and yet gesturing as if he saw something in depth. Unless the other person gestures convincingly, we see from our side view that he is deluded. But perhaps the mirror has real depth when I myself stand before the mirror in the spot where the other now stands. How do I know that the mirrored depth is no more real when I see it than when the other person sees it? I know, because man is mirror for man; the other person standing before the mirror is himself a mirror in which I see myself standing before the mirror. Or perhaps I actually do stand in front, but place another mirror off to the side where I stood as an outside onlooker; without another person present, I can look to the side and see myself standing before the mirror which I see from the side, but into which I do not see myself looking, since I am looking to the side and not to the front. With three mirrors, I can look straight ahead into the mirror before me and see in its depth a mirror which reflects me in profile looking into a mirror reflected at a very oblique angle, almost from the side. We can stand outside and look at the mirror from the side, but we still see from the inside; the mirror image is the instrument through which we see our bodily outside from the inside; if we could not see depth in any mirror, then we would scarcely know that the mirror is flat. Of course, without any mirrors at the side, and without another person as a mirror, we can move around to the side and view sideways the mirror before which we formerly stood. But, standing at the side, we imagine ourselves standing around front, and the imaginary person standing before the mirror is a mirror in which we see ourselves. Although we would not know very well that the mirror is flat unless we could see the mirror from the side, we would still know, because we can see the flatness from the front. If we touch the mirror surface with our hand, we see that the hand does not touch the body seen in the mirror; my hand leads my gaze to a surface so diaphanous that I often do not see it with my eyes alone. But I can manage to see the surface without touching it; I can look at the surface, or I can let my gaze go through the looking glass until it stops at the face which I see looking back from the depths. The mirror is so clear that my gaze sinks into depth with hardly any resistance; I have seen so many opaque bodies that I slip into the mirror unawares. But I can withdraw my gaze to that surface which I touch with my fingers. If I let my look rest lightly against the glass, I see that the glass has enough density to support my gaze. I look at a somewhat dusky surface; I see through the glass darkly. But confronting a clear surface, I easily see myself face to face, unless my gaze settles upon some dust specks more opaque than the faint darkness underneath. On the surface beneath the dust, I see pinkish pools shaped like that face over here which I feel with my hand, though the face over which I run my hand has volume, whereas the face floating on the mirror is flatter than a lily pad. The mirror can be seen as flat even from the front; but this flatness leads our gaze toward the flatness seen from the side, and the flatness seen from the side leads us back around front, where our gaze slips into depth, if our body still has the habit for penetration.

The Cartesian learns not to see beyond the surface. Or if his gaze should slip, the image which he sees inside is not his own face. In the mirror the Cartesian sees a "dummy."[75] The dumb face is an "outside"[76] without inner life. The objective thinker sees his face as just a surface which shows forth nothing beyond itself. He believes that other people see this outside in the same way that he sees it in the mirror, but the outside which others see is not "a body in the flesh,"[77] any more than is the outside which he sees. The surface which the mirror shows is an effect produced mechanically by the rebounding light. If suddenly the thinker sees himself in the mirror, the image "looks like him."[78] His thought sees a similarity between the images on the yonder side of the glass and the outside here on the hither side; he does not see this similarity through his bodily eyes, and he does not see the mirror image as veritably his own.[79] The apparitional dummy is the objective body; science investigates, not my own body, but that empty doll, that exterior projected outside my sensitive flesh. The scientist, while thinking, is a disembodied mind; objective thought is disembodiment; the mind becomes an inside without an outside, while the body appears as an outside without an inside. But unbeknown to the thinker, our original body is double sided, an inside with an outside, which can be objectified as sheer externality. Our body is a flesh which is reversible between inner and outer; the inner is the body sensing, and the outer is the body sensed.[80]

The scientific sensibility is derived from preobjective perception, an ambiguous experience containing divergent perspectives. The original mirror phenomenon is polyvalent. Gazing into superficial polish, we can see depth, and in that depth we can see an inside behind the outside, an interiority which exhibits the specular reflection as my own body, not a dummy. Nonetheless, standing before a looking glass, we sometimes do see just an outside in the mirror, if we are caught up in thought. The Cartesian is not only caught up, he is caught so that he cannot descend, unless he stops thinking altogether; up in heaven he sees down below

210

an outside which looks uninhabitable, but which appears to be his own when he engages in daily activities.[81] Standing abstractedly before the mirror, we may indeed see just an outside in there. We may even not see inside the glass, but see merely a glassy surface with a pinkish pool floating in breadth. Our abstracted stance may mean that our mind wanders elsewhere, in private images; absent-mindedness need not mean that we reflect upon our mirror image and see that our mind is absent. The Cartesian however is an absent-minded man who gazes abstractedly into the mirror and reflects from above that he is absent down below. The mirror image appears on that open circuit which runs from my seeing body to my visible body; the mirror makes my body visible from over there. But I do not always look along this circuit; other routes are open. I can look into the overhead mirror which reflects my body as an outside moving mechanically. Or, without the least scientific reflection, I can short-circuit the route into the mirror by stroking my chin, or rubbing my brow. The stroking and rubbing is a reflective process on the hither side of the mirror surface; my hand is a sensitive surface which from the inside reflects my cheek or brow. The intentional current flowing through my eyes reroutes itself and flows through my hand; through the eyes gazing abstractedly only a weak current now flows. If I rub my brow so intensely that I gaze sightlessly, then I see only those lights which strike my eye; with passive vision, I see only what can be seen without looking. The intentional current can be divided, however; if I look into the mirror while feeling my forehead, I suddenly feel my forehead over there where I see; from over here I feel that the hand over there has an inside through which I feel the imaginary forehead whose outside I see from here. Or, if I smoke a pipe, I feel the burning bowl in those merely visible fingers which I see in the mirror.[82] When suddenly I

211

feel myself over there inside that outside which I see, I experience that outside as inhabited. Just as I can feel myself over there, I can see myself over there looking back. Perhaps, though, I never experience this particular mirror image as inhabited; I frequently witness reflections in shop windows and polished walls which I could see as my images but do not. Yet I nearly always perceive the depth phenomenon somewhere: if I do not look along one circuit, I look along another; if I do not look along the visual circuit, then my intentional current flows along the tactile circuit. My inside prolongs itself until it runs against an outside, an external siding which the exploratory gaze can penetrate. We gradually indwell whatever we look at, seeing depth in surface; and seeing human interiority in depth, if the reflected external is my own body.

Creative vision as mirror play. The artist is further fascinated with the mirror, because he sees that his own eye is a mirror. He sees himself in the mirror, and sees that the eye visible in the glass is another mirror, a pool of brightness swimming in a shining lake. The artist is a mirror which sees. Or does the mirror too see? Certain paintings show an empty room which is " 'digested' by the 'round eye of the mirror.' "[83] Does the silvered glass witness the surroundings, before the room is inhabited? No, the mirror is an outside without a living interiority; any life we see in the mirror merely prolongs the inside which we live here on the hither side. Only in a human body does the mirror see the denizen who stands in the room. Mirror vision is a narcissistic seeing which reflects our hither-sided vision back upon our bodily outside.[84] When our back is turned to the mirror, the glass no longer has a hither side which views our surface; when we turn our blind surface to the mirror, the looking glass is blinded. When we turn toward the mirror and see our face, we prolong our gaze into a surface which already views our surface, but with a prehuman gaze, a ray which does not see. We look back at our outside along the unblinking look which the mirror directs at us from over there, on the wall. The living look which inhabits the silvered glass radiates from an organic speculum with a human inhabitant. In the eye of the mirror we see our reflective eye.

What happens when this human looking glass looks at a looking glass? He projects his reflection, as a graven image, or an engraving. The artist along his look reflects upon the glass and reflects the reflection he sees in the glassy depth. Having reflected, the artist projects his reflection upon paper along his drawing arm. Through the drawn projection he sees the glassy reflection which he saw with his creative gaze. And the drawn projection becomes a reflection which projects back into the eye the reflection which he projected upon the paper. In this mirror play, our dazzled eye soon loses the track along which the reflection becomes reflected and the thing reflected becomes a reflection. But we easily see that artists are fascinated with mirrors, because we see paintings which depict mirrors upon which the painter has reflected. And we see paintings in which the artist is seen looking into a mirror, painting himself painting.[85] The mirror itself may be depicted in the painting, or the artist depicted as painting may merely look as if he were looking into a mirror, so that we suspect a mirror being used for the portrait. Since the painter depicts himself as reflected in mirrors, and depicts mirrors as reflective eyes which see while no human is present, we see that the painter mutely reflects upon his activity. These reflective paintings are a "figured philosophy of vision."[86] They are an "iconography"[87] which philosophy can decipher and express in written and spoken figures. Philosophy is a literature which

213

reflects upon straightforward painting, and upon the iconography in reflective painting, and upon the literature in which the painters themselves reflect upon painting.

What do we see when we decipher the reflective icons? If a painting shows an empty room reflected in a mirror, the painted mirror is an icon in which we philosophically see that the mirror reflection is a prehuman vision, and we see that the painter sees as the mirror does. The mirror is an artifact which anticipates within things the human vision. The mirror, together with other technical contrivances, appears within "the open circuit [that goes] from seeing body to visible body. Every technique is a 'technique of the body.' "[88] My own body is a visible thing which sees other things, and sees itself. In my body the visible reflects upon itself. My eyes are potentially visible organs through which I can see my body, without a mirror; the mirror simply prolongs this reflective circuit; my visible outside is seen further outside, over there in the mirror; everything inside my body goes into the reflected outside, that ghost; I inhabit a ghost outside my body. Just so, I can inhabit other bodies. "Man is mirror for man."[89] The looking glass is one instrument within a more general bodily technique; working through the looking glass and other reflective instruments is "a universal magic that changes things into a spectacle, spectacles into things, myself into another, and another into myself."[90] Mirroring is not a mere "mechanical trick."[91] Artists see in this mechanism a "metamorphosis"[92] which operates in our body during natural perception and artistic gesture; artists express this insight when they draw themselves as seen during their painting activity; in such a drawing, the artists add "to what *they* saw then, what *things* saw of them."[93] The artist sees the things, and he sees himself in the things; he sees the things looking at him; he sees himself looked at in the things; he sees himself looking at himself in

214

the things. Deciphering the figured philosophy, we can say that artists see "a total or absolute vision, outside of which there is nothing and which closes itself over them."[94] The artist with his totalitarian vision inscribes images, which create a merely visible world. An engraving, a reflection, a face, is a carnal essence which magically captures our body, and incarcerates our mind in a temporary totality.

VISIONARY RECOMPRESSION

We easily understand how we see through the light, since the medium is so clear. With more difficulty, we now understand how imaginal light leads our gaze into depth through sensuous intermediaries. How can we see through a solid cube, whose illuminated surface is so obviously opaque; how can we see through a solid wall? Our gaze can penetrate because vision is stereoscopic. The cube is seen as solid in the place where the transparent images pile up. Binocular vision exhibits the process wherein something opaque becomes transparent and merges upon something more opaque farther on beyond: a cube seen through one eye looks impenetrable; but we open the other eye, and the cube splits into two transparent monocular images which merge upon a cube that looks more solid than the cube seen through a solitary perspective. Visual perception is a process which opens new eyes, until we see from innumerable viewpoints. We are a creature with compound eyes. When we move around a cube, the cube becomes more solid because our views become diaphanous. From a single side, the polyhedron looks solid, but we move around back and the front view becomes a thin film which overlaps upon the back view.

Do we look "through" the things, or "between" the things, or "around" the things? We look all these ways, and we also look "at" the things. Consider the stereoscope. If we look at this mechanism from above, we see two lenses side by side, set apart at a width which lets us look through the glass to the other side. At a calculated distance from the eyepiece, we see fixed a card, which has affixed to its surface two photographs side by side, perhaps pictures of a cube. The pictures are taken from two slightly different angles. The card showing these divergent views is a flat objective at which we aim through the eyepiece. From above the eyepiece we see two views, each with a certain apparent depth. When we get behind the eyepiece and look through the lenses, we experience convergent disappearance, as the two views on the objective slide together and recoil upon an objective farther on. The new objective has more apparent depth and solidity than the two views seen separately. The binocular view appears somewhere "between" the monocular views. But also we look "through" the monocular views, so that the binocular view which appears "between" also appears "beyond." Also, each eye looks "around" the view seen through the other eye. And we look "at" the binocular image seen in the background, until such time as this too becomes translucent for vision.

Binocular vision is already creative; the physical is already metaphysical; stereoscopic assemblage exhibits ontological creativity. Creative vision decompresses material reality, letting the things express themselves in our sight. Natural expression, this invisible decompression, impresses the human eye. The sensible influences, the layered effluences, pile up in vision, become sedimented in the seeing body, cram our sensitive core, until the heart becomes overfull. We decompress our accumulated impressions in human expression, relieving internal pressure, generating external display. Gesticulating in the clearing, our body makes a pact with the world. In the clear zone before our

216

face, at the interface between inside and outside, we create a sensuous face, a deep surface, that decompacts the sedimented sensory impacts. Our gestural symbolism presses out the human meaning of compacted reality, modifying unmodulated positivity, aetherializing airless materiality.

Reality having been decompacted in our spiritual pact, decompressed in human expression, the images, the intermediaries, are recompacted, recompressed, as a solid reality, a solidity which emerges in our vision, as our views find a focus, and converge upon a common aim. Reality is decompacted and recompacted, decompressed and recompressed, pressed and packed into a new reality, as we impress the world, make our impact upon our surroundings. Our expression makes an impression, our differentiations make a difference, our pact with the world produces imaginal reality. Our divergent views merge upon something solid, something discoverable only in these visionary coverings. Shrouded in our clinging dreams, reality is revealed through veils. The world cloaks itself in our phantasies, makes itself phantasmal without becoming a phantasmagoria, because we serve the light, lend our personal expression to the natural process, to the encompassing reality which receives glorification in human guise.

NOTES

[1]An expressive image is a "symbol" or "metaphor." These images we could also call "signs," since "meaning" means "signification," and whatever has meaning is a "sign." But speaking less broadly, a "sign" is a sensible thing which leads us toward something else which is utterly absent from its indicator, whereas a

217

symbol makes present the thing toward which it directs us. The thing symbolized is always farther on beyond its symbol, but nevertheless is really present. The symbol is a sensible thing in which the latent is manifest, while remaining hidden. Signs are indicators which trigger habitual associations, or else occasion a thought. Our gaze strikes a sensible object which automatically carries our gaze toward another sensible thing altogether isolated from the first. Or else our gaze stops at the sign and leaps from there in thought. The sign then is a sensible signal for thinking. The symbol gives us a view through, whereas the sign gives us an intellectual overview, or gives us another sensation through blind association. The sign is a signal or a stimulus, whereas the symbol is a sensuous sensible which lets us see farther than we see, without taking flight from the earth. Through a symbol we perceive the world as easily as through a monocular image, but across a greater distance, as through a telescope.

2 *PrP*, p. 164.
3 *PrP*, p. 164.
4 *PrP*, p. 164.
5 *PrP*, p. 164.
6 *PrP*, p. 164.
7 *PrP*, p. 178.
8 *PP*, pp. 203-5.
9 See *VI*, pp. 241-43.
10 *PrP*, p. 180.
11 *PP*, p. 267.
12 *PP*, p. 267.
13 *PP*, p. 267.
14 *PP*, p. 267.
15 *PP*, p. 267.
16 *PP*, p. 255.
17 *PrP*, p. 180.
18 *PrP*, p. 180.
19 *PP*, p. 263.
20 *PP*, pp. 262-63.
21 *PP*, p. 262.
22 *PP*, p. 263.

[23] *PP*, p. 263.
[24] *PP*, p. 263.
[25] *PP*, p. 264.
[26] *PP*, p. 264.
[27] *PP*, p. 264.
[28] *PrP*, p. 184.
[29] *PP*, p. 265.
[30] *PP*, p. 265.
[31] *PP*, p. 265.
[32] *PP*, p. 265.
[33] *PP*, p. 265.
[34] *PP*, p. 265.
[35] *PP*, p. 265.
[36] *VI*, p. 242.
[37] *PP*, p. 264.
[38] *PP*, p. 264.
[39] *PP*, p. 264.
[40] *PP*, p. 264.
[41] *PP*, pp. 264-65.
[42] *PrP*, p. 164.
[43] *PrP*, p. 188.
[44] *PrP*, p. 172.
[45] *PrP*, p. 172.
[46] *PrP*, p. 172. See pp. 180-82.
[47] *PrP*, pp. 183-84.
[48] *PrP*, p. 183.
[49] *PrP*, p. 183.
[50] *PrP*, p. 183.
[51] *PrP*, p. 172.
[52] *PrP*, p. 172.
[53] *PrP*, p. 172.
[54] *PrP*, p. 172.
[55] *PrP*, p. 171.
[56] *PrP*, p. 170.
[57] *PrP*, p. 170.
[58] *PrP*, p. 170.
[59] *PrP*, p. 170.

[60] *PrP*, p. 170.
[61] *PrP*, pp. 170-71.
[62] *PrP*, p. 186.
[63] *PrP*, p. 171.
[64] *PrP*, p. 171.
[65] *PrP*, p. 171.
[66] *PrP*, p. 171.
[67] *PrP*, p. 171.
[68] *PrP*, p. 186.
[69] *PrP*, p. 170.
[70] *PrP*, p. 171.
[71] *PrP*, p. 168.
[72] *PrP*, p. 170.
[73] *PrP*, p. 170.
[74] *PrP*, p. 170.
[75] *PrP*, p. 170.
[76] *PrP*, p. 170.
[77] *PrP*, p. 170.
[78] *PrP*, p. 170.
[79] *PrP*, p. 170.
[80] *VI*, p. 136.
[81] See *PrP*, pp. 175-78.
[82] *PrP*, p. 168.
[83] *PrP*, p. 168.
[84] Compare *VI*, pp. 255-56.
[85] *PrP*, p. 169.
[86] *PrP*, p. 168.
[87] *PrP*, p. 168.
[88] *PrP*, p. 168. Brackets in original translation.
[89] *PrP*, p. 168.
[90] *PrP*, p. 168.
[91] *PrP*, p. 168.
[92] *PrP*, p. 169.
[93] *PrP*, p. 169.
[94] *PrP*, p. 169.

Chapter V

THE INTERCHANGE BETWEEN INSIDE AND OUTSIDE

The imaginary is inside our body, and the real is on the outside. The inside can be turned out, and the outside can be turned in. The imaginary becomes real when our body is turned inside out, and the real becomes imaginary when our body is turned outside in. My insides are turned out, so that I am inside something outside; the things over there are turned in, so that the things become my insides. The outward turning is expression; the turning inward is impression; the expressive things impress my body, and my body turns back upon the things, pressing out the impression, leaving my impress out there in the things. This turning about, this interchange between my body and the things, lets the inside and outside interpenetrate. My inside is turned out while the outside is turned in, so that the inside on this side joins with the inside on the other side, creating a joint body, an imaginal reality.

The crossing, the "chiasm"[1] where my body and the thing intertwine, is also an intertwining within my own body,

221

because my body is a thing in the world, but a thing which perceives itself, handles itself, looks itself over. Because my own body turns back upon itself, and approaches itself from outside, my body is "an *exemplar sensible*,"[2] where I see the mutual encroachment between myself and the world. Because I inhabit a body, I already dwell outside in the world, and because I dwell in the world, I remain enclosed within a body. This opening and closing, tying and unbinding, is our fleshly generativity, a "natal secret"[3] which we now disclose.

THE INSIDE ON THE HITHER SIDE

I am on the inside; I am the inside. My center is a spatial zero, and at a given distance from this center I see outsides spread out in breadth. These outsides which I see before me are the outside of my inside, as seen from my center; my inside extends from my spatial zero unto these outsides, and no farther; on the other side of these outsides are potential outsides; these surfaces spread out before me are the separations between my side and the other side. The other side is an outside, in the sense that it is outside my visual body; but the other side is not an outside actually confronted and seen as a surface; the depth on the other side is an external outside. This real depth is an outside, a depth outside my body, and in this depth is the reality which has not yet become a surface, confronted from my side. The depth on the other side is an inside, but an inside beyond that inward depth which is mine.

Depth and Breadth
A "side" can be a certain breadth. But "side" can also mean a certain depth. The surfaces which I see spread out in breadth before my gaze are "sides;" they are the outside

surfaces of the things on the other side, and they are also the inside surfaces of the subject on this side. These "sides" have depth on both "sides;" the depth on my side is a "side," and likewise the depth on the other side is a "side"; between this side and the other side is a "side" which separates my depth from the depth yonder. This separation between the hither and yonder sides is a side which can be seen as the inner surface of my inside or the outer surface of the things yonder. The depth on my side is a separate side, because a side, a superficial membrane, or siding, separates my depth from the depth beyond my depth; the depth beyond is on the other side of the slice which separates me from the real world. The depth on my side we can call the "hither-sided depth"; this depth extends from my spatial zero unto those surfaces which I confront at a given distance from my center. My center is the "here" which prolongs itself by degrees up to those surfaces over "there." Beyond those surfaces is a further depth, which we can call the "yonder-sided depth." The hither side is the inside over here, while the yonder-sided interior is the depth over there beyond those outer surfaces yonder.

Hither Breadth as Inside Surface

The inside here on the hither side has a depth, and also a breadth. The hither breadth is an outside; it is my outer limit as seen from over here; this outer limit is that inner surface unto which my inner depth extends from my degree zero. My inner world is a sphere; my degree zero is the center, and the breadth which I confront at a certain distance from my center is the inner surface of this sphere. The confronted surfaces build up the sphere while I actually confront them. The surfaces spread out before me shade off toward the sides, so that the things which appear laterally I do not clearly experience as surfaces, though I experi-

223

ence them as things which could be seen as surfaces, if only I turned my face to the side and confronted them. The clearly lighted surfaces shade off toward the sides and direct my gaze around behind my back; if I turn full circle and sweep the horizon with my gaze, I see that I am enclosed within a virtual sphere; but when I face forward without turning, the sphere remains merely potential behind my back; the shining actuality before my face shades off into a twilight at the sides, and then enters the darkness around behind. The things behind me do not confront me any more than I confront them, but back me up as I back up against them; the things behind are a background which grounds me while I confront the things in front. The things behind have no actual outside, nor does my back have any actual outside when it is not seen; the things behind are dark insides which merge with the darkness inside me; my body and the things behind merge, without the things being turned inside out and then outside in, because the things have no actual outside; no surface separates us. The things in the background support me like the ground upon which I stand; my background backs me up during the confrontation which drives the things before me back against their background yonder.

Hither Breadth as Outside Surface

The surface which I see spread out before me during frontal experience is an inner breadth, but also a breadth which is an outside, an inner surfacing which is also an outer siding. The inside surface of my hither-sided depth is the outside surface of the yonder-sided depth. The depth yonder is that outer depth which extends from my inner surface into the bottomless beyond; this abyss opens toward the cosmic horizon. Within the world are things which have their own centers; the distance between my degree zero

224

over here and their degree zero over there has finite degrees, whereas the distance between my degree zero and the cosmic horizon is infinite; my center over here and the yonder center have their places within the outermost horizon, which encircles the natural cosmos. Situated within boundless surroundings, we experience an inside and outside depth, and an inside and outside breadth: the inside depth is the depth on the hither side which extends from my degree zero to the surface which I confront over there; the outside depth is the depth on the yonder side which extends from that surface to the degree zero farther over there behind the surface. The surface which isolates the hither-sided depth is an inside breadth, which can be seen as the outside surface of the yonder-sided depth. The surface which separates the hither side from the yonder side is twice a side, operating as both the inside surface of the hither side and the outside surface of the yonder side; we experience this duality from the hither side, when we reversibly experience the separation as an inside breadth and an outside breadth; we experience the separation as interchangeably my outer limit and the outer limit of the things which radiate toward me.

Here, There, and the Here Yonder

My "here" and the thing's "there" are both spatial zeros, from which we both radiate a sphere into depth. My place is a here, and the thing's place is a there; from my place I radiate experiences, while the thing from its place radiates appearances, producing between us a phenomenal reality. The thing is a being whose there is not a here; when I see a thing, I experience no here over there, or hardly any. A mere there is a place from which nothing is experienced, unless my here prolongs itself yonder; a thing is a mere there without a here. But when I perceive another person, I experience something over there which is also a here, and I experience myself as being experienced from over there as a there, and a here. I understand how I can be seen from over there as a thing, because I can experience myself as a there from over here. A "here" is a place from which something can be experienced as over there; a person is a here which is also a there, and a there which is also a here; a person can experience another person as a here, and can experience himself as a there; a person can become a thing, and a thing can become personal, when lived from here. We experience things becoming personal and persons becoming like things, because a person is not a pure spirit, which lacks a there. A person is a spiritual body and an embodied spirit; the spirit of a person is incarnated, not incarcerated. Matter is yonder-sided depth without a here, and thus without any hither-sided depth; while a pure spirit is a hither-sided depth without a there, and thus without any yonder-sided depth; a person has both a here and a there, and has both a hither-sided and a yonder-sided depth. Persons dwell in a material nature, a maternality not originally experienced as a material object; an object is something spread out over there without a deeper there from which further appearances could emerge. The objective thinker has an inner surface without imaginal depth; he is spread out before himself, so that he is nothing but what he thinks; the thinker cannot dream. But a person gets drowsy, and dreams about the things which he perceives, until inspiration depersonalizes his body; along the outer light, the dreaming spirit becomes a dreaming matter, a place where the earth dreams, and becomes world. The world is in our heart, "at the heart of our flesh;"[4] matter too has a hither side, in us.

Insides on the Yonder Side

The thing which we see over there radiates its appearances rhythmically along its radii, establishing an apparitional style. The sense presentations form an outer surface which can be seen only from a here somewhere outside the thing; the breadth yonder can be seen only from the hither side; and thus the presentational spread is a hither-sided breadth. The appearances which the thing radiates outward are also inner experiences, when perceived from over here; the outer surface on the thing faces outward and also faces inward as our hither-sided surface. This hither-sided surface facing us yonder we should distinguish from that yonder breadth which some things have inside, hidden from sight, the inside surface of hollow things. A box is a thing which is hollow inside, facing outward toward my here and also inward toward its there; the side on a box is a partition with a surface on both sides. However, if the box is closed so that the inner surfaces are hidden from sight, this yonder-sided breadth is merely potential. A closed box is different from a solid cube, because the former is a thing into which we could look and see surfaces, whereas the latter does not have this potency; we cannot see surfaces inside a cube unless we hollow it out. When we look inside a box, our here becomes situated in there, and we see the partitions facing outward toward that central viewpoint; the box faces inward through its partitions, which face outward toward the inside, as well as outward toward the outside. Thus we can say that a thing always faces outward unless the thing is hollowed out and inhabited, and then the partitions face outward toward the internal viewer. When a box has no domestic spirit, its sides radiate their surfaces invisibly toward the inside; these invisible surfaces belong to the yonder depth, until they are actually seen. We must

227

speak about the yonder-sided depth without speaking as though its apparitional contents were already spread out before our gaze.

The human body is a box stuffed solid with organs. But our body is a sensing sensible which hollows itself out on the hither side, so that the sensible appears yonder across a clearing. The bodily appearance over there is both a hither-sided surface and a yonder-sided surface; the yonder surface faces out and the hither surface faces in; the outward-facing surface and the inward-facing surface are both the same side, the same surfacing. Thus, if I look at my hand, this planar thing faces out from its degree zero and also faces in toward my degree zero over here behind my eyeballs. My palm is an outside surface when I look; my palm is the outside of my hand over there and the inside surface of my visual body over here. My gaze penetrates along the light until it strikes my palm; my hand radiates its visual appearance without visually experiencing itself, except through my eyes. The colored pellicle which I see over there is my own skin. "Color is the 'place where our brain and the universe meet'. . . ."[5] Color is a universal skin.

THE CORPOREAL ENCLOSURE

My body is enclosed in a skin, an outer covering which binds together my internal organs. Beneath this membrane is my yonder-sided " 'interior horizon,' that darkness stuffed with visibility of which [the] surface is but the limit."[6] My skin is a shifting superficies: the outer layer sloughs off when I bathe; hairs fall from my head; the nails grow on my toes and fingers. Finally I cut my nails and discard the clippings among the orange peels. The savage buries his nail parings in a secret grave, lest his enemy eat them. When does my body become something outside my body? When I cut my nails they are no longer mine; my nails discontinue my ownership even before I cut them; I use the scissors when I experience my nails as alien; with a clipper I cut off from my body something which has already put itself beyond the pale. The savage experiences his nails as still his even when cut off; the savage who has trimmed his nails must cut them again with a burial ceremony; clipping my horny growths is not for me such a long process; when I clip, I usually have other things on my mind, and clip absent-mindedly. Considering how my skin shifts about in daily life, I see that my epidermis is not the outer limit of the lived body, nor the inner limit. Sometimes I feel my body contracted into my eyes while I look down upon feet which wear my shoes, but which appear outside my perimeter; my feet seem alien because they are outside my eyeballs where the visionary resides. Sometimes my body expands into my motor vehicle through the pedals and steering wheel, so that the wheels become rotary appendages through which I tread the road surface. The various bodily expansions and contractions establish a level, with reference to which the expansions and contractions appear as deviations; this level is an experiential average. Because expansions shift my average skin outward and contractions shift it inward, the bounded body is a relative absolute. The various deviations from the overall level are innumerable, but ordinarily I do not attempt to number them, just as I do not count my heartbeats, nor measure the systole and diastole; the variations average themselves in my experience without requiring a calculation. On the average, I experience myself as this body bound in a skin which is gradually becoming parchment, whether I express myself upon paper or simply sit in the sun.

Without utilizing objective knowledge, we want to describe the bodily enclosure from our degree zero here beneath the skin. We can understand the skin which is our own, only if we stand under our skin and look from the interior standpoint; we can understand our outer covering only if we live our skin from the hither side. Let us describe some essential situations in which we perceive our superficies shifting outward, releasing us from bondage, but binding us again.

Hand and Handle

This hammer lying on the workbench is a material thing, radiating appearances from its spatial zero over there. I perceive its visual appearances from over here, and if I reach out my hand to the hammer handle, I experience its tactile appearances. The gleaming steel and polished wood, which I see and touch, are sensible surfaces which I can reversibly experience as the outside surface of the hammer and the inside surface of my visual and tactile spheres. The gleaming steel and polished wood compose the inside wall of the home which I inhabit, and also the outside wall of the hammer which has an inside yonder, but no inhabitant. Extending my arm, I grasp the handle, take the hammer firmly in hand, and use this tool for driving a nail. As I pound upon the nail head, I look with my visual equipment at the spot which I want to hit; I feel the nail head through the hammer handle, which prolongs my arm through the striking surface, so that the surface on the hammer head becomes the outside of my arm. The hammer is now inside my body, and the nail head is the hither-sided surface of my bodily home, when the hammer head makes contact; the hard and shining nail head is the outside of the world over there which I do not yet inhabit. Armed with the hammer, I attack the alien materials.

Personal appropriation. My bodily prolongation is a personal appropriation of the impersonal externals; the impersonal properties of the material thing become my personal properties. I hammer with the hammer, and the tool with which I have labored gradually becomes my own hammer; the more I use the tool, the more it becomes an imaginal reality. If the hammer were not real, I could not release it from my grasp and lay it down again in the external world; when I lay the hammer down on the workbench, my tool becomes again something separate from my body; but I still haunt the unused hammer. The hammer when I lay it down does not die; the unused tool remains mine, much as my weary bones remain mine when I lay them down to rest. When I fall asleep, I keep in touch with my hands, even though my hands are no longer in use; I keep my hands ready to hand, so that I can take them in hand when I awake. Likewise, I keep the hand tool within reach, so that I can use it when my task calls for it. I may indeed put the hammer out of reach, but the hammer remains reachable somewhere on the tool rack within my home. The tool rack is a tool for keeping the hammer handy; my bed is likewise a rack which keeps my body ready to hand for use in the morning.

I incorporate the hammer through my labor. The glossy wood becomes invisible when I take the hammer in hand, and then becomes intangible when I hammer the nail; the hammer over there has a glossy surface which becomes an inner surface as my palm approaches; when I grasp the hammer and drive the nail, this surface disappears inside my body; the surface which caught my eye when I was looking about for the proper tool becomes transparent to the hard and shining nail whose head I strike. When I take the hammer in hand and drive the nail, the hammer turns

231

outside in; the outer surface turns in toward my outer surface; our outsides touch and gradually become transparent as my hither side prolongs itself to the degree zero over there, and radiates from that center toward the nail. When I lay down the hammer after using it, I again see the outside of the hammer, but this outside is now mine; the hammer comes out into the open, and I see myself turned inside out before my eyes; my own body now has a gleaming surface yonder. The hammer handle is a bone clothed with my flesh; that hand-rubbed gloss on the wood is my palm turned inside the hammer and then turned inside out, so that I face myself from over there on the workbench. I haunt my hammer in those tasks which I recollect and in those which I anticipate.

Interpersonal appropriation. More than one human body can prolong itself into the same impersonal external, generating interpersonal property where the personal spheres interpenetrate. Personal properties become common property through the impersonal properties in the thing, when the thing is jointly appropriated by another person and myself. My hammer is something which can pass from hand to hand among persons who are handy with their hands. The hammer handle is a wooden bone which we pass back and forth; within the interpersonal field, the hammer can become a bone of contention or a token of friendship. When I lay down the hammer and lay bare this bone by withdrawing my hand, I see my body available yonder for another hand. When someone else lays a hand upon my hammer, I see my bodily sphere overlap with his; my property becomes his property; my own body joins with his body proper, as he grasps the handle and turns my outer surface in toward his hither depth. My hand is a hand in general, because the other person has a hand like mine which makes the hammer common property. My upper arm is joined to my lower arm through a joint, and my forearm is joined to the hammer through a jointed coupling, my hand; my hand comes uncoupled from the hammer and reaches for another tool, leaving the hammer available for general use. Anything which my hand can grasp becomes my property when my coupling closes upon the handle, and general property when another hand shares the work. When my hammer passes from my hand into another hand, the other body proper gradually assumes the same glossy surface that mine has. While the other and myself work within the same sphere, the worker who uses my hammer can become my right hand, if my hand directs his toward a nail I want driven. When another person takes my hammer in hand and drives a nail, he and I clasp hands, if he handles my tool with respect; we join hands only if he works without exorcising my ghost from the wood and steel, only if he handles my body proper with propriety. Exorcism uses various incantations, but the most efficacious are those objective formulae which let us view the hammer as just a quantity of wood and steel. The exorcist does not feel the hand which rubbed the wood to glossiness, and does not see the eye whose aim dulled the striking surface; my bones grow cold on the workbench as the other person warms to his task; his disrespectful hammering drives a nail into my coffin, unless I can shrink back in time.

Handling the Hand

Grasping handles and manipulating tools, the hand makes the external world a human habitation. The hand handles things outside the body; but also, the human hand is a handle; the hand is something outside which can be handled; I can handle my own hand; I can grasp the hand of another person; the hand yonder is a handle which I can grasp with the hither hand. The human hand is equipped for handling other things, but the hand too is something yonder which can be handled; the hand is equipment which can be manipulated from the hither side. Bodily motion is the tactile medium through which my living body moves from its degree zero into the world; when I grasp a hammer handle and swing its head against the nail, my life moves along this arm motion into the hammer; from over here I inhabit the degree zero over there, so that my experiences radiate from that center along with the material appearances; the hammer becomes an apparition of my living body. When I grasp the hand of another person, and shake his hand, my life moves along our common motion and enters his body, so that I inhabit his upholstery.

Personal appropriation of another hand. Another person approaches; I grasp his hand, and shake. His hand is a handle, but the spatial zero yonder is a here from which radiate bodily motions directed toward my own body. From over here I can feel my hand being shaken from over there; I need not stand on both sides of the handshake to know that my hand is being shaken by a here over there, and not by a pumping machine. When I shake a hand, my bodily motion prolongs itself into his arm so that his equipment becomes mine; while I shake, I let my hand be shaken, so that his bodily motion can penetrate my arm; through our clasped hands, my bodily motion passes into his body, and his motion passes into mine. Through his arm I feel his whole body as an opacity beyond the limb which I move, and I feel my own body as an immobile center toward which the other penetrates as his bodily motion runs up my arm. I experience his arm as mine, and my arm as his; my bones become clothed with his flesh and his bones come under my

234

skin. While we move together, our clasped hands function as a material through which spirit penetrates from both sides; his prehensile arm is a real limb which becomes imaginal while I shake; and my limb is a reality which becomes his imaginary; our clasped hands become a joint flesh through which the leading element in the tactile medium penetrates hither and yon. My bodily motion leads my life into his body; but the leading element is also a receptive element; my bodily motion animates his arm, but becomes there an element which leads his bodily motion into my body; my shaking motion can penetrate into his body with a seductive modulation which draws forth his motion to my side. Mobilizing immobility, the handshake personalizes the hands which clasp.

Personal appropriation spiritualizes reality. The real hand which I feel when I touch his palm becomes an imaginal reality through which I feel a reality beyond. His palm becomes intangible, and my palm too becomes intangible against his palm. I feel that the other person is shaking hands with me personally; he is not just feeling the limberness in my arm, or feeling the calluses on my palm. Perhaps I feel a rough palm when our hands touch; and when our hands clasp I feel a knobby hand; and when we shake I feel a supple arm; but this roughness, and knobbiness, and suppleness become intangibles which overlap upon the person himself whose hand I shake. Once I have released his hand, I can reflect upon our handshake and feel again these qualities; I can separate the roughness from the knobbiness, and I can separate these qualities from the person himself, who also has visual qualities; but these reflected qualities were not separately touched while we shook hands. The handshake is essentially a communication, but there are numerous variations which diverge from the essential. With a frozen grin, I can mechanically pump his hand while secretly analyzing the texture of his skin; my treachery strips away his sensible properties, leaving his body naked, shorn of my sentiment. Or, I can resist communication by actively immobilizing my arm, or by making my movement work against his. The handshake is a communication nonetheless, and the open hand is a welcome. When another person reaches forth and takes my hand in his, my spirit is made welcome in his body, unless I am received with violence. He may grasp my hand in a crushing grip which immobilizes my hand, so that I cannot grasp his hand in return; his violent spirit penetrates into my body and imprisons me inside; my overpowered soul is driven back into my heart; my arm becomes a pump handle. Or, the other person may greet me, not with violence, but with reluctance, reaching forth a limp hand which I grasp without feeling any life there; he gives me his hand as though handing me meat; he withdraws from his hand while reaching it forth.

Personal appropriation of my own hand. My hand is a handle through which another person can grasp me personally, but I can grasp my own hand, and handle myself. When my right hand touches my left hand, a "spark is lit between sensing and sensible."[7] Consciousness flares at the interface, between touching surface and surface touched. The spark jumps the gap between my hands, and the grounded energy circulates through the yonder hand, back into the sensorium which generated this intentional current. The sensing hand is the positive pole, the sensed hand the negative. This sparking mechanism lights "the fire that will not stop burning until some accident of the body will undo what no accident would have sufficed to do."[8] The fire is the inner light, spurting into space.

I who sense am something sensible; the human body is a

236

flesh which sees itself, and touches itself. I can touch my own hands, using my bare hands as instruments; my right hand touches my left hand, my left touches the right; my left hand touches my right hand while the right touches things beyond my body. My hand can touch my eye; my eye can see my hands; my eyes can see themselves, in the mirror. My eyes might have been located so that one eye could look directly at the other, positioned on stalks, just as my hands are positioned on arms. If my hands were set in my shoulder sockets without arms, my hands could not touch each other, except through a reflection; I could press my right hand against a clay tablet and then feel the impression with my left hand; or I could grasp with both hands a stick held across my chest, and with one hand feel the movement of the other hand, as reflected in the moving stick. Suppose that our hands were positioned so that we could touch the things but could not touch our own body; and suppose that our eyes were positioned so that we could not see our hands; suppose that our eyes were positioned laterally, like the eyes of certain animals, so that our two visual fields did not overlap; and suppose that in the world were no mirrors in which we could see ourselves reflected, and no tablets in which we could feel ourselves impressed. Such a body, in such a world, "would be an almost adamantine body, not really flesh, not really the body of a human being."[9] We are fully human only when we turn back upon ourselves and experience our body from the outside, turning inside out, and outside in. "There is a human body when, between the seeing and the seen, between touching and the touched, between one eye and the other, between hand and hand, a blending of some sort takes place. . . ."[10] My body is not really my own unless I can handle myself in the way that I handle a hammer, and in the way that I feel the other person handle me. I handle my own body even when I

237

shake hands with another, even when I drive a nail, because the hammer and the hand over there reflect my hand over here; after I use the hammer I see my own hand over there turned inside out; after I have shaken hands, I see the hand over there as my own hand seen from the outside.

I can touch my sensible body, but I can never quite touch my sensitivity; I am a sensing sensible which never quite perceives its perceptual action. I never quite touch myself touching, or see myself seeing; my senses cannot reverse upon their sensitivity. If my left hand touches my right hand, my tactile perception can reverse direction, so that my right hand reverses from touched to touching; but my right hand does not quite touch my left hand touching. I can close the gap between touch and touched, but not between touch and touch. With my right hand I can passively feel myself being touched by my left hand, or I can actively touch my left hand, which then becomes something touched; but my right hand cannot actively touch my left hand touching my right; from the hither side, my right hand cannot touch frontally the hither side yonder in my left hand. Because the touch cannot confront its touching when my left hand touches my right, and my right the left, there is a gap in the circuit; this gap also appears when my left hand touches my right hand touching the things. "My left hand is always on the verge,"[11] never quite contacting the touch. When my left hand touches my right, the right becomes something touched, and no longer touches the things beyond the body; or else, my right hand remains in touch with the world while my left hand touches merely the surface on my right hand; the surface becomes something touched, but the right hand beneath this surface touches the things in the world and remains untouched.[12]

Frontally, my left hand cannot quite perceive my right hand touching a material thing, whether that thing be my left hand or something beyond my body. Frontal experience of perception is always negative.[13] The touching which we want to touch withdraws, or the touching which wants to touch our touching misses the goal; we miss our aim, the aim withdraws, and we touch the touched. This gap within our tactile sense is an intangible, or invisible; this gap is the space where the cogito appears.[14] Consciousness of consciousness appears in the hiatus where unreflective consciousness originated. Consciousness, understood as direct sense experience, takes rise in the place where touching contacts the tangible; across a gap my hand touches a thing yonder. This contacted external is a tangible which does not touch, or else a human flesh which touches, but whose tactile experience I cannot feel. Suppose the person whom I grasp is myself: when my left hand touches my right, I close the gap between my left hand and my yonder tangibility; but I never quite close the gap between my left hand and the tactile activity in my right hand; my right-handed touching withdraws beneath the tangible surface of my right hand. But precisely in this gap I experience myself as a touching which I never quite touch; and thus I experience myself as a certain nothingness. I never quite possess what I am, and thus I am conscious of myself, conscious of my consciousness. This personal absence is a clearing across which I experience myself yonder as a hither side which I never quite reach.

Although I never confront the hither side yonder, I do perceive the hither side on this side of the gap. While looking I feel the ocular strain, while touching I feel the muscular effort, while speaking I feel the vocal contortions. "Like crystal, like metal, . . . I am a sonorous being," but unlike a bell, "I hear my own vibration," and I hear it "from within."[15] If I make no audible sound, "I hear myself with my throat."[16] I always perceive myself as the hither depth, but perceive this depth longitudinally, not frontally. "I do not hear myself as I hear the others."[17] My voice, when I speak out, is poorly heard from my side. I hear an "echo," because my voice "vibrates through my head rather than outside. I am always on the same side of my body. . . ."[18] Since I have outer ears, I can hear myself speaking outwardly, as I would hear another speak, but mostly I feel my throat and mouth operating, and I hear the sound which reverberates through my head, not the vibrations in the air which other people hear through their outer ears. I can record my voice, with a tape recorder, and hear my voice played back, but while speaking I can never quite escape my body and hear myself from yonder. Suppose that I silence those sounds which echo through my head, and make just the anticipatory movements in my throat and mouth, movements which would become sonorous if I were to speak more forcefully. When I speak inwardly, I do experience myself yonder; the yonder side emerges inside my body; I perceive myself over there in the throat, yonder in my own body. Nevertheless, I cannot confront my vocal chords as successfully as I can confront my hands when I see my hands yonder, or touch that hand yonder with my right hand. I cannot back away from my vocal chords. Whether speaking inwardly or outwardly, my yonder voice is poorly heard from my side; my voice is mostly an inner agitation which I perceive longitudinally. This inward voice is so intimately my own that it never quite emerges yonder as material for personal appropriation.

Lateral and longitudinal interpersonal communication. When another person handles my hand, and I handle his, our confrontation becomes interpersonal communication, as each person appropriates the hand of the other. Uniting frontally, the other person and myself can also communi-

240

cate laterally and longitudinally, if I handle my own hand, or handle his hand handling mine. When I and the other clasp hands, I feel myself being touched, but I do not touch what he touches; I touch his outside while he touches my outside; from the hither side I touch his outside, and from here I also feel that he is touching my outside. I do not touch the same outside he touches; however, employing my left hand, I can feel the right hand which he touches; when he touches my right hand with his right hand, I can touch his right hand with my left hand, and feel him touching me. When my left hand first touches his right hand, the hand which I feel is his; but then I feel my own right hand through his right hand, which has become intangible; his bodily motion leads my touch through his hand to my hand; I experience his hand longitudinally, while I experience my hand frontally through his hand. I can feel my hand through his only dimly, since the tactile medium is quite opaque; I can feel my right hand most vividly if I directly touch my right hand with my left hand, without using his hand as an intermediary; touching my right hand with my left, I feel the same tangible surface which I obscurely felt through his right hand. Perhaps I move my left hand alongside his hand while I touch my right hand, so that I experience his right hand laterally while I experience my right hand frontally. Or perhaps he withdraws his right hand from my right hand and grasps with that hand my left hand, which he moves over my right hand; I let him move my left hand over my right hand, so that I experience his right hand behind me directing my left hand toward my right hand. I feel that he feels my right hand longitudinally through my left hand, because he moves my hand with the same motion which I experienced laterally when I moved my left hand alongside his right hand, and with the same motion which I experienced frontally, and longitudinally, when I touched with my left hand his right hand touching my right hand. I best feel my right hand as he feels it, if he guides my hand from the side or from behind. But I feel well enough what he feels, if he withdraws his right hand and lets me advance my left hand to the place where I with my right hand felt him touch that hand; I feel what he feels, because I feel from the outside what from the inside I felt him feel from the outside. Moreover, the surface on my right hand solicits a certain movement from my left hand; unless I move my left hand with the proper style, I cannot adequately feel my right hand; I must move my left hand with the style which my right hand solicits from my left hand. And from within, my right hand feels the motion which its outside solicits. And I feel, from inside my right hand, whether my left hand moves with the same style that his right hand exhibited; if his hand moved with a different style than mine, I can alter my style, letting my left hand move with his mannerism, so that I feel the solicitations which he apparently felt.

During longitudinal communication, I personally appropriate my own hand through the hand of another who is appropriating my hand for himself, or I let him appropriate the hand of mine which is appropriating my other hand. If with my left hand I grasp his right hand while his right hand touches my right hand, I with my left hand weakly feel through his right hand my right hand, which he strongly feels through his right hand. His right hand prolongs my left hand and becomes my own; the circuit which runs from my right hand through my body to my left hand now prolongs itself into his right hand and flows a short distance along the circuit which runs from his body toward my right hand. If my left hand, while grasping his right hand, actively moves his right hand across my right hand, then my intentional current leads his current through our

242

shared circuit. But if my left hand grasping his right hand is otherwise passive while his right hand actively moves across my right hand, then his intentional current leads my current through the joint circuit, guiding my hand which has relinquished its leadership. Again, if he with his right hand grasps my left hand while my left hand touches my right hand, he with his hand weakly feels through my left hand the right hand which I strongly feel through my left hand. My left hand prolongs his right hand and becomes his property, without ceasing to be mine; the current which streams from his body toward my right hand prolongs itself into my left hand, and runs a short distance along the circuit which runs from my right hand through my body into my left hand. If his right hand grasping my left hand actively moves my left hand across my right hand, then his intentional current leads mine, but leads from behind at the point where the circuit running through his right hand hooks onto my circuit. If his right hand grasping my left hand is passive while my left hand actively moves across my right hand, then my intentional current leads his, but leads from in front at the hookup point.

Employing longitudinal communication I can lead the other person from behind during his appropriation of my hand; from behind I can incorporate his clasping hand into my appropriation of myself, helping him take me for his property, without letting him take me away from myself. When the other person clasps my right hand with his right hand, I can clasp his right hand with my left hand, so that his hand becomes an intermediary between my left hand and my right; I catch his clasping hand between my hands so that my hands nearly clasp themselves. My left hand touches his right hand, and the surface on his hand becomes intangible as I direct my touch along the bodily motion which courses through his right hand into my right;

243

my left palm touches the back surface on his right hand and my left hand backs him up, and merges into his background at the point where my left hand touches his right. I can merge from farther back in his background if I lengthen the circuit, extending my left arm and clasping his right shoulder. In this handshake, my fingers extend behind his back and partially separate the other person from his background, but also my left hand backs him up as I draw him into the foreground. From behind his back my touch is directed down his whole arm while his right hand shakes mine. I separate the other person from a background which we do not share, and make my body his background. Here the handclasp is becoming the embrace, which closes the distance between our front sides so that our surfaces become intangible. Pressed together, we touch around behind; we wrap our arms around each other and separate one another from our backings.

Personal and Interpersonal Appropriation as Impersonal Process

The process wherein I personally appropriate my own hand is an intrapersonal activity, a process wherein I handle my own hand as the hand of another; intrapersonal appropriation becomes an interpersonal process wherein my own hand yonder becomes for me the hand of another person. Perhaps then, interpersonal communication is an intrapersonal union; perhaps the other person yonder is the one who reaches forth my hand here. Is the natural world a vast intrapersonal transaction? Does there exist "some huge animal whose organs our bodies would be?"[19] Does the world have two right hands and two left hands; does an animal touch itself in me when my left hand touches my right hand, and again touch itself, but in us, when his right hand touches my right hand? The other bodily subject and myself would be two organs in this larger body, just as my right and left hands are two organs in my own body. The suggestion is too bizarre.

If not an animal, what exists instead? There exists a synergy. My two hands work together, so that I feel a single thing when I grasp something with both hands, even though each hand can feel a separate tactile sensible; my two eyes work together, so that I see the same thing when I look at something with both eyes, even though each eye can see a separate visual sensible; and my two eyes work together with my two hands, when I grasp something with both hands and view it with both eyes; I see the same thing that I touch, even though my eyes perceive visual sensibles, not tactile sensibles; when my left hand touches my right hand, my left hand works together with my eyes, which see the hand I touch; my body is a common sensorium through which my various specialized sense organs work unitedly. "Why would not the synergy exist among different organisms, if it is possible within each? Their landscapes interweave, their actions and passions fit together exactly. . . ."[20] During interpersonal communication the natural world becomes a synergetic system, a filigreed opacity where finite clearings open and close. Other hands and eyes work together with mine; I can see a landscape from my own viewpoint, but if I verbally point out the landscape to another person, and he turns his eyes toward the spot where I direct mine, our bodies work as one; "what I see passes into him, this individual green of the meadow under my eyes invades his vision without quitting my own, I recognize in my green his green."[21] When we look in the same direction, I do not wonder whether the other person sees what I see, "because it is not *I* who sees, not *he* who sees, because an anonymous visibility inhabits both of us, a vision in general."[22] The other person and myself are both flesh; flesh is a here and now which radiates everywhere and forever; flesh

245

is an individual which becomes universal in mutual perception. Flesh is something sentient, and something sensed; the other person and myself radiate visual experiences, while the fleshly landscape radiates visible appearances, just as our bodies radiate tangible appearances when the other person and myself stand forth from the landscape and clasp hands.

Interpersonal communication, synergetic union, is not intrapersonal appropriation, but an impersonal process which binds persons in carnal community. We do not favor denominating the synergetic system an animal, because nature is largely inanimate. "Hylozoism is a conceptualization" which falsely thematizes "our experience of carnal presence."[23] The thematization is false, because matter is not yet the living being which perceives itself; matter is merely the precondition for self-perception. The world with its denizens is an "intercorporeal being,"[24] which has "no name in traditional philosophy."[25] This being is not a "group soul" but the "connective tissue" between myself and the others.[26] We still have our own viewpoints and standpoints while the world sees and touches itself through our eyes and hands. The world is flesh, but this material is not entirely human and animal; the inanimate world does not sense itself as does my own flesh; the world senses itself only in man and his brethren. The inanimate world "is sensible and not sentient"; we nonetheless call this world "flesh," because it is "a pregnancy of possibles."[27] The world is not an object spread out with all its apparitions actualized before a consciousness; the sensible world always has hidden in its womb appearances which we have not confronted yet; the world holds potentially those clearings across which we confront surfaces; the pregnant world calls for our perceptual activity. The world becomes animate only when we press out its carnal essence during perception; the inor-

246

ganic becomes animate in animals and men. The latent lifeworld includes the machines which men construct, and includes the natural things which can be imagined as mechanical. The mechanical can become organic: my hammer is clothed with my flesh as I drive a nail. The organic can become mechanical: my arm is denuded during the handshake when the other person operates my arm like a pump handle. The natural world is mechanical and organic, lifeless and living, and in the derived cultural world is spiritual, working organically through human contrivance. In all synergetic operations, the human body is the measure, because the world perceives itself in us.[28]

Communal perception can be understood, if we no longer make sense perception the private operation of a personal consciousness, if "we rather understand it as the return of the visible upon itself, a carnal adherence of the sentient to the sensed and of the sensed to the sentient."[29] The personal consciousness is a perceptual life which closes in upon itself, taking the impersonal properties yonder as my private property, as personal possessions not shared with material things, and not shared with other persons. The personal consciousness becomes bound up in its privacy; I perceive the material properties yonder as my hither breadth, I take the external apparitions as the inner surface of my mental sphere. But my perceptual possessions are private appropriations of common property. From my standpoint, from my center, I grasp the material externals, which others grasp from their standpoint. I internalize a material thing as a personal vision, and other visionaries, other voluptuaries, likewise internalize the outer reality; but our visions remain perspectives upon common property. My personal appropriation is not an isolated act, but a singular event within community activity; inhuman nature perceives itself interpersonally, through its human inhabitants.

247

Perception is a circular process which personalizes the impersonal, making the material qualities our personal property, incorporating the externals into our body proper. I appropriate impersonal properties when I handle a tool, when I handle the hand of another person, when I handle my own hand as a handle not my own. During interpersonal communication in the handclasp, I handle the hand of another person, and appropriate his impersonal properties as my own, while he grasps my hand and appropriates my impersonal properties for himself. I lend him my body while he lends me his; my impersonal properties become his personal properties while his become mine; I internalize his externals while he internalizes mine. During interpersonal communication, my impersonal properties, my outward appearances, can become not merely personal properties, but interpersonal properties, if, during the handclasp, I grasp with my free hand the hand which the other person holds in his. Touching my right hand with the left, I personally appropriate my own impersonal properties for myself, while he personally appropriates the same externals for himself; the outward surface becomes interpersonal, something both mine and his, since we touch the same hand yonder. Impersonal properties again become interpersonal, if I and the other person handle, not my right hand, but some instrument beyond both our bodies. If I and the other work together with some inanimate tool, or together look at the same scenery, the viewed panorama, or the touched surface, becomes my personal property and also becomes his; the impersonal apparitions become interpersonal possessions, because the two persons join in perception; their looks converge; they both touch the same surface. Whether the impersonal properties are the apparitions of my body, or the apparitions of something corporeal beyond my body, these appearances are yonder surfaces presented for personal appropriation. The yonder surfaces, the material externals, become personal when appropriated by a single subject, and interpersonal when jointly appropriated. This personal and interpersonal appropriation is fundamentally an impersonal process, an operation wherein nature perceives itself across the clearing, opening perspectives upon itself through the human perceptual apparatus. The sensed body and the sensing body are "two segments of one sole circular course"[30] which goes across the clearing unto the sensed body yonder, and then goes from the sensed body, through the earth, back to the sensing body. The intentional current goes across the clearing in one direction, and circulates back in the reverse direction; the current runs from the hither side through the yonder side, back to the hither side; this back and forth intentional flow is "one sole movement in its two phases."[31] This circle operates throughout the sensible world, circulating intentional energy through the small body which is mine, and through that boundless body which we all hold in common, and which holds us, enmeshed in its toils.

ESCAPING THE ENCLOSURE FROM WITHIN

Our body is an enclosure, bound with skin, located in the external world. The mind is enclosed within the body, and the body is enclosed within the surrounding externals. Matter surrounds mind; the world is a box which encloses the body, and our bodily integument is another box, enclosing the mind; the body is a box within a box, a boxed-in box; and the mind is doubly boxed-in, walled-up within a double enclosure.

Is the mind within the body? Where in the body can we locate the visionary? Inside we discover only " 'shadows stuffed with organs,' that is more of the visible."[32] Is not the mind outside the body in the world? When the animate body prolongs its life into the external world, the world too becomes a sensing sensible, a flesh with an inside and an outside. "Since the world is flesh,"[33] we cannot designate our skin as the fixed limit between the lived body and the lifeless world. The mind is the hither side of the body and the world is the yonder side. The body and the world are both flesh, a place where the inside and outside reverse. The body turns inside out, so that the mind enters the world; and the body turns outside in, so that the world enters the mind. The body turns inside out and outside in, both inside the body and outside the body, because there is a world inside the body, and because the lived body prolongs itself outside.

The Descent from Above

When we look inside the bodily enclosure, we discover more visible externals; we discover the external world inside the body; we cannot find the mind. The mind is merely a ghost which haunts the machinery, a ghost which external reflection can banish from the world. Objective thought makes man a machine, and makes the objective thinker a little man somewhere inside who can rise above his situation and look down at our hands and eyes moving toward the world. The visionary who hovers overhead, looking at our eyes from outside, can descend into our head, where he becomes the little man who looks through our eyes from the inside. While living within, the little man seems more closely connected with the body than a sailor with his ship; but when he abandons the body and looks from overhead, this intimacy is unintelligible. Hovering above, the little man sees the body and the world spread out below, and he sees that the body is an enclosure which the world surrounds.

250

Seen inside the body is a cubicle into which the little man can descend, a cranial enclosure where the mind, operating the controls, looks through the portholes and drives the body around in its environment. Where is this body and world which the aviator sees before he descends into the head? The boxes down below are just outsides, one inside the other, and all these outsides are inside surfaces of the mental sphere which is centered overhead. The objective thinker has no body, and hence all the visible outsides are surfaces which mark his outer limit. The mind hovering overhead is a degree zero, and the mental distance from this viewpoint to the world spread out below is his inside depth; the world below is his inside breadth. Beyond this breadth is no apparent depth, because anything hidden underneath the things seen from above is not seen, or is drawn from its hiding place and viewed frontally. From overhead, the body is seen as something surrounded; this bodily inwardness is an inwardness seen in breadth, a yonder-sided interiority. The body is boxed inside the world, and the body is seen as inside yonder, not inside over here where my vision is. The body too is a box, or several boxes; one box is the cranium where sits the driver who operates the controls; the birdman overhead sees the operator as an external object boxed inside the control cab. Again, inwardness is an interiority seen in breadth. The operator is called the mind, but the relation between the mind and the body is external; the mental inwardness is altogether yonder-sided, and thus not truly mental. A box seen from the outside has a yonder-sided inside; a thing inside a box seen yonder does not inhabit the box; habitation is hither-sided inwardness. The cranium seen from outside is a machine for living in which no one lives. The overhead subject sees yonder-sided insides and outsides; but when the subject moves from his overhead viewpoint into the head below and installs himself there, the yonder-sided inside becomes a hither-sided inside; the world seen through the bodily eyes remains an outside seen yonder. Behind the outside yonder, the world has an inside which radiates toward my degree zero from depth; this worldly inwardness is an inside seen yonder, but not spread out in breadth. When overhead, the subject sees material things enclosed within the world, and sees the body as a thing among things. When the subject descends, and inhabits the body, the uninhabited interiors are still seen yonder, but the yonder inside becomes a deep interior, not just an inner breadth, or a broad outer limit.

Is my body a machine? I look at my hands resting on my workbench. Yes, those hands down there are instruments which I am careful not to break, when my right hand is coupled with the hammer handle and my left hand holds the nail. But, if I carelessly strike my thumb, I do not feel like the sailor whose ship has struck a rock; I do not look over the railing and see that my vessel needs a patch down there. When hammering a nail, I feel solicitude for my thumb, and I suffer with my thumb when that appendage is struck; and my hands enjoy their work when my work goes well. I learn, of course, to keep a stiff upper lip when I feel pain, and suffer; I bandage my thumb and staunch the flow; I put my thumb in drydock and take a shore leave. But even the sailor has solicitude for his ship, in deep water and rough weather; like the sailor, I fear that I may go down with the boat. When my hands lie motionless on the workbench alongside the hammer, and I look without touching anything, I at least have solicitude for the eyes with which I look; when something darts toward my eyes, my hands fly up protectively; when my thumb is struck, my eyes water sympathetically; the little man inside my cranium drives carefully, because he has solicitude at least for himself.

When the operator really drives, and does not simply speculate, he has solicitude for his machine, and the little man prolongs himself into my limbs, becomes the large man which we see in the external world. How does the little man grow larger? I see a corporeal mechanism down there on the workbench; my hands lie dispirited while my eyes muse upon the spectacle; my hands are externals spread out before my gaze. Vision can turn these outsides inside itself, so that my hands become merely seen hands, hands which look handy. The little man who has withdrawn his tactile sense, and has become a visionary, still feels a phantom limb; my tactile hand hovers somewhere near those lifeless instruments yonder; as I become a visionary, the phantom slowly shrinks until it dangles at the shoulder; finally the limb is absorbed into my brain, from which it may sprout forth at any moment. While musing, I am suddenly inspired; I grasp my hammer and get set to drive a nail, my eyes riveted upon the striking point. But stop; my eyes widen in surprise; I see that my hands have sprung to life; my arm is inhabited; my phantom limb has returned, and now lives inside my hand. Why in my hand, and not somewhere else in another body? Because my hand was handy, lying on the workbench, ready to hand. My hand fits like a glove, as if my hand were made for this tactile sense which stirs now in the flesh. When I grasp the hammer, I work hand in glove with my hand; the man in my head is handy with my hands. These tools, which looked handy, feel handy; the tactile sense goes inside their visual outside, so that my tools, which feel handy, feel as if they would look handy too. Suppose this animated body still says, "I am a machine." Neither a machine nor a ghost can speak; the machine can only make sounds, and a spirit cannot make sounds at all; thus the spirit must haunt a voice box; only a

253

haunted speaking mechanism can say, "I am a machine," in a tone which haunts us; these words make sense in our ears because the sounds issue from a sensitive body.

The embodied soul is a ghost which cannot be exorcised without killing the body. The mechanical body is a dead body, or an uninhabited body. The lived body is a man my own size who sees with these eyes which other people see from the outside, and which I too see from the outside when I look in a mirror. We are describing "not that possible body which we may legitimately think of as an information machine but that actual body I call mine."[34] Along with my body we describe those other bodies with whom I live in the world. The others are not those fellow creatures which the zoologist studies, "but the others who haunt me and whom I haunt; the 'others' along *with* whom I haunt a single, present, and actual Being as no animal ever haunted those beings of his own species, locale, or habitat."[35] Our description does not exorcise the ghost, making the body a machine, but prolongs the ghost into the external world, so that my spirit inhabits the externals, and wanders into the bodies of others. We banish the "little man inside the man."[36] We banish the inner man, not to heaven, but into the outer man. The ensouled body is imprisoned within the exterior world, a realm of soulless externals, and we want freedom. If the soul breaks out above, the body too becomes an external; the soul flies free, but has lost its body. Remaining embodied, the soul can break out into the external world. The externalized soul haunts the externals, utilizing the body so that the embodied soul indwells the physical surroundings, releasing the soul from its inner alienation.

The Exit from Inside

Once the soul is embodied, we can prolong the soul into

the world, through the bodily enclosure, and we can draw the world into the soul, since the ensouled body is already an external in the outside world. How does the soul escape its enclosure and haunt the outer world? Consider the tactile sense; and suppose that I don a glove. As I pull the glove over my right hand, I feel the inside surface sliding against my skin. Once I have situated my fingers in their casings, I stretch and flex my hand, enjoying this covering which encases my epidermis; I experience the glove as the inside surface of my tactile world. No more than the visual sphere is this tactile world actually spherical; the tactile sphere is ameboid; our fingers are pseudopodia which in their probing tend toward a sphere which remains virtual; our actual reaching and grasping fleshes out a potential world. The sensory sphere is a bag which evaginates when we reach out, and invaginates when the things press in upon us. A model for this bag is the skin sack with which our body is naturally upholstered; our skin is only a model, because the tactile sphere can expand far beyond our epidermis, and can contract from the epidermis toward our degree zero; the glove is another evaginated bag, for whose construction a cow was excoriated. Once my hand is well situated in its new skin, I reach forth and grasp the hammer on my workbench; the glove leather which so enjoyably lined the inner surface of my tactile sphere effaces itself before the hammer handle, and the nail to be driven. I can touch the outside surface on things in the real world without jumping out of my skin; I touch the things through my skin, from inside; my skin and the glove, which protects me from barking my knuckles, become dimensional, opening me upon the routes which run through the world; my glove has invisible nerves dangling, which my hand knows how to hook up with the instruments leading toward the work to be done. I feel the glossy hammer handle through these soft

255

leather gloves, just as I feel the cushioned leather palm when I double back my fingers; from inside the glove I feel its outside. "There is no need of a spectator who would be *on each side*. It suffices that from one side I see the wrong side of the glove that is applied to the right side, that I touch the one *through* the other. . . ."[37]

This reversibility between the external world and human interiority is a depth reversibility between figure and ground, an interchange wherein real depth displays a forward surface and then disappears into imaginal depth. Spatially our body moves forward while the things come forth, and temporally too there is a perpetual oncoming and going forth. The material thing which figures as the focal point somewhere in the middle distance is a temporarily opaque skin separating the foreground from the background; this opaque separation is a sensation which becomes sensuous as we move farther forth. The sensation which stopped our focused gaze moves into the foreground through which we look into the middle distance and beyond; the things in the temporal foreground come inside our experiential body; when they advance deeply enough into our body, they enter the dark background which trails away behind our back as we move forward. Thus the things come forth from their background and enter our background, from which we step forth when we move toward the things that figure in the middle distance. The background yonder merges into the hither background as the things come across the clearing to our side; but farther on beyond the clearing there is always a further background, a horizon whence further things come forth. The background yonder and the background over here, which backs me up, are backings which base themselves on the common ground where the things and I stand. The things on the hither side of the focal separation between background and

256

foreground are imaginary things, which become less clear as they come toward my degree zero, until they become invisible in the darkness at my center; this hither depth, where the world no longer confronts me, is the imaginary. Beyond the thing which we imaginally perceive from over here in the dark is real depth which extends to the world horizon, the horizon of horizons. The clearly seen separation at the focal point in the middle distance is the inside surface of the visual sphere within whose depth the things are imaginary; this separation, this inner siding, is also the outside surface of the real world beyond our sphere thus far.

Between the imaginary foreground and the real background we see a shining surface; this superficial separation is something external right in the middle of the middle distance where we see things best. But if we focus also upon the surfaces in the middle zone where our gaze ranges hither and yon, we can imagine that place where the creatively seen thing is located. Anything creatively seen is an imaginal reality located in a depth carved out between a hither and yonder separation. The hither separation is the surface which first clearly figured in the middle distance as the single separation between the hither side and the potential appearances yonder which had not yet come to the fore; as the single separation comes farther forward and becomes sensuous, the appearances farther on come forward and figure in the far middle distance where the hither separation first stood. One after another, lighted surfaces appear across the clearing and move into the middle distance where they overlap and pile up; within this middle distance emerges a layered locality with a certain depth. These peelings, or layers, expressed across the clear zone are films which the creative visionary presses together as a single imaginal reality. Our gaze can range back and forth across this layered middle distance from the hither separation unto the one yonder, and we can focus on any layer in between. As our gaze ranges back and forth, working over this interstitial material, we see a reversal back and forth between figure and ground, until our gaze comes to the hither side of the hither separation where the foreground has no figures, or goes to the yonder side of the yonder separation where the background has no figures, except in breadth. The appearances pressed together in the background peel off in layers as the world decompresses across the clearing in the middle distance. As these feelings come across the clearing into the foreground where we stand, they pile up in our body and become again pressed together as a sediment which backs us up when we step forth. We advance toward the yonder side, carving from the intermediate matter a carnal essence, an interiorized externality.

Let us isolate a single shining surface, a siding which separates the foreground from the background. Focusing upon this surface, we must fix our gaze so that vision no longer wanders hither and yon. The surface located at our focal point becomes clear and distinct, while the visual field becomes obscure forwards, backwards, and laterally. Looking at this lighted surface, we experience a surface reversibility where the yonder depth joins the hither depth; the lighted surface is reversibly the inside surface of our visual sphere and the outside surface of the things beyond; the lighted surface is reversibly a figure seen through the foreground and a figure seen against the background. If we can stabilize this surface as a figure seen through the foreground, we experience the actually visible world as something in our mind which has its being only for us; if we stabilize this surface as a figure seen against the background, we experience the actually visible world as something outside our mind, having its being in itself. We stabilize a surface which fluctuates; originally we experience a reversal which leads our gaze hither and yon into depth; the lighted surface leads my gaze onward into the background, and also back through the foreground toward my body; I experience this leading force even when I keep my gaze fixed upon the focal surface and do not let myself follow the lead. I may stabilize the lighted surface by counterposing the opposing directional forces, or I may simply clarify the superficial figure until the obscure ground disappears from view, until the guiding forces too disappear. But when I let my gaze wander hither and yon, I experience a fluid reversibility, not yet stabilized in the idealist and realist theses which contradict one another.

Reversal in the Vortex

Perception operates in a vortex, where flesh turns back upon itself, perceives its exterior yonder, and turns outside in, reversing the outer siding to inner surfacing; perception is reversal in a vortex. The body here, in hither-sided depth, faces the body yonder in outer depth; the external body confronts the hither body across a clearing. The embodied soul breaks into the outer world through the bodily enclosure, toward the surfaces perceived yonder. The hither body, together with the body yonder, is flesh, a substance with a hither side and a yonder side, a substance which perceives itself from over here as something over there, a substance which hollows itself out, and fills itself up, opening interiority within external plenitude. Flesh is a sensing sensible, a substance whose outside is always yonder, and whose inside is always here, opening between inside and outside a clear zone across which the outside is perceived from the animate body here. The clear zone is no longer in the body, enclosed within bodily outsides, but is beyond the body, between body and yonder background.

The clear zone is the locus of intellectual illumination. The light dawns, no longer within my skin, but beyond, at the interface of hither body and soulless corporeality yonder.

Flesh is a sensible which can touch its outside from the hither side, because flesh folds back on itself, making a complete circuit. The intentional current which courses the circle can turn around and circulate in reverse direction, so that the flesh which senses turns into something sensed, while the sensed becomes sentient. This turning back, and turning around, takes place within outer depth, where surfaces come forth from across an open space, turning the real into something imaginal; reality comes out into the clear and turns outside in. The real is always becoming imaginal, perpetually coming forth from the background; the ground yonder stands outside my body, unless my body turns back upon itself; when I look at my hand or touch it, my own body appears yonder, and advances toward me from there. On the hither side my body is imaginal, a phantom whose substance radiates from the world; on the yonder side my body is real, something dense and solid whose appearances fill my inner emptiness, making my mind a dreaming spirit. The crossing from the real to the imaginal takes place within a complete circuit; in the vortex gleams a gap, always closing, but always opening, so that we stand in the clear. The gap closes as the apparitions pour across the clearing, becoming sedimented as a hither background, a ground which makes my behavior habitual; but the gap opens again as I step forth from my backing, venturing toward the unperceived, a yonder depth which may be my own body or the world beyond this nearby exterior. The background yonder decompresses and becomes imaginal, dissolving in the sensory media, making my outer interiority a spirit which dreams in the light. Personality is a dreaming but also a waking spirit; a person is the vacuum in

260

the plenum, the gap in the circuit, the clear zone across which sensations are clearly displayed. The person is also the touching which nearly touches itself. The intentional energy which flows from my right hand toward my left can turn around and flow back through my body toward my right hand; my body turns back upon itself when my left hand appears yonder as something which my right hand touches; and turns back also when the touching in my right hand turns around, returns through my body, and flows through my left hand, so that I almost touch myself touching. I am the touching, the sentient spark which darts across the gap, and also I am the touched which I perceive yonder; I am the plenum and the vacuum. Fundamentally I am flesh, a substance which turns, "in the patient and silent labor of desire." [38] The visionary becomes a voluptuary, a spiritual sensuality which makes the sensational sensuous. Flesh manipulates itself with hands and eyes, molding from its own mass a "strange statue,"[39] an outside which expresses the inside. Flesh labors upon itself, becoming its own spectator, inscribing in itself a specular reflection. Spirit labors in the vortex, as flesh turns and turns.

NOTES

[1] *VI*, p. 130.
[2] *VI*, p. 135.
[3] *VI*, p. 136.
[4] *VI*, p. 136, n. 2.
[5] *PrP*, p. 180.
[6] *VI*, p. 148.
[7] *PrP*, p. 163.

261

[8] *PrP*, pp. 163-64.
[9] *PrP*, p. 163.
[10] *PrP*, p. 163.
[11] *VI*, p. 147.
[12] *VI*, pp. 147-48.
[13] *VI*, p. 255.
[14] See *VI*, p. 257.
[15] *VI*, p. 144.
[16] *VI*, p. 144.
[17] *VI*, p. 148.
[18] *VI*, p. 148.
[19] *VI*, p. 142.
[20] *VI*, p. 142.
[21] *VI*, p. 142.
[22] *VI*, p. 142.
[23] *VI*, p. 250.
[24] *VI*, p. 143.
[25] *VI*, p. 139.
[26] *VI*, p. 174.
[27] *VI*, p. 250.
[28] See *VI*, p. 249.
[29] *VI*, p. 142.
[30] *VI*, p. 138.
[31] *VI*, p. 138.
[32] *VI*, p. 138.
[33] *VI*, p. 138.
[34] *PrP*, p. 160.
[35] *PrP*, p. 161.
[36] *VI*, p. 208.
[37] *VI*, p. 263.
[38] *VI*, p. 144.
[39] *VI*, p. 144.

BIBLIOGRAPHY

Merleau-Ponty, Maurice. *In Praise of Philosophy*. Evanston: Northwestern University Press, 1963.

—————. *Phenomenology of Perception*. New York: Humanities Press, 1962.

—————. *The Primacy of Perception*. Evanston: Northwestern University Press, 1964.

—————. *La prose du monde*. Paris: Gallimard, 1969.

—————. *Résumés de cours*. Paris: Gallimard, 1968.

—————. *Sense and Non-Sense*. Evanston: Northwestern University Press, 1964.

—————. *Signs*. Evanston: Northwestern University Press, 1964.

—————. *The Structure of Behavior*. Boston: Beacon Press. 1963.

—————. *The Visible and the Invisible*. Evanston: Northwestern University Press, 1968.